The Liminal Loop

The Liminal Loop

Astonishing Stories of Discovery and Hope

Edited by Timothy Carson

The Lutterworth Press

The Lutterworth Press

P.O. Box 60
Cambridge
CB1 2NT
United Kingdom

www.lutterworth.com
publishing@lutterworth.com

Paperback ISBN: 978 0 7188 9583 9
PDF ISBN: 978 0 7188 4845 3
ePub ISBN: 978 0 7188 4844 6

British Library Cataloguing in Publication Data
A record is available from the British Library

First published by The Lutterworth Press, 2022

You are in this time of the interim
Where everything seems withheld.

The path you took to get here has washed out;
The way forward is still concealed from you.

"The old is not old enough to have died away;
the new is still too young to be born."

You cannot lay claim to anything;
In this place of dusk,
Your eyes are blurred;
And there is no mirror …

What is being transformed here is your mind,
And it is difficult and slow to become new.
The more faithfully you can endure here,
The more refined your heart will become
For your arrival in the new dawn.

John O'Donohue, "For the Interim Time," *To Bless the Space Between Us*

Table of Contents

Acknowledgements

As we discover in Gabriel Garcia Marquez's novel, *Love in the Time of Cholera*, pandemics change much of life as we know it, even as much remains the same. In the time of Covid-19, I have been especially thankful that whatever else was lost or limited, the writer's art endured. For some, this involuntary time-out even added fuel to their creative fire.

This is not the first anthology based on liminality published by the Lutterworth Press. The first was *Neither Here nor There: The Many Voices of Liminality* (2019). Like its predecessor, *The Liminal Loop: Astonishing Stories of Discovery and Hope* gathers a remarkable community of authors, all writing out of their own contexts, experiences, and disciplines. I have been humbled by the warm and enthusiastic reception to my invitation to participate. They dared to stand where their own pursuits and liminality intersect. The resulting magic has made this collection what it is. I am so very appreciative.

Of course, we never navigate alone during such a project. I was ever encouraged by the ready prompting of the Lutterworth Press staff. The careful copy-editing of my editorial assistant, Nancy Miller, kept me on track; and friends and family encouraged me throughout the long process.

The creative process depends on an imagined conclusion and the passion to head toward it. Along that way, however, we encounter inevitable surprises. Enough surprises, we hope, to stimulate improvisation but not so many that we become disheartened. For that balance, too, I am thankful.

No book really matters without a readership to take it up, read, think, learn, and respond. As you are reading these words now, I can only imagine what brought you to this space, this enchanted garden between the page and your life. Were you captivated by the notion of liminality itself, an experience so very characteristic of these times? Have you discovered a new handle, a clue, that connects your greatest concerns with tangled mysteries? Did your professor require it for class? How did your small group decide to read it together? Whatever brought you here, I want to acknowledge *you*. In the end, you are why this book exists.

Timothy Carson
Editor

Foreword

Carrie Newcomer

Liminality

So much of what we know
Lives just below the surface.
Half of a tree
Spreads out beneath our feet.
A tree lives simultaneously in two worlds,
Each half informing and nurturing
The whole.
A tree is either and neither,
But mostly both.

I am drawn to liminal spaces,
The unruly and wild
Where the forest gives way
And my little patch of garden begins.
Where water, air and light overlap,
Becoming mist on the morning pond.
I like to sit on my porch steps, barn jacket and boots
In the last long exhale of the day,
When bats and birds loop in and then out,
One rising to work,
One readying for sleep.

And although the full moon calls the currents,
And the dark moon reminds me that my best language

Has always emerged out of the silence,
It is in the waxing and waning
Where I most often live,
Neither here nor there,
But simply
On the way.

There are endings and beginnings
One emerging out of the other.
But most days I travel in an ever-present
And curious now,
A betwixt and between,
That is almost,
But not quite,
The beautiful,
But not yet.

I've been learning to live with what is,
Be more patient with the process,
Love what is becoming,
And the questions that keep returning.
I am learning to trust
The horizon I walk toward
Is an orientation,
Not a destination,
And that I will keep catching glimpses
Of something great and luminous
From the corner of my eye.

I am learning to live where losses hold fast
And grief lets loose and unravels
Where a new kind of knowing can pick up the thread,
Where I can slide palms with a paradox
And nod at the dawn,
As the shadows pull back
And spirit meets bone.[1]

---

[1] The poem *Liminality* is used with permission of its author, © 2021 Carrie Newcomer.

Introduction

Timothy Carson and David McGee

Suspended between Heaven and Earth

David McGee

We love you, Bill. These were the words I pronounced as I poured the ashes of my friend, Bill Rotts, out of a tiny canvas bag. The location seemed appropriate because Bill had been at that exact spot nearly forty years earlier. The wind blew the ashes upward, into the face of my climbing partner, Todd Johnson, who was with me. The place where that wind swirled was called the Wild Stance, the last stopping point on the over-3,000-foot granite monolith called El Capitan in Yosemite Valley, California. At that moment there was nothing but air between us and the ground nearly one kilometer beneath us.

As one stands at the foot of El Cap and looks upward, before ascending, it is like peering into an endless, vertical ocean of rock. For days during the climb, the sensation is one of being lost at sea, tossed by the wind, the summit never in plain sight, and a view of the ground that never reveals your height. Objects below simply shrink. People seem like ants, cars like metallic slivers, and helicopters like flies; and, even though the Captain looms so large that it dominates every view for observers on the ground, they can barely see climbers on its face with the unaided eye.

When you cross the threshold into the space of this strange vertical world, what you have is what you need, because *it has to be*. It is survival in its most basic terms. In many instances, once climbers pass a certain point on the route, retreat is not an option; and, though

Ashes to Ashes. Photo by David McGee.

climbing requires an insane amount of physical agility and hard work, there are moments in which it seems much more like a science project, evaluating the situation and solving problems while trying to maintain your composure. It is all right to yearn for the summit but what is most important is attending to the process of getting there.

In the end, there is no conquering a rock wall. The only thing to be conquered is the ego, which is one of the primary things that can get you killed. Only a reality check provided by the enormity of the wall reveals how small, how fragile, and how limited we are. The ambiguity and chaos of the rock face has the power to help leave behind the person we thought we were even as it helps us to find the one we are meant to be. The definitions of ourselves from the horizontal world disappear and we become granite astronauts, dangling in a kind of space/time warp, dangling in a breezy cathedral of the sky.

Even sleeping on the wall can feel other-worldly. There is something mystical about waking up in the middle of the night, positioned on your porta-ledge, several thousand feet off the ground, breathing the cool, clean air, blanketed with stars and floating in space.

The disorientation that occurs on a big wall is immense. You long for the feeling of simply putting one foot in front of the other in the horizontal world. Your entire reality has been turned 90 degrees; and the best you can do is crawl upward to an ambiguous goal; but progress is hard to measure. The ground does not seem much farther away, and the summit does not seem any closer. How tall is this thing, anyway? The goal is to somehow feel at ease with uncertainty, incompletion, and not knowing yet.

What appears to be exceedingly difficult sometimes becomes easier than we thought, and what appears to be easy on your map can become nightmarish. It is misleading to say that we enjoy every moment. Pleasure is mixed with fear; and fear is healthy, fear is good. Since climbing is a sport with obvious and inherent dangers, our fear makes us vigilant.

If you are the lead climber, for example, it often feels like casting off from the safety of an island and entering a great abyss with nothing more than a rope tied to your waist, some gear on your belt, and your hands, feet, and mental fortitude.

The View from Wild Stance.
Photo by David McGee.

Much of that fear causes you to review all your safety protocols. You check and double check your belay, hauling system, knots, and back-up knots. Am I tied in properly? Have I backed up the haul bag? Does my partner have me on belay?

However, other fears relate to unpredictable chaos. What if a sudden storm strikes? What if a mass of rock decides to flake off the wall while we are climbing it? What if an earthquake hits?

During a typical climbing season, multiple parties of climbers would be on El Cap, many on the Nose, which is widely considered to be the best rock climb in the world. Many of those climbers will make the several-day slog to the top while others attempt speed ascents in less than 24 hours. In 2020, when my partner and I decided to climb the Nose of El Cap, with the pandemic in full force, there were no other climbers to be seen anywhere. The park limited capacity; and the smoke of California wildfires had recently billowed into the valley. After nearly twenty years since our last big wall together, we would return to El Cap, the sole climbers with perfect weather and visibility.

We arrived at the Wild Stance fulfilling more than one aspiration. Of course, we were crossing the wild granite sea of El Cap for ourselves. However, we were also making a pilgrimage, accompanying our friend on the last ascent, giving him back.

For us, this climb solidified a key conviction that could only be received in such an extreme environment as this: the key to climbing big things in life is to find contentment without complacency. We must find a way to be content where we are, but unafraid to endure the hardship that is required. Complacency will hold us back and allow discomfort to turn us aside from the full potential and greatest capacity to which we are called. Traversing liminal terrain requires acceptance of ambiguity, drive for discovery, passion to dig deep, and the singular conviction that the rocky road to happiness lies far beyond what is most comfortable.

The Liminal Loop and Its Strange Power

Timothy Carson

Though very few of us will cross a threshold into the strange vertical world of a rock face, we do, nevertheless, know what it is like to be suspended in time and space, dangling between what was known and what is entirely yet-to-be-known. This reality can only be described as uncertain, ambiguous, and laden with confusion. The past coordinates of structured life seem to have melted away, as well as ubiquitous and arbitrary rules that defined the land we left. This is a dimension defined by danger as well as unusual consolations. Unexpected traveling companions and guides join us in that territory, and we discover unimaginable sea monsters that rise out of the deep.

Liminality is this in-between state of being, a strange loop in which individuals or groups find themselves in both voluntary and involuntary ways.

The loop of liminality is the transition phase within rites of passage, something explored through anthropological studies in the early twentieth century[1] and refined, expanded, and adapted by the next generation of researchers.[2] Rites of passage, especially as found in agrarian, pre-industrial tribal societies, mediated the dramatic shifts, movements, and developmental phases of the whole of society. The passages were often predetermined and utilized over and over for repeating patterns of renewal. They were also employed in great moments of unpredictable urgency and emergency.

The insights of liminality have been adapted and applied to many disciplines of study, employed in almost every context that requires a dynamic lens to interpret change and transition, as I have argued

---

[1] Arnold van Gennep, *The Rites of Passage* (London: Routledge & Kegan Paul, 1960).

[2] Victor Turner, *The Ritual Process: Structure and Anti-Structure* (New York: Aldine Publishing Company, 1969).

elsewhere.[3] This lens helps us to see phenomena freshly, describing what is already there and suggesting a way to move with the forces in play and not against them. When employed as a hermeneutical method, we peer through the liminal lens and pay close attention to context, social position, narratives and patterns, and universal images and symbols of transformation. In addition to the social sciences, liminal studies now make an important contribution to the various arenas of literature, film, art, education, spirituality, therapeutic models, and organizational change.

Moreover, this present historical moment includes vast social dislocation, collision between cultures and world views, and the simultaneous benefits and harms of technology. All of these are wrapped in an unparalleled ecological crisis. If there exists a broadly shared disorientation in our time, it may be traced to deep liminal sources, and the arts in their many forms are serving in the roles of seers and prophets. If nothing else, pandemics such as that of Covid-19 make made it abundantly clear how an extended liminal time may shape and reshape almost everything.

At our best, we are becoming mindful of the danger and potential of this liminal moment. If existence itself may be characterized as a series of liminal moments, we have become certain that we are living in at least one of them, a liminal moment of outsized intensity. Many are discovering new life-giving communities of the in-between, tribes of the transition. At the same time, we are becoming polarized by the same tribalism, as different alliances spin us ever more to opposite sides of the ring. Only wise liminal guides may assist individuals and groups in traversing such a fearsome landscape as this. These guides are already initiated into the liminal mysteries, having passed through them in one form or the other before. They have discovered the deep wisdom that is to be found within the powerful loop of transition. On those who draw from the deepest places of spirit, our many fates may hang. Like hanging on a great rock wall, we must find our contentment where we are without becoming complacent, without losing track of the pathway that appears as we climb it.

[3.] Timothy Carson, Rosy Fairhurst, Nigel Rooms and Lisa Withrow, *Crossing Thresholds: A Practical Theology of Liminality* (Cambridge: The Lutterworth Press, 2021), pp. 67–68.

The Path of Initiation

Timothy Carson and Suzan Franck

The call to move to a new state of being often comes first in dark whispers: actions that begin to feel empty and staid, and laughter that seems neither as deep nor as joyful. Like a hint of fall that makes an appearance on a late summer's eve, we sense that our energy is beginning to dry up and those tried-and-true ways do not seem to work anymore. No matter how hard we resist the unsettling moments of rising awareness, the verdict becomes unavoidable: the rules and structures that used to hold us securely in place are beginning to crumble.

For many of us, we are first prompted to make a shift by a perplexing sense that something has not been quite right. An invitation beckons from just outside our reach, calling us forward to something we cannot quite put our finger on. Something is trying to happen, but we are not quite certain what it is. Our old ways just do not seem to fit the new self that is wanting to become. The horse we rode in on is beginning to tire; it has taken us as far as possible and is coming to the end of its power. Soon it will be time to mark and mourn its passing. So, we are being asked to cross a threshold,[1] to let go of an old world even before a new one rises to take its place.

[1.] The concept of *threshold* is central to rites of passage and liminality. One crosses out of the structure of the known territory of the past by crossing over a boundary into the unknown territory of the future.

This threshold is the entryway of a process as old as time. It is a process we recognize in our bones, yet perhaps cannot name, especially in the modern world, tamed as it is of all mystery and aliveness. This is the threshold of initiation.[2] Unless we release our grip on the old world, accept the invitation and give our consent to cross this threshold, we shall not move toward a new state of being. This pathway requires more than simply tinkering with the machinery, shoring up the foundations and making adjustments. It comes as the result of entering a powerful process of transformation, and transformations emerge through the sacred process of initiation.

What we usually do not realize early on is that the invitation to let go is also and at the same time an invitation to a new way of being. There is new life on the other side of all initiatory great rites of passage,[3] even if we cannot see or visualize it. Like the caterpillar entering the cocoon, we must first liquify before we feel our emergent wings. That liquid transitional space between worlds – liminal time and space[4] – holds the greatest potential for transformation to a new life of wholeness, one that was not possible before.

As we cross the threshold, entering this liminal space, we die to an old world to make room for the rebirth of a new one. If we are unable to allow this death, we not only delay the process, but also invite additional suffering. We may even begin to feel chased. In dreams, this can show up as pursuit; we are pursued by an emerging reality we cannot outrun, a reality we do not want to face.

[2.] In its social dimension, *initiation* is a process of passage into a deeply held mystery of a tribe or group. It is often accompanied by traditions of passage, rituals, and story-telling. In Jungian thought, initiation is also applied to the inner passage from the ego self into the deeper realms of unconscious life.

[3.] Indigenous societies rely on prescribed *rites of passage* safely to transition people and groups from one actual or symbolic place to a new state of being. Communal rituals mitigate disruption to ongoing life and provide a powerful language of change.

[4.] The Latin word for threshold – *limen* – is the root of the English adjective *liminal* or noun *liminality*. This is the state of being that is betwixt or between, an unknown dimension following the crossing of a threshold which lacks familiar coordinates and structures. The liminal domain is at once full of uncertainty and potential, an in-between time and space in both social and psychological dimensions.

In our waking life, we may try to avoid this encounter with the unknown other than through substance abuse, compulsive work, or just staying busy. We convince ourselves that, if we remain sufficiently distracted, we can avoid the persistent stranger who keeps knocking at our door. Unfortunately, that strategy neither works well nor indefinitely. The interior call to transformation is often so strong that it summons us with or without our permission. With our consent we are certain to enter a most daunting and uncertain journey. Though some will arrive at the longed-for destination, others will start and abort the journey, unable to maintain the rigorous and necessary stamina. They are like Thoreau's oft-quoted "lives of quiet desperation" who choose to die a little every day instead of forging ahead on their unique date with destiny. However, without our consent, the pull to change often emerges unconsciously, in tumultuous ways that are certain to gain our attention.

If we begin to listen and allow for this ending to take place, if we submit to our necessary losses and begin our mourning process, we shall begin to move toward an encounter with a new life-giving reality. Before we get there, however, we must navigate the disorienting challenges of liminal space; and answering the call to cross the threshold into the transitional liminal container requires grace, courage, and no little curiosity.

As we enter this wilderness, this domain of the desert, we find it full of fearsome landscapes, wild beasts, and unanticipated peril. What previously seemed normal no longer works or has become irrelevant. Old tools become useless in the face of new challenges. Former ways of perceiving and understanding dissolve within a dream time that is replete with the most unusual and confounding cast of characters. Perplexing and paradoxical questions arise. Time and our sense of its passage become fluid. Yet, we also discover a realm of deep mystery, filled with its own consolations, strange beauty, sudden epiphanies and enchanted traveling companions.

We are not meant to be alone as we trek through these unknown landscapes. In times past, sojourners were accompanied by a community. Initiated elders escorted pilgrims and helped them to understand the archetypal[5] nature of their experience, walking beside them through the liminal spaces, serving as experienced conversation partners who

---

[5.] Universal *archetypes* are symbolic representations of the deep structures of the collective unconscious. They reveal themselves in dreams, literature, art, and religion and can take the form of characters, stories, and mysterious

interpreted tradition and helped the pilgrims to explore deep questions, fears and aspirations. Sacred mentorship allowed initiates to birth anew into a world transformed, carrying with them the wisdom and new sense of identity they gained from their time in the liminal container.

Though many today do not have these same built-in communal and ritual[6] structures in our secular, industrialized, and technological culture, we nevertheless retain a strong need for them, or at least for their equivalents – inspired and gifted mentors, guides, therapists and advocates who will accompany those who enter the dramatic and ritualized passages of life.

In the broadest sense, this universal arc of passage is five-fold and includes many different aspects within each movement:

Old World → Threshold → Liminal Womb → Rebirth → New World

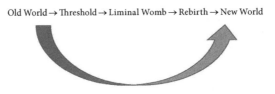

Universal Arc of Passage.
Graphic by Timothy Carson.

Although not taking place in all lives, this journey of initiation has been traversed by millions of people in many different times and places. Though form and cultural particularity may differ, the essential pattern of transformation remains strikingly constant. Whatever ways we choose to describe this time and space – a collapse and remaking of the self, a spiritual awakening, the call of the pilgrim into the wilderness – it remains a recognizable experience, one that has been shared by individuals and collective groups throughout the millennia.

Each person must locate a personal story within this archetypal pattern. Some may find themselves at the beginning of the passage, the first intimations of new thresholds to cross. Others may already be deep

---

symbols. Archetypes are central to Jungian thought and often revealed in the liminal domain.

6. *Rituals* are socially designed dramatic enactments that pass on the wisdom of the group. They are highly symbolic and depend on myths, stories and wisdom teachings. Central to the rites of passage, rituals are frequently employed in sacred ceremonies and provide a non-rational language to express transcendent truths.

into the exploration of the liminal passage. For those well along the road, reflection may provide a retrospective, an exercise of meditation on a journey already taken, with new thoughts of mentoring others.

The epic journey we enter often requires relinquishing our analytical ways of thinking. It requires entrance into an internal, enchanted mythic world rich with sacred spaces, artifacts, story, drama, dance, music, and ritual. If we can open ourselves to other ways of knowing, we often sense the beckoning aliveness and new energy that mysteriously fills our awakening consciousness. We cast off from shore, wind-filled sails pulling us toward the open sea and worlds of as yet unknown possibility.

* * *

This archetypal journey of initiation has manifested itself in the sacred stories of many traditions, such as from the three following myths of initiation.

Jonah and His Watery Passage

The short, enigmatic story of Jonah describes one of several biblical watery passages and introduces us to a man who is running from his destiny. Jonah is engaged in the greatest absurdity, the attempt to flee from the all-present God. Instead of going as instructed to Nineveh, he flees in the opposite direction, making a water crossing. In the midst of this watery flight, a storm arises. The crew is petrified and the sailors pray to their gods; but Jonah knows that the storm is for him. Realizing he can evade the force of the deeps no longer, he volunteers to go overboard. The stormy weather of his subconscious has prevailed; he is propelled into the sacred deeps.

Jonah is swallowed up by a great fish where he simmers in its belly for three days. This is Jonah's womb, cocoon, and alchemical vessel. From this place of despair, desire, and longing, he prays and is united with his deeper nature, with the transcendent. After three days he is unceremoniously spat up on the shore where his journey began.

It has been said that everything that goes around, comes around, and so it does for Jonah. He has passed through the watery birth canal and is reborn into a place he used to be, the same place, though a different person. He still has much to learn as he surrenders ego to transcendent truth, and the story leaves us with a man who is far from perfect. However, he has crossed over. There is no going back.

As Avivah Zornberg puts it, "He has been a small figure, overwhelmed by gigantic forces, a child who shrinks to fetal size as he withdraws into his stupor in the ship's hold. Now, for the first time, he experiences great forces *within* him.... He powerfully describes the experience of drowning, of the downward plunge to the depths of the sea, and he thanks God for restoring him to life.... These are the inner depths that God desires: hard to reach, obscure, alive with currents and crosscurrents. Crying from this place of frailty, [the human being] transforms pain into intimacy with God. From the depths of his heart, Jonah cries to God of his dis-ease."[7]

Every unfolding watery birth requires some sort of dying on the way to rebirth, a releasing of the former world that defined us, overcoming the resistance fueled by attachment to old certainties, passing through the womb that carries us to new life, awakening consciousness and our very own next calling.

The womb of transformation receives and transports the one who surrenders to its liminal passageway. Whereas external physical landmarks may remain the same, the interior space of the psyche has shifted, reoriented, and the self is positioned differently in relationship to the demands of conscious life, seeing them differently.

Inanna and Her Descent and Rebirth

Yet another image of death and transformation through initiation is found in the ancient Sumerian story of Inanna, Queen of Heaven.[8] Inanna decides to leave the heavens to visit her sister Erishkegal in the underworld. Knowing that this descent could prove dangerous, she alerts her faithful servant Ninshubar to seek help if she does not return. Encountering the gatekeeper to the underworld, Inanna finds that, in order to make the descent, she must pass through seven gates, submitting a piece of her royal garment at each, thus arriving at her sister's throne room naked and vulnerable. Erishkegal is furious, and Inanna is judged and found wanting. In her impotent state she is turned into a corpse and hung on a meat hook.

---

7. Avivah Gottlieb Zornberg, *The Murmuring Deep: Reflections on the Biblical Unconscious* (New York: Schocken Books, 2009), pp. 80, 93, 104.

8. Sylvia Brinton Perera, *Descent to the Goddess: A Way of Initiation for Women* (Toronto: Inner City Books, 1981).

After three days and three nights, Ninshubar, realizing Inanna is not coming back, enlists the assistance of the god Enki in securing Inanna's return. Enki then fashions two sexless beings from the dirt under his fingernails and they witness Erishkegal moaning, as though in labor. Erishkegal is moved by this empathetic witness and grants them a boon. They take the opportunity to set Inanna free. As with any good myth, however, there is a catch. Inanna must secure a replacement. Inanna considers her followers, but all of them are faithfully mourning her passing. It is only when she stumbles upon her consort Dumuzi, seemingly unconcerned with her supposed death, that she realizes she has found her replacement. Dumuzi, sentenced to the underworld, is spared in part when his sister agrees to split the year with him, sharing his sentence in the underworld.

This tale is quite similar to the later Greek story of Persephone, who is captured by Hades and pulled into the underworld, except in one respect: Inanna chooses to enter the underworld. Because this choice is voluntary, our protagonist can now bring consciousness into the process. Inanna takes precautions (Ninshubar is conscripted) as she makes preparations for the dangerous journey to visit her dark sister.

Few examples of voluntary initiation exist in our modern world, averse as it is to darkness and death, both literal and metaphorical, but many exist in indigenous cultures. In these cultures, more connected to the earth and its cycles, it is known that with death comes new life. Whether it is the piercing of the chests in the Lakota sun dance, the separation and fasting in vision quests, or the literal sickness and purging that follows the ingestion of ayahuasca or other entheogens, voluntary descents often include an element of danger, pain and at least a metaphorical death. Thus, a preparation is necessary. One crosses the initiatory threshold with a sense of reverence, acknowledging the potency of such a journey.

One example in modern culture is undertaking the voluntary descent into a deep psychological process with an analyst. Feeling the old life no longer working, we can feel called to explore in ways that often unravel the threads before they are rewoven together. Moreover, if we are to enter such a process with a knowledge of its initiatory nature, it behooves us to take great care in the selection of the person who, like Ninshubar, will be there to call the Gods if we do not return.

So, like Inanna, we go down, gate by gate, removing the items that display our power in the upper world. We cannot remain defended if we are to open ourselves to being fundamentally changed. We must disrobe, one garment at a time, in order to allow for the vulnerability that invites transformation. It is the death of the old that paves the way for the rebirth and resurrection that is already unfolding. The ability to bear witness and bring compassion to our very own suffering brings with it a renewed wellness that allows us to leave the underworld for good. As in the myth, however, parts of us remain forever in that lower world. Our waking consciousness thus has attained a new balance and with it a fuller awareness of both the upper and lower worlds. This is also the price paid and gift received on the next leg of the path of initiation.

The Conference of Birds

A final allegory of ritual awakening through a rite of passage comes from a little-known tale about an auspicious conference of birds. Around 1177 CE, the Sufi mystic Farid ud-Din Attar wrote an extended narrative about 1,000 birds of all kinds who were challenged by a great bird prophet to engage in a life and death pilgrimage through seven realms to find the sacred Simurgh, the mythical sovereign.[9] This was part of a larger cycle of spiritual instruction.

Many make excuses to avoid the perils of the journey. Many others perish along the way or give up from exhaustion or disillusionment. In the end, only 30 birds prevail and arrive at the great threshold of the Mystery. After pleading with an angelic gatekeeper to allow them inside the great sanctuary, the holy of holies, they are finally admitted. The light of the throne is so bright they can barely look into it. A scroll drops out of the glory at their feet and it reveals the half-forgotten story of each traveler's life in an instant. When they dare look again into the blaze of the throne, they behold an unimaginable surprise, an eternal mirror:

> *And in the Centre of the Glory there*
> *Beheld the Figure of – Themselves – as 'twere*
> *Transfigured – looking to Themselves, beheld*
> *The Figure on the Throne en-miracled ...*[10]

[9.] Farid ud-Din Attar, *The Conference of Birds*, trans. Afkham Darbandi and Dick Davis (Auckland, New Zealand: Aziloth Books, 2011).

[10.] Ibid.

As they gaze into the mirror, they behold the visage of themselves, searchers of a Mystery they carried all along. Only a perilous quest to the sacred center allowed them to discover that which they possessed all the time, a reflection of self, divinity within.

Like the journey of Dorothy and her companions to the magical land of Oz, whose encounter with the Wizard is also an encounter with themselves, they are informed that they already possess that which they sought. It is the necessary journey, however, that reveals what has been hidden.

This rite of initiation requires separating from the structure of the familiar and known and embarking on an uncertain and even perilous journey. Not everyone is willing to surrender to such a quest and, when that person is unwilling, he or she often finds him- or herself stuck and distracted from the great call of life. Those who do let go and cross the threshold into the great womb of transformation, however, find themselves shedding the skins of old ways by degree. By the end of the journey their feathers have been lost and lesser preoccupations abandoned. All that remains is the object of the pilgrimage, the destination of their longing.

What is found, of course, are sacred aspects that have been hidden from normal perception. The journey has shifted the consciousness of those who search. They have descended from the shallows of consciousness into the deep end of the unconscious pool, to a mystery beyond their own personal unconscious; and at the center of the sacred labyrinth is a reflection of the holiness that permeates every creature who will see: I am what I see.

Conclusion

Our story began with a call, a summons, to move from the shallows of the present way of things, the old world, across a threshold into deeper, riskier and transitional waters. The liminal container into which the initiated fall holds danger and surprising truth, a kind of truth unavailable in the old world. This process of initiation requires a metaphorical death and rebirth, one that is often resisted. However, without a perilous journey, we shall never find the new level of being that we secretly long for.

Initiates are best accompanied by wise mentors, liminal guides, and communities who escort them through the wilderness and its accompanying mysteries. Liminal time is dream and story time, a realm that includes new language, rituals, and imagery. That is why it is often best expressed through the truth-telling tales of the great world traditions.

Like Jonah, we flee the dangerous call that is ours, only to find ourselves swimming in the currents of the unconscious womb which remake us for a greater destiny. Like Inanna, our death and rebirth require passing through multiple thresholds, releasing our defenses, exposing our nakedness, and transforming by way of empathetic witness. And, like the pilgrim birds, the perils through which we pass refine us, leaving the bravest and deepest parts to encounter the light which we have carried all along.

The destination of this sacred journey is the deepest well to which we could have traveled, the result of total immersion, birthing, dying, and rebirthing in the womb that holds us all.

Wayfinding to Freedom

Lisa R. Withrow

Prospective Immigrants Please Note

Prospective Immigrants Please Note
Either you will
go through this door
or you will not go through.
If you go through
there is always the risk
of remembering your name.
Things look at you doubly
and you must look back
and let them happen.
If you do not go through
it is possible
to live worthily
to maintain your attitudes
to hold your position
to die bravely
but much will blind you,
much will evade you,
at what cost who knows?
The door itself makes no promises.
It is only a door.

– Adrienne Rich

Each of us is on a journey through this life, encountering doors at particular intervals on the path. In some ways, we are all immigrants, wayfaring into new territory as we evolve personally and collectively. The doors we face allow for choices – is this the right one, or do we move on to the next? We can never be sure. Indeed, Adrienne Rich's door makes no promises. If we move through the door into an unknown space, carrying with us what we have learned before proceeding, we are on high alert for what we might encounter. Some choose to turn away from the door, others decide to move forward; but most of us now have been thrust through the door into liminal space on a global scale as we recount the pandemic times. How we travel determines how we come out the other side.

The phrase "liminal space" has found its way into common parlance worldwide through the many months of living in the Covid-19 pandemic. Huge populations found themselves forced to let go of "normal" life in the workplace, school, and home without a clear sense of what post-pandemic life might look like in each of those realms. The entire world felt "in-between" the past and future. Some welcomed the change, perhaps yearned for it, and ran toward innovative living and working despite various public health restrictions. Others held back or resisted, hesitant to encounter a strange and dangerous space. Still others had a forced choice between continuing on-site work that was likely to expose them to the Covid-19 virus and inability to pay rent and bills if they took leave for safety reasons. Some decided to hold the anticipation of a different kind of future and fear of change in tension, waiting to see what unfolded. Whatever the approach, we all are still learning and shall continue to learn how to walk again through difficult terrain, one step at a time, into what is emerging on the horizon. There are as many opinions about the quality of that future as there are human beings in the world; nevertheless, we must keep walking.

Those of us who choose to look toward a new emergence with a willingness to depart from old norms and expectations that became destructive (always rushing, efficient performance at the cost of sleep, giving away life for work, living in destructive personal mental prisons of our own creation, environmental destruction) find that difficult times invite self-reflection about what is essential for living a meaningful life. It is in the choice to dwell intentionally in liminal space, where the acts of "letting-go and letting-come"[1] evolve, that we initiate a threshold

---

[1.] See Otto C. Scharmer, *The Essentials of Theory U: Core Principles and Applications* (Oakland, CA: Berrett-Koehler Publishers, Inc., 2008), pp. 103–106.

of deep work fostered by uncertainty. During this transition time, we meander into questions of significant importance, discarding what no longer is true for us while yearning for what brings a new depth of meaning to our lives. This liminal path spirals through a variety of thoughts and images; we choose or choose not to pay attention to what rises in our awareness.

Liminal space is threshold space, often a path into the wilderness without a map. The trail is visible at times during the trek and all-but-covered at other times, requiring an intuition or sensing about when to move and when to stop and notice surroundings. This journey holds both adventures and different kinds of dangers. Some of these dangers bring us to a full-stop, stuck in space that harms us. Other dangers are part-and-parcel of deep transitional work, which ultimately lead to a new kind of freedom. The former danger, stuckness, can lead to permanent distress or destruction. The latter, dangers of deep work, are essential for growth, and may evoke distress, but with a promise of something new unfolding on our paths. Ultimately, to traverse these paths well, it is important to have wise, committed accompaniment while wayfinding to avoid stuckness and negotiate other dangers we may encounter.

Closed Systems – Stuckness

Those who study systems, such as organizational behaviors, environmental cycles, or biological flows, understand that there are open, semi-open, and closed systems. Closed systems rely almost entirely on themselves, generating their own energy or beliefs with little input from external sources and little output to systems outside their own impermeable boundaries. In biological terms, a closed system has an impermeable membrane, unable to take in nourishment or expel waste. Open systems have permeable membranes, taking in information or nourishment from external sources and exchanging their own information or nourishment with these sources, while keeping a boundary to hold in what they need and guard against what they do not. For example, the carbon dioxide-oxygen exchange of plants and animals is one way to think about an open, symbiotic system that nourishes self by taking in just the right amount of what it needs and expelling what is useful to the other. This exchange creates a system where nothing is wasted and both plants and animals benefit. Semi-open systems occur when there is an element of stress present, where the exchange of information or nourishment flows with greater volume in one direction than the other;

the attempt is to re-equilibrate or re-create balance but, in the moment, stress inhibits flow in one direction. For example, when countries are at war, foreign information may flow into internal command centers, but responses are kept secret; information does not flow outward. In the end, long-term, chronic stressors often lead to a system closing. Cancer cells show this process of moving from health, to relative unhealthiness, to closed systems that eventually starve the body of healing capabilities. The same holds true for organizations that pay attention only to their internal messaging without engaging external stakeholders – their work soon becomes irrelevant to the outside world.

Liminal space can be fostered as an open (full internal-external movement), semi-open (protective but still allowing some movement at least in one direction) or closed (only internal movement) system. If closed, the space no longer can be liminal; a stuckness occurs that becomes a permanent dwelling space unless a new disruption to the system presents itself. After all, as Adrienne Rich says, entering the threshold is walking through a door, but it makes no promises; so, getting stuck in the doorframe is always possible if we are not intentional about liminal wayfinding. Such an inability to move through liminal space, getting stuck in one place on the path, can occur for several reasons, ranging from communal cultural choices about how we encounter grief and pain to how we personally choose to face challenge and difficulty.

First, we in the West have a cultural tendency to avoid deep grief work. We "allow" grief for a short time, especially with the loss of loved ones or in situations of natural disaster, but there is pressure to "get over it" and "move on" pretty quickly. The time and space necessary for grief work differs from person to person, but social acceptance of a longer-term cycle of grief remains low. Deep griefs of generational trauma resulting from ongoing hate speech/acts against races and genders are all but invisible to the wider, dominant-culture society and little understood. Further, a series of personal traumas or losses occurring for an individual, family, or organization, built up over a long period of time without safe grief expression, are buried. Compounded grief rises again each time a new loss or vicarious trauma occurs, only to be buried on top of the other feelings already percolating beneath the surface. In time, ungrieved grief can be debilitating emotionally, then physically, without a sense of being able to move forward – individuals, groups, and organizations become captive in what should have been a liminal space of grief and cannot heal. In time, our permeable, flexible systems begin to close and decisions automatically become reactive, based on the internal, subverted grief that drives us.

Second, closely related to buried grief, is an addiction to seeking personal peacefulness and harmony without tending to the discomfort of difficult feelings, bringing us into a disconnected, trance-like way of being in the world. Peace and harmony are essential for well-being, but the industry that promotes these to the exclusion of dealing with inner work can preclude deepening maturity, which again renders us stuck. An *exclusive* focus on creating a happy interior privatizes our spiritual work and can anaesthetize us from the pain in ourselves and experienced by others.

To deal with our painful feelings well, we need community, whether it be caring people surrounding us, the community of nature, or even the collective unconscious or sense of ancestors accompanying us. Indigenous wisdom traditions know that emotional maturing (become true adults) cannot occur without the collective.

Healthy mindfulness practices pay attention to the discomfort as well as the comfort in our lives with a balance of engagement and detachment; however, disassociating from all things negative or hurtful and calling this disconnection "mindfulness" is a subtle path toward stuckness. This dissociation is a way of polarizing oneself, closing one's own system to the rest of the world, contrary to our deeper need for community as we grow.

Third, there are tricksters among us. Unfortunately, we might not recognize them or be attuned to their intentions. The trickster archetype appears in mythologies and stories throughout the ages, including the snake in the Garden of Eden in Judeo-Christian tradition and the wolf in the fairy tale, *Little Red Riding Hood*. Some cultures have gods[2] associated with characteristics of the trickster: forward-thinking strategy to achieve certain outcomes, a cunning intelligence that "reads" situations and people well, and a propensity for mischief and deceit with self-serving intent.

Modern-day tricksters invite us to change in a way that looks very helpful to us, guaranteeing a positive outcome. Often this goal is one that the trickster knows we already want, such as belonging to a close-knit community of like-minded people, safety, certainty, greatness, or non-stop adventure. The trickster invites us to move into what looks like liminal space, where we break from our past and adopt a path toward what *appears* to be a promising future. However, the trickster controls

---

[2] For example, the Polynesian god Kaulu, the African god Esu, and the Pacific-Northwest Native American god Blue-Jay.

this future rather than inviting us to discover what is emerging. We are asked, if not obliquely coerced, into forgoing past rituals to form new ones that serve the trickster's purposes. While liminal space does indeed call for new rituals (addressed in another chapter), in this case the trickster is the leader of rituals that often are hypnotic (constantly repeated words or slogans), cult-like (we are to become all alike for our success), and anaesthetizing (don't pay attention to anything external; pay attention to what I am telling you to think – it's for your own good). We have unwittingly entered a closed system. Personal identity becomes hostage to the trickster's power and control and, as a result, we cannot move through liminal space without significant, often painful, intervention and disruption. In fact, people who leave cults or other closed systems find it very difficult to shift back into open systems again and may not have the capacity to do so without a great deal of support.

Fundamentalist religion, extremist politics, colonizing mindsets, cults of any sort, and patriarchal control over defining "correct" body images and racial or gender-based behaviors all fall into this immovable state of being. For example, think of a polarized society. Each pole has a self-righteous quality to its purpose and messaging. Each side wants change – either to a prescribed new reality or back to what is perceived as a good, old reality. Internal grief work, either focused on loss of potential, because change is not happening quickly enough to alleviate problems, or loss of what used to seem like a good life, is neglected. Instead, entrenchment into certainty about what is right and wrong for the future becomes extreme – two closed systems battling each other. In the middle, there are two other events occurring. One is paralysis, a stuckness that keeps people from making any decisions at all. The other is a successful holding of the tension between the poles, where liminal space includes the co-creation and gestation of a positive, emerging future despite high pressure from each extreme. The path (threshold space) between the poles is what might be called "Third Space." It takes resilience, fortitude, flexibility, and community support to hold such space.

The desire to lose the difficult, uncomfortable tension is where the liminal journey gets derailed, and people capitulate to "going back to normal" or to a trickster who shows up. And one will. Tricksters surface quickly and publicly when liminal dwelling is forced and widespread. People who succumb to the trickster no longer live "in between." They become polarized, stuck in a new life where liminal wayfinding falls away; they are complacent and compliant, not dealing with grief or disorientation inherent in a healthy liminal journey. In other words, their new normal cannot be penetrated; they cannot move forward, and they entrench in their "rightness." There is no Third Space, and the system closes.

Fourth and finally, if we are forced into liminality by unexpected, sometimes tragic circumstances, we may freeze, flee, or fight. Shock automatically sends us into our prehistoric, survival-based limbic system where our innate self-protective reactions are triggered. One of these three reactions is completely normal when we are threatened. When we stay too long in the limbic reactivity rather than easing up and looking around at our new circumstances or space, we block ourselves from traversing further into the unknown. I suspect that we all know our own typical reactions or have observed people who repeatedly try to become invisible (freeze), avoid conflict (flee), or behave belligerently (fight) when stressors arise. They may be reacting to trauma that occurred in the past, but they have not altered their way of being in the world from that first trauma reaction. Or they simply learned how to feel safer when employing one of these habitual reactions and do not think about possible alternatives when conflict comes knocking. Therefore, this automated response prevents them from growing deeper, becoming increasingly free people through liminal journeying; they do not know how (or are not willing) to move forward. Their fear has metastasized into chronic, often unexamined reactivity and self-protection, symptomatic of stuckness.

In liminal space, we can become stuck when we are overcome by that which we do not understand, when we undervalue or overvalue the experience, or when we are injured or threatened beyond our capacity to cope. To move through it without being caught by these dangers, we simply express what we are learning in the midst of community, perhaps in symbols, song, art, and thanksgiving as new awareness emerges. From this awareness, we learn our next step, which may bring us to a different kind of danger, one that is helpful to our formation.

Open Systems – Freedom

Dwelling in liminal space is in itself a scary prospect. Disorientation and disconnection from habits, norms, and belief systems can manifest with uneasiness and, more often, fear. If we cannot see the end point of the transition, we experience stronger disorientation than if we have an inkling about what is on the horizon. Either way, to re-orient ourselves, we need to slow down, look around at this new space and, if possible, find some degree of familiarity as our anchor. Of course, the more grounded a person is in community, the easier it is to anchor in the midst of stormy chaos. However, in some situations, there is no anchor. Our past does not help us. Our families resist our change. Our peers think we are crazy. In these cases, we need to rely on imagination rather than succumb to negative messaging and/or a debilitating level of fear.

Having said that, let's pause for a moment to think about embracing fear as one aspect of journeying through liminal space by facing dangers well. Acknowledging our fear without succumbing completely to it (freeze, flee, fight) is essential in order to deepen our interior lives and our communal connections. Experiencing fear tells us that something significant is happening. Our focus is not to eliminate fear by trying to create comfort, but to choose to face it and walk through it. It is at this decision point that courage is born and, with it, the will to move forward. As we move through fear, we develop a greater sense of confidence that we shall survive. With such confidence, we may be free to look around this liminal space and find some very interesting thoughts, images, ideas, and adventures. We may even invite wise people to accompany us, or notice others walking a path that crosses with ours.

This new path, if we face forward taking only what we need for the journey, has the capacity to teach us about meaningful living. We ask important questions: What really matters? What is life-giving and worthwhile pursuing? What gets in my way? What/who needs to be let go? What does grief teach me? What adventure and experiments might be interesting? Who do I choose to be in this world? What does my imagination require of me? How do I connect with others deeply? All these questions and more rise in us as we transition from the past to the future through the threshold of letting go and letting come.

Use of imagination about the future – an imaginary – helps us navigate uncertainty and disorientation as we journey toward our deeper selves, inviting us to try on a new identity or way of being in the world. The ways we experiment with our choices and identities connect with a necessary feedback loop, found in community. We learn what is connective and what is isolating. We learn who supports us and who wants us to change back to the old Self for their own comfort. We learn to foster our permeable membrane so that it is life-giving in two directions. In other words, community holds us in the face-to-face connection like a safety net. Here, we are invited to find our courage because we know that, with community, we have witnesses for our journey even as we witness ourselves. Likewise, if we are traveling with companions, we are witnesses for them. It is in the witnessing, the seeing and being seen, that we form *communitas*, an equitable and kind community of co-travelers in liminality. If we stumble on the journey, participants in *communitas* tighten the holding space until we are on our feet again; then the hold loosens. We begin to build stamina for the uncertainty, walk through fear, and face an emerging future with greater curiosity. We can move forward because we are *held* in connected presence together, immersed in imagination, held by *communitas*, and are called to be courageous to be open to our own vulnerability so that the Spirit or Source can move within us.

As a global example of invitation to *communitas* for the journey, I am instructed by indigenous leaders in Australia who are naming the current, destructive state of the world an opportunity to reclaim our true humanity. In a 2020 online seminar that addressed the dire state of planetary ecosystems, one of these leaders, Noel Nannup, said that the ancestral drums are beating to call us back to the hearth fire, the place where we once again connect as community with ancestors, nature, dwelling spaces, our loving compassion for the world, and our true, human Selves. We are invited to descend steadily ("steady, steady," he said) and deeply back into our true Selves at this crucial time of planetary destruction and illness.[3] To do so requires that we cross the threshold into liminal space, deepening and widening our awareness of all the gifts and wisdom from the ages, laid at our feet. These leaders and other religious practitioners know that meaningful, well-practiced holding of community is what calls us both back and forward, anchoring us in long-held tradition in ways that, paradoxically, invite us into the future. They are experts at holding this tension for human movement into our best Selves.

This notion of holding in *communitas* surfaces in many other places. For example, Croatian-born theologian Miroslav Volf offers a description of being held, quite literally, in his four movements of a hug. His work counters exclusion and hatred of the other (and I would add polarization based on fear) with the invitation to embrace as an act of human reconciliation rather than relying on social systems to lead to greater connection. Likewise, countering stuckness in entrenched beliefs that cause us to step back from the threshold of transition requires these four movements. Volf describes these movements this way:

[3.] Noel Nannup, "A Piece of the Path," Gaia Journey webinar, Presencing Institute Global Forum, 9–11 July 2020, http://www.presencing.org/gaia (accessed 9–11 July 2020).

The four structural elements of the movement of embrace are
opening the arms, waiting, closing the arms, and opening
them again. For embrace to happen, all four must be there
and they must follow one another on an unbroken timeline;
stopping with the first two (opening the arms and waiting)
would abort the embrace, and stopping with the third (closing
the arms) would pervert it from an act of love to an act of
oppression and, paradoxically, exclusion. The four elements
are then the four essential steps of an integrated movement.[4]

Arguably, an embrace, figurative or literal, is an act that strengthens
connections. Volf details why these movements matter; they indeed
create an anchor in the midst of liminality. For example, opening the
arms is a reaching for or a desire for another, a desire to open a closed
space of self or personal identity (closed system) to create space for
another person, thought, or belief (open system). A permeable boundary
presents itself as invitation. Waiting with open arms as invitation
honors the boundary of the other without coercion or manipulation,
with hope of reciprocation so that each enters the space of the other.
Closing the arms mingles the presence of each equally felt in a two-sided
"soft touch" that does not seek to dominate. Finally, opening the arms
again allows for the preservation of identity in each person (thought,
belief) while having offered and been offered part of each Self, and a
shift or change has occurred in relationship.[5] Such is the building block
of *communitas* for the journey.

This metaphor for traversing liminal space is important for the
necessity to anchor oneself, to be held well, and, at the same time,
to invite companions for the journey. Embracing the unknown,
the different, perhaps the unthinkable or unimaginable in extreme
situations, requires an actual movement of mind, body, or both toward
an emerging future without complete loss of Self (anchored in what we
know). The embrace is one way to think about the integrity of our being,
held for us and within us, as we journey into the threshold between past
and future with open minds and hearts.

[4.] Miroslav Volf, *Exclusion and Embrace: A Theological Exploration of Identity,
Otherness, and Reconciliation* (Nashville, TN: Abingdon Press, 1996), p. 141.

[5.] Ibid., pp. 141–47.

I have often encountered situations in my life in which I have sought to claim freedom *from* something or someone – relationships, sick systems, and beliefs – that bound me too tightly, and freedom *to* move toward something or someone – life-giving people and learning postures – as I strive to contribute well to the world. For me, freedom is the opposite of stuckness, the cages that we build in our minds and spirits or choose to inhabit with our bodies. I acknowledge that, for some, freedom of body and mind are not possible, particularly those whose bodies and minds are controlled by others. For others of us, we often create our own mental maps that hold us hostage: negative messaging absorbed from our society or context; repeated focus on failure; self-berating; staying in jobs that are destroying our health; staying in relationships that cause us to live in reactivity all the time; or hearing the negative tapes in our minds planted long ago.

As discussed, to travel through liminal space is to dwell with disorientation and sometimes danger. The danger of stuckness is always a possibility but, if not stuck, there are other fearsome dangers we encounter such as grief, resistances, failures, misinterpretations, losses of old relationships or old belief systems, and rejections. Even so, if we travel faithfully and with companions guiding or holding us, despite our fears we shall find our inner courageous warrior, meeting the other dangers directly and living into our courage for what is coming to us. The point is not to be free of fear, but to be free of that which binds us to fear and creates the stuck place. Freedom to choose who we wish to become, what we pay attention to, and how we go about that journey is the greatest freedom of all.

On the search for freedom to become what we are called to be, we travel along paths that take us deep into our dangerous inner messaging. Freedom often requires a rebellion at some level, a resounding "no" to unwarranted expectations conjured from habits, inner voices, or outer pressures. As a result, the danger rears its head; we shall no longer fit into our culture, our tribe, our family, or our group. We may have to say good-bye. Further, with the pursuit of freedom comes the knowledge that a battle may be forthcoming. So at the crux of our choice to move into liminal space toward new freedom or regress into the safety of the known is integrity, the sense that our exterior and interior lives match and are consistent. For example, if a person speaks about honesty and transparency and quietly embezzles money to become astronomically rich, he or she lives in irreconcilable incongruity that eventually turns into cover-ups and lying, which in turn carries him or her into a stuck state of dishonesty and polarized persona. Emotional life begins to shut down until there is no more room in the closed container. Many people who choose to be dishonest finally make what almost seems like a deliberate mistake so that they are caught; they cannot live with the pressure of an inner self at odds with an outer façade. Others shut down one part of themselves, justifying their actions and creating a new, secretive mental map that walls off the voice calling for integrity (unless they live with pathologies such as narcissism, or personality disorders where voice never surfaces). They close their own system, attempting to pursue what they perceive they want.

One might argue that choosing freedom to live wholly is a privileged or advantaged option. Having traveled the world and spoken with people living in deep poverty, I would disagree. The economically and politically marginalized certainly live with disadvantage. However, they may foster a mindset that sets them free. The Shackdwellers Association, an organized group of women living in a township in Namibia, told me that they were not interested in being victims, waiting for the government, post-apartheid, to bring them running water or basic services. They, as *communitas*, created their own cottage industry and made a living to support their families and their surrounding community. They were pleased to show me their fine work, and they had deeply moving and sometimes highly amusing stories to tell about life in the township. They were not materially free, but they were mentally and spiritually free, both of apartheid scars and the victimhood mindset that stays frozen, disconnected, or perpetually violent. They lived a life of integrity and were able to advance their community because of it. In that sense, they rebelled against expectations more prosperous people hold of people coping with poverty: the classic projection, "they're happy because they don't know anything else." The freedom these women fostered in themselves invited others into it; there was a clear sense of *communitas* in that township. In contrast, some of the most advantaged, prosperous people in the world are not emotionally, mentally, or spiritually free – they are not whole.

French philosopher Albert Camus once said, "The only way to deal with an unfree world is to become so absolutely free that your very existence is an act of rebellion."[6] This journey to freedom is our inner work in liminal space. The path is rocky and treacherous at times as we let go of old handholds and cannot quite see around the next corner,

---

[6.] Albert Camus Quotes, BrainyQuote, http://www.brainyquote.com (accessed 2 April 2021).

but even with rest stops along the way, we must keep moving toward what is ahead of us. We prepare as best we can. We keep moving toward what is ahead of us. Our *communitas* holds out its hand to help us on the path.

What We Know

So, here is what we know. Adrienne Rich tells us that the door into liminal space makes no promises. There is uncertainty and perhaps pain in that doorway to deeper space. We often have the fortune of choosing whether we walk through, and many choose not to do so. Sometimes we are pushed through if we wait too long or if we encounter unexpected change. We know that liminal space can be traversed, or it can render us stuck. If we choose wise companions to hold us and accompany us, and if we face our fears with courageous small steps forward, we know that we shall find the handholds as they appear along the pathway. We know we can let go to make space for what is yet to come. We grieve honestly and deeply. We watch the horizon closely. There are no promises except one: if we walk with intention, we shall be surprised. In our surprise, we choose who we shall become as we re-enter our hearth fires, changed and ready for our work.

Indeed, the second, third, fourth time we move into or are thrust through to liminal space, we shall have a better sense of the journey itself. We pay attention differently. We discover some familiar uncertainty. We know that dwelling there is temporal and that there will be movement. Finally, over time, we too may become wise companions as others walk their journeys. The cycle continues as we evolve into the best of whom we are called to be, immersing in liminality as a natural part of initiation into ever-deepening wisdom and integrity.

Clarissa Pinkola Estés, author of *Women Who Run With the Wolves* (1992), is a *cantadora* story-teller[7] and Jungian analyst. In her now-classic book, she focuses on the Wild Woman archetype, moving deeply into the liminal space of the psycho-spiritual journey toward

---

[7.] *Cantadora* story-tellers hand down wisdom stories from the ancestors, often leaving space in the telling for the presence of forebears to be acknowledged in the story-telling circle.

deep inner knowing. One of her short wisdom stories taken from the Jewish tradition illustrates the choices we make to stay stuck or move to freedom when we move into liminal space:

> One night four Rabbinim were visited by an angel who awakened them and carried them to the Seventh Vault of the Seventh Heaven. There they beheld the sacred Wheel of Ezekiel.
>
> Somewhere in the descent from *Pardes*, Paradise, to Earth, one Rabbi having seen such splendor, lost his mind and wandered frothing and foaming until the end of his days. The second Rabbi was extremely cynical: "Oh I just dreamed Ezekiel's Wheel, that was all. Nothing *really* happened." The third Rabbi carried on and on about what he had seen, for he was totally obsessed. He lectured and would not stop with how it was all constructed and what it all meant … and in this way he went astray and betrayed his faith. The fourth Rabbi, who was a poet, took a paper in hand and a reed and sat near the window writing song after song praising the evening dove, his daughter in her cradle, and all the stars in the sky. And he lived his life better than before.[8]

The choice for stuckness or freedom is before us.

---

8. Clarissa Pinkola Estés, *Women Who Run With the Wolves: Myths and Stories of the Wild Woman Archetype* (New York: Ballantine Books, 1992), p. 32.

Liminality and the Event

Jonathan Best

Liminality is an enticing word, one full of potential and mystery, but also fraught with the real-world pains of transition and transformation. It is hard to characterize and describe, especially academically, as it seems to resist the parameters that a textbook definition might offer. The best teachers and explainers of liminality are generally not philosophers and other academics, but normal everyday people caught up within the transitional "stuff" of everyday life. Of course, this places me in an odd and paradoxical place. How does one write about something that is best learned from experience? We typically come up short when describing meaningful and life-changing phenomena, especially so in the case of liminality, which can evoke simultaneous feelings of clarity, confusion, and frustration. Yet, it is this very quality of indefinability that makes liminality so appealing. We usually play catch-up when it comes to portraying liminality, giving words to an experience we come to see as liminal, "after the fact," so to speak. However, meaningful phenomena incite the imagination in important and sometimes clarifying ways. The search for an adequate description of or, rather, response to liminality is part of the journey of discovery.

Liminality's experiential nature means that it is both individual and communal. It is individual in the sense that every liminal experience is unique, communal in that we all share in life-changing transitions of some sort. Bjørn Thomassen states that: "Liminality is a universal concept: cultures and human lives cannot exist without moments of transitions, and those brief and important spaces where we live through the in-between."[1] He continues:

> Liminality is both social and personal. Liminality reminds us of the moment we left our parents' home, that mixture of joy and anxiety, that strange combination of freedom and homelessness; that pleasant but unsettling sensation of infinity and openness of possibilities which – at some moment, sooner or later – will start searching for a new frame to settle within. And if it does not, the void will perpetuate, and anxiety with it ... endless liminality.[2]

The liminal experience comprises more than just the feeling of being in-between, however. The search for words, ideas, and imagery to describe the liminal state means that liminality remains relevant long after the event. Moreover, in the case of "endless liminality," as described by Thomassen, liminal effects become a general state of being which blurs the lines of one's experience in and out of liminality, *being-liminal* if you will, which haunts us during and after the liminal experience. Liminality does not just linger; it is perpetual. As Michelle Trebilcock describes it, "When there is no demarcation of a pre-liminal and post-liminal experience, there is no journey from one world-of-life to the next, and therefore no progression, no growth, no maturation for the individual in terms of his or her relationships."[3] Liminality spooks us, surprises us with new emotional battles, unearths old mental wounds, and exhausts us with the aftershocks of transition and change.

We cannot forget that liminality exacts an enormous emotional, mental, and even spiritual toll, one distinctively and uniquely generated from crossing a threshold and enduring a transitional time of flux, uncertainty, and insecurity. Recognizing the transitions and reacting to them in a way that is positive, constructive, and hopeful is vital.

[1.] Bjørn Thomassen, *Liminality and the Modern: Living Through the In-Between* (New York: Routledge, 2018), p. 4.

[2.] Ibid.

[3.] Michelle Trebilcock, "Hope in a Dark Passage," in Timothy Carson (ed.), *Neither Here nor There: The Many Voices of Liminality* (Cambridge: The Lutterworth Press, 2019), p. 62.

Liminality, at both the individual and communal levels, represents important moments for study, understanding, and clarity as to who we are and what we might become. Liminality, in all its stages (pre-liminal, liminal, post-liminal) necessitates our questions and searches, including space for exploring the fear and anger that such a liminal experience might have incited within us. That being said, it is important to also remember that on its own, "Liminality explains nothing," as Thomassen puts it. He continues, "Liminality *is*. It happens. It takes place. And human beings react to liminal experiences in different ways."[4]

Liminality does not generate or create meaning; that task is up to us to do as we reflect, consider, and ponder liminal experiences. There is provocation and we respond (or not). Liminality "opens the door to a world of contingency where events and meanings – indeed 'reality' itself – can be molded and carried in different directions."[5] Meaningful experiences require that we probe and challenge them, in order to reflect and act upon the *event* we have just experienced or are currently in the midst of. It is this consideration of the event that helps us to recognize the process of metamorphosis we have just undergone or are still undergoing.

In this sense, liminal experiences carry a kind of *invitation*, but not the kind of invitation we are accustomed to receiving. Invitations typically invite us to attend an occasion at a specific time and place – dinners, birthday parties, weddings, and so on. We are asked to enter into a definite moment in time, a moment that includes an assurance that the occasion, whatever it might be, will end. However, the liminal invitation announces our stepping forward into indeterminacy, into the openness of possibility and change, the what might-be and could-be moments of life, where we face unknown choices and undetermined paths. It is also an invitation into discomfort and strangeness that throws us out of our places of ease, especially places of privilege. The invitation might be one of discovering hope, particularly for those enduring and struggling within perpetual liminality. This is a cautious hope-against-hope within liminality itself, inviting those who are merely surviving a liminal state (being-liminal) into a place of possible post-liminality.

The liminal invitation is not one we expect or want.[6] However, it does signal and point to a remarkable chance for personal and spiritual growth, the kind that comes from those trying and scary moments that bring us to the brink of mental and emotional exhaustion. The liminal invitation is not one we can create or incite on our own; it grasps us while we are lost within life's transitional fog. The liminal invitation seemingly arrives at moments when all seems incoherent, disjointed, and fragmented, when there does not seem to be a way out and meaning has long since been abandoned. Even for those in a post-liminal state – the feelings of disorientation, searching for what it all meant – the invitation can be one of reframing liminal experiences with a different light or seeing it using a new pair of lenses.

To carry this imagery of the liminal invitation a bit further: because this invitation could suggest disaster to a way of life which has become comfortable and to which we have become accustomed – particularly if it invites us to make a drastic change in the way we live our lives – this is an invitation read with fear and trembling, rather than one we open in excited anticipation, the kind that comes from an encounter with a coming event (that word again), that which is going on *in* what is happening, happened, or continuing to happen. This event is not liminality itself, but what is happening within liminality and our experience of it; and this encounter is one that (in all likelihood) we are not ready for.

This is a good moment to pause and talk a bit more about what I mean by the term *event*, specifically within the context of liminality. The term is actually one that I have borrowed from American philosopher John Caputo (who himself borrowed it from Jacques Derrida). According to Caputo, "An event (*événement*) is something 'coming' (*venir*), something 'to come' (*á-venir*). As something futural (*l'avenir*), an event is something we cannot see coming that takes us by surprise, like a letter that arrives unexpectedly in the mail with news that changes your life forever, for better or for worse."[7]

---

6. This is something Thomassen makes clear, he writes that liminality "is not something simply to be celebrated or wished for. Quite the contrary: liminality needs to be duly and carefully problematized." Ibid., p. 8.
7. John D. Caputo, *Truth: Philosophy in Transit* (New York: Penguin, 2014), pp. 74–75.

Events cannot be ignored, cannot be refused (though we can try), and cannot help but change our lives. They announce points in time that signal a point of divergence from a prior way of being. Many of these occasions are easily recognizable: marriage, starting a family, beginning a new career, moving to a new city. Others are less recognizable but nonetheless immensely important (perhaps even more so) – an unexpected and life-altering conversation, a moment of charity, words of encouragement from a stranger. Then there are moments of calamity, undesirable and frightening episodes that forever change, maybe even haunt, our lives – an unexpected death, failure, loss of a job. Simply put, events mark the coming of something that shatters our expectations, signaling the arrival of unexpected and life-changing news, a moment of clarity or realization, or even a provocation that challenges old ideas and prejudices.

It is crucial to clarify that an *event* is not what happens but, as Caputo says, "something going on *in* what happens, something that is being expressed or realized or given shape in what happens; it is not something present, but something seeking to make itself felt in what is present."[8] Events happen within things, they shake and tremble within places, names, and particularly moments in time. Caputo distinguishes between a *name* and the *event*. According to Caputo, "The name is a kind of provisional formulation of an event, a relatively stable if evolving structure, while the event is ever restless, on the move, seeking new forms to assume, seeking to get expressed in still unexpressed ways."[9] To put it another way, names represent the historical and conditional, something that happens at a particular time and place. Events are something altogether different. Events have no specific time or place of their own but find realization within specific and contingent things. Events "stir the pot," so to speak. They often arise within something stable and remake it into something unstable, even unpredictable. However, this is not unpredictability for the sake of unpredictability. Events move us to consider and reflect upon new possibilities, reach different conclusions, even open us toward others – especially those different from ourselves.

---

8. John D. Caputo, "Spectral Hermeneutics: On the Weakness of God and the Theology of the Event," in John D. Caputo and Gianni Vattimo, *After the Death of God*, ed. Jeffrey W. Robbins (New York: Columbia University Press, 2007), p. 47. Italics in the original.
9. Ibid.

Let us reframe this using some different imagery. Events, while chaotic and sometimes unsettling, also plant tender and vulnerable seeds of new life, new understandings, and new perspectives meant to shake up old and oppressive ways of being, doing, and thinking. They draw us into the future, helping us to break free from a shackling present and past.[10]

So far, we have characterized events as happening within the conditional, something occurring within a time and/or place. As is often the case, our minds typically conceive of events as occurring within "sacred" and "profound" moments like a service of worship or a grand ceremony. These types of activities are candidates for events; but I have something more mundane in mind. I am thinking about what can occur in the midst of everyday life: a conversation with a friend, an encounter with a stranger, a walk in the park, a bus ride. Even having a bad day can offer a moment of in-breaking, of insight, that forever changes our perceptions. Our lives are full of life-changing moments coming from oh-so-ordinary moments, striking when we least expect it. Events are off-putting because they upset from within seemingly normal and predictable points in time. They come upon us when we are unprepared to deal with what has suddenly been thrust upon us, shaking us to the very core of our being. Caputo describes events as "the way we reinvent our lives, or better, the way our lives are reinvented for us, since an event arises from an exposure to the future over which we have limited control. *We cannot make events happen, but we can make ourselves available to events.*"[11]

Herein lies a crucial point: events cannot be solicited or provoked, they solicit and provoke us. Further, while certain situations, especially of the liminal variety, might be candidates for the event, nothing is guaranteed. Not every meaningful conversation will be life-changing, nor will every walk in the park bring a much-needed moment of clarity. Sometimes a bad day is just a bad day, the vast majority of which never bring anything other than disappointment. However, sometimes, in the mystery of the moment, the event grabs us and sets our sights toward a new and scary future. We cannot do anything about the timing but we can remain ready, open, and available to what may come. It is a saying "yes" to the future, specifically, the promise of the still-to-come wonder

---

[10.] Caputo puts it this way, "In terms of their temporality, events, never being present, solicit us from afar, draw us on, draw us out into the future, calling us hither." Ibid., p. 48.

[11.] Caputo, *Truth*, p. 75. Italics mine.

and terror contained with every future, both personal and collective.[12] We have been given the invitation; it is up to us to reflect and act upon the event.

Therefore, according to Caputo, we have two choices. "We can maintain ourselves in varying states of openness to the coming of what we cannot see coming. Or we can try to prevent the event. This is usually the aim of the powers that be who think the present order serves them well."[13] Events are about shaking up the status quo, haunting powerful structures and institutions, and bringing awareness to injustice. At both the social and personal levels, events can make us extremely uncomfortable. The invitation is not the joyous announcement we were expecting; rather it confronts us to make a difficult but much needed change. Of course, we can also try to put it in a drawer or throw it away altogether. Nevertheless, in much the same way that events cannot be solicited or coerced, they cannot be stopped. The restlessness will just continue, festering and burning within us until it finally emerges, often destructively so.

> The irreducible event is what reduces us to tears, to prayers and tears, for its coming. The event is what destabilizes all such relatively stable structures [that] attempt to house it, making them restless with the future, teeming with hope and promise, even as it is in virtue of the event that things are haunted by the past, made an occasion of dangerous memories, which are no less unnerving and destabilizing.[14]

Our world is full of people and institutions whose first impulse is to hold the event captive and restrain it, in order that harmful and oppressive structures can continue. As individuals we are often fearful of the future, afraid of what a change might mean for our status, position, and privilege. Institutions, especially old and powerful ones, carry similar fears. Governments, corporations, legal systems, and even religious institutions can harbor conservative impulses that are stifling

---

[12]. Caputo writes that the "event is what is simmering in the present but is still to-come ... whose destination is radically concealed, a venture or adventure in which we cannot see what is coming." Ibid., p. 76.

[13]. John D. Caputo, *The Folly of God: A Theology of the Unconditional* (Salem, OR: Polebridge Press, 2016) (Kindle), ch. 2.

[14]. Caputo, "Spectral Hermeneutics," p. 55.

and limiting, leading to nasty consequences for those on the margins of society. Some rejoice and welcome the event, others "pray and weep over its arrival."[15]

The invitation is both a warning and a guide. An invitation lets you know that something is on the horizon, that we are approaching a significant threshold moment. The invitation offers a "heads up," making us aware of a critical juncture happening in our lives; and, though it is a warning, the invitation is not asking us to stop or turn around. The invitation is honest and genuine. Our presence is requested and desired. It invites us to say "yes" and step toward the threshold event. What we do with our invitation can have long lasting effects on the future.

Every event also involves risk. At every event we embark upon a path that could lead to success or failure. At each instance, the invitation is one that encourages us to consider what "perhaps" might happen. For Caputo, "perhaps" represents the risk we take for the future. It is the willingness to leave the safety of the known for the "fluid milieu of undecidability in which every radical decision is made."[16] Caputo describes "perhaps" as a choice that abandons predictability, principle, and power for unpredictability, flexibility, and weakness. "Perhaps" is not a risk for further certainty, trading one certainty for the next, but a risk that "unhinges us from the real, making the impossible possible."[17] What Caputo is describing is an insistence that leaves us open to the impossible, considering ideas and considerations we deemed improbable and even ridiculous. "Perhaps" brings a bit of extra courage to open and accept the invitation, so that we might take a risk, step forward, and walk across the threshold into the unknown. Moreover, though we might recoil in fear, wishing to close the invitation, "perhaps" is a whisper that urges us to reconsider and keep ourselves open. It insists and causes us to wonder, "What if?"

So, to return to liminality, why does all this talk of invitations and events matter? To reiterate Thomassen's sentiment, "Liminality does not and cannot 'explain.'"[18] Here Caputo's imagery is useful. Liminality is itself a structure, one that shelters the possibility of the event, but

---

[15.] Ibid.

[16.] John D. Caputo, *The Insistence of God: A Theology of Perhaps* (Bloomington: Indiana University Press, 2013), p. 5.

[17.] Ibid., p. 7.

[18.] Bjørn Thomassen, "The Uses and Meanings of Liminality," *International Political Anthropology* 2, no.1 (2009), p. 5.

liminality is not the event. Liminality is the name that harbors the event, carries it, and brings to us an invitation for reflection, consideration, action, and ultimately change. As Thomassen explains, "In liminality there is no certainty concerning the outcome. Liminality is a world of contingency where events and ideas, and 'reality' itself, can be carried in different directions. But for precisely these reasons, the concept of liminality has the potential to push social theory in new directions."[19] Liminal experiences are great candidates for the arrival of the event, moments that attempt to "form or formulate, nominate or denominate"[20] the invitation and take the risk for those "new directions" Thomasson describes. Liminality is the space to do all of this, a space to explore unknowns, consider opportunities, and experience the impossible.

We must also keep in mind, however, that liminality itself, precisely because it exists as a space, is also deconstructible. Liminality does not hold exclusive rights to the event, it is not the only space where we might receive an invitation.[21] We can consider, analyze, and think about liminality in space and time in a way that is not possible with the event. Liminality is conditional, it occurs in certain frames, some initially manufactured, others spontaneously so.[22] That manufactured space (created, spontaneous, or otherwise) can be broken down and analyzed to a degree. I am thinking here of the tripartite liminal form (pre-liminal, liminal, post-liminal) and its ritualistic underpinnings. The event itself cannot be bound to any sort of structure or form. The event will always run ahead of us, eluding our attempts to contain and explain it. We can deconstruct and pick apart the moment of the encounter, but the event will always be more than our interpretations, explanations,

---

[19] Ibid.

[20] Caputo, "Spectral Hermeneutics," p. 48.

[21] As Caputo explains it, "The event can never be held captive by any particular instance of the event, never reduced to any present form or instantiation." Ibid., p. 55.

[22] According to Thomassen, "Liminal experiences can be 'artificially produced' as in rituals, or they can simply happen, without anyone planning for it, as in natural disasters or the sudden disappearance of beloved persons. In a similar way, individuals can consciously search for a liminal position, standing outside normality." Thomassen, "The Uses and Meanings of Liminality," p. 18.

and rationalizations. However, we can still look at the spaces where such encounters with the event take place. Spaces, such as liminality, offer important and unique chances for "playfulness," whereby:

> the most basic rules of behavior are questioned, doubt and scepticism as to the existence of the world are radicalized, but the problematisations, the formative experiences and the reformulations of being during the liminality period proper, will feed the individual (and his/her cohort) with a new structure and set of rules that, once established, will glide back to the level of the taken-for-granted.[23]

Liminal space is an opportunity for restlessness, for upsetting and breaking down old structures – both institutional and personal – and this restlessness, provoked by that which solicits and calls from afar, offers to us a special invitation to give the event the flexibility to work within us. Instead of constraining the event, working against it, we must *release* it, learning how to let liminality become space for freedom, opportunity, and growth in the right sort of ways – ways that are mentally and spiritually healthy, emotionally supportive, and open to diversity and change. It is important to keep in mind that this is an ongoing process. As restlessness slowly shifts back to stability, it is easy for profound transitions and hard-fought moments of clarity to stagnate, thereby allowing old oppressions and injustices to creep back in. It is our responsibility to take liminality seriously and look for the invitations that might come our way. The event just might (and probably will) need to "stir the pot" again. That spells "trouble," the kind that is always lurking right around the corner.

No two journeys are alike, even in instances when individuals participate in the same ritualistic experience. How we respond to liminality will vary from person to person. Some experiences will be more profound than others, and some may barely register any sort of change. I think this has a lot to do with how we respond to the invitation contained within liminal experience. A liminal experience does not necessarily mean that we shall come out of it as better and more insightful people. We cannot expect that simply participating in a ritual or going through a transitional time will automatically change us in ways that are meaningful. A full consideration and

---

[23.] Ibid., p. 20.

reflection of the liminal journey, and the willingness to immerse oneself in the liminal space, has much to do with our reaction and response to the liminal invitation.

Perhaps what makes liminal experiences so transformational and memorable has less to do with structure and the ritualistic language we have become so accustomed to with van Gennep and Turner and more to do with something that is unnameable and wholly mysterious – something that does not lend itself to easy characterizations or identifiable stages. This something is unsettling and restless, provoking and haunting, hopeful and promising. What I mean to say is this: there is great value in seeing liminality as a shelter for the event, as a space offering a safe harbor for the release and experience of a coming promise. This is not a promise that everything will work out and be okay – a "happily ever after." The event is a promise of the future, that there *will be* a future – not a future that anyone can name, control, or manipulate, but one that remains *open*, both individually and collectively. This in turn gives us all the reason to be hopeful. What then is required of us? How do we respond to this promise? It is as easy as saying *yes* to an invitation.

The Body Leads the Way

Mary Lane Potter

At the beginning of God's creating of the heavens and the earth,
when the earth was wild and waste,
darkness over the face of Ocean,
rushing-spirit of God hovering over the face of the waters –
God said: Let there be light! And there was light.

Genesis 1:1-3, tr. Everett Fox[1]

Embodiment has long been central to my way of thinking. Though my mind has been disciplined by analytical thought, I remain, at bottom, a kinetic learner. I think with my body. We all do, of course, as we must, given that we are earth creatures and not angels. For me, however, the physicality of thinking, a moving body-mind, is vital. When my body is engaged, I know more deeply, think more creatively. It is often my body, not my mind, that leads me into new ways of thinking, new ways of acting, new ways of being; and what has facilitated that attitude for me has always been ritual, which engages and moves the whole person, body, mind, and spirit. That is why I began my academic career studying the History of Religions, concentrating on the work of Mircea Eliade and Victor Turner. And why – though I trained as a theologian and later became a creative writer – ritual and embodiment still ground my work. It is only recently, however, that I have begun to understand

---

[1.] Everett Fox (trans. and commentary), *The Five Books of Moses* (New York: Schocken, 1997), pp. 11, 13.

how liminality plays into my work as a creative writer. What I want to explore is the nexus of embodiment, ritual, liminality, and creativity that I experience as a working artist.

By way of orientation before setting out on this journey of exploration, let me offer my current approach to ritual, drawn from anthropology, philosophy, spirituality, and art: ritual is an intentional sequence of acts or gestures or body movements, performed individually or in community, that sanctifies space and time, carves out a moment from the endless flow of time, and erects a temporary shelter in the vast expanse of our world, a moment and a shelter that we can step into to cross over from the profane to the sacred. You might say rituals create liminal spaces or moments that give rise to creativity and help us to make our human existence, this created world, more habitable. Now comes the challenge: to articulate the connections suggested here. The path sketched in this essay is not a straight line heading toward a fixed destination. To paraphrase Paul Klee in his *Pedagogical Sketchbook*, this essay is an active intuition going for a walk.[2]

Ritual Is an Intentional Sequence of Symbolic Gestures or Body Motions that Enact Meaning

Growing up in a Dutch Calvinist community, I was formed by a constant stream of communal rituals – praying before and after every meal, reading the Bible after dinner, singing psalms of praise in unison, hearing the Word of God read and interpreted several times a week, witnessing the solemn ritual of communion once a month. We had our dramatic rites of passage as well – baptism and confirmation – but it was the rhythm of the everyday rituals that sculpted my inner landscape and made me a ritual-dependent person. I do not feel whole without ritual. I do not feel alive. This is why, wherever I find myself in the world, it is not museum or temple art that draws me, but the living art of rituals – Sun Dancing on Rosebud Reservation, sacrificing goats to Kali in a sacred valley outside Kathmandu, burning offerings to ancestors on the streets of Hanoi, floating burning boats down the Mekong during *Lai Heua Fai* in Louangphabang, Laos. It is also why the two mornings a week I wake up with my grandson, I wrap us together in a blanket and we step

---

[2.] Paul Klee, *Pedagogical Sketchbook*, trans. Sibyl Moholy-Nagy (New York: Prager, 1972), p. 16.

outside to recite *Modah ani*, a prayer of thankfulness for the soul being restored to the body – ending with our own song-dance, *boom boom boom boom*. If I wait too long, Ruben Zev crawls to the door we always step through and puts his hands on the threshold. At twelve months, he already knows the ritual of sharing a repeated sequence of acts.

Ritual involves the whole being, body-mind-spirit, in action, *in motion*. You cannot read or speak ritual; you must *do* ritual; and that doing generates a surplus of meaning, which enables individuals to experience the same ritual anew at different times in their lives and different individuals to each participate in his or her own way in a shared ritual. As the ancient midrash imagines, manna tasted different to each of the 600,000 Israelites, depending on his or her unique situation and need – to young men like bread, to the elderly like wafers made with honey, to babies like mother's milk, to the sick like fine flour mingled with honey, and to those lacking faith as bitter as linseed.[3] Words recited over and over or shared with others – sacred texts, prayers, liturgies, creeds – invite multiple meanings too. The Kabbalists speak of "the seventy faces of Torah," which, Gershom Scholem explains, "simply represents the inexhaustible totality and meaning of the divine word."[4] Words are miraculous. They create worlds. Yet – even when they are used poetically and not demotically – words are not enough. We embodied beings, earth creatures, require the receptivity, the openness and movement, the unity and flow of gesture as well as the distinctions and precision that words, naming, offer. As the rushing-spirit hovering over the face of the waters flows into "Let there be light!", so gesture and word go hand in hand in the creation of meaning.

Meaning, as Maurice Merleau-Ponty emphasizes in *Philosophy of Perception*, is not a product of the mind, but a creation of the body-mind. It arises from our interactions with the world; meaning is embodied. "Truth does not 'inhabit' only 'the inner man,' or more accurately, there is no inner man, man is in the world, and only in the

---

[3.] "Midrash on Exodus 5:9," in *Genesis Rabbah*, in Hayim Nachman Bialik and Yehoshua Hana Ravnitzky (eds), *The Book of Legends: Sefer Ha-Aggadah: Legends from the Talmud and Midrash*, trans. William G. Braude (New York: Schocken, 1991), p. 40.

[4.] Gershom Scholem, *The Messianic Idea in Judaism: And Other Essays on Jewish Spirituality* (New York: Schocken, 1971), p. 296.

world does he know himself."[5] The body, then, is not a thing or object bumping up against others, or a vehicle for expressing concepts, ideas, or experiences, but our way of engaging the world. "My body appears to me as an *attitude* directed toward a certain existing or possible task," he writes. "And indeed its spatiality is not, like that of external objects or like that of 'spatial sensation,' a *spatiality of position*, but a *spatiality of situation*."[6] Gesture, therefore, understood widely as bodily motions, including speech, acts or language, is not bodily movements that express pre-conceived thoughts; gesture, by situating us in the world, *enacts* meaning. The gesture itself – whether linguistic or non-linguistic – brings meaning into existence. When confronted with an angry face or gesture, Merleau-Ponty explains, "the gesture doesn't make me think of anger, it is anger itself."[7] Gesture is fundamental to meaning; and, as Mark Johnson emphasizes in *The Aesthetics and Meaning of Thought*, "meaning is not dependent on language." There is meaning "beyond and beneath language," for example, in two people dancing slowly to soft music in low light.[8]

As besotted as I am with words, it is gesture understood in the narrower sense, as non-linguistic bodily motions, that fascinates me. Perhaps because gesture evokes meaning beyond and beneath the sharp distinctions and control that words bring. Perhaps because gesture feels less distancing than words, closer to the immediacy of experiencing the differentiated yet unified whole that is our world. Perhaps because, like visual images, gesture shares more directly in the physical world, the realm of bodies and movement, and allows for an even wider scope of interpretation and participation than words, offering greater inclusion with greater diversity. Whether these felt comparisons are accurate or not, it is the creation of meaning through gesture that intrigues me. For me, that comes down to ritual. Ritual actions situate us in our world, they orient us. In rituals we move our bodies as attitudes directed toward an existing or possible task. Ritual choreography, such as circumambulating the Dalai Lama when praying, or facing east or north, Jerusalem or Mecca, is designed to facilitate this orientation of

[5] Maurice Merleau-Ponty, *Phenomenology of Perception*, trans. Colin Smith (New York: Routledge & Kegan Paul, 1962), p. xi.

[6] Ibid., p. 100, original italics.

[7] Ibid., p. 184.

[8] Mark Johnson, *The Aesthetics of Meaning and Thought* (Chicago: University of Chicago Press, 2018), pp. 86–87.

the body, to evoke a certain attitude toward the task at hand. Ritual spaces are designed to situate the body as well. Gothic cathedrals lift the body toward the heavens. Many contemporary churches open toward the natural world. The Sun Dance circle centers on a cottonwood tree, the *axis mundi* around which all action occurs, and dancers enter and exit from the east. The temple in Jerusalem opened to the east, with an outer court, sanctuary, and the holy of holies guiding bodies toward the ineffable and shielding them from it. These choreographic and architectural directives or nudges are born of the wisdom that ritual enacts meaning and the body leads the way.

Much of why I was drawn to Judaism and converted when I was 40 was that it is purposefully embodied and action-oriented, so gesture-affirming and ritual-rich. Jews may be known as a "people of the book" but we communicate faith and traditions through a treasury of shared rituals. Part of the genius of Jewish tradition is that it transforms *everything* into gesture or ritual. Laws are perforce enacted – wearing a *tallit* and *tefillin* for morning prayers, not wearing wool and linen together, cracking each egg carefully to see if it contains a blood spot, lighting Shabbat candles and sanctifying wine and bread every seventh day – every table an altar around which the kin-dom of priests gathers. The community's history and sacred narratives are also enacted, so that Jews in every generation, in whatever culture they find themselves, may experience them "as if they were there," as the *haggadah* teaches. Shabbat practices reenact the Creator resting on the seventh day and glorying in the goodness of creation. The kashrut practices and *seder* of Passover enact the Exodus from Egypt, the candles and latkes of Hanukkah the Maccabean revolt, dwelling in *sukkahs* the wandering in the desert, refraining from eating leg of lamb the story of Jacob wrestling the angel.

The philosopher Marc-Alain Ouaknin calls Jewish ritual "gestural memory," or "the third way of transmitting myth," alongside oral and written transmission. His definition of gestural memory as "the concrete textual memory *expression* and *objectification* of myth in the human body and gesture,"[9] could be read as Cartesian, perpetuating a dualism in which mind and body are separate and mind takes precedence over body. I believe it is more accurate, however, to understand his notion of gestural memory along the lines of Merleau-Ponty's view of gesture as enacting meaning, in which meaning is inseparable from the act.

---

9. Marc-Alain Ouaknin, *Symbols of Judaism* (New York: Assouline, 2000), p. 10. Emphasis mine.

Gestural memory does not express or represent or re-enact the meaning of an event or thought that has already happened: it enacts fresh meaning for the doers. The doing is not an aesthetic add-on or a dressed-up idea; it is essential to meaning. As many commentators, ancient and contemporary, have noted, Israel's response to the revelation of the Torah at Sinai, *Naaseh v'nishma*, "we will do and we will hear" (Exodus 24:7), underscores this emphasis on action leading to understanding. The body leads the way.

Rituals, then, as intentional sequences of symbolic acts or gestures or body movements enact meaning and create connections across time and space for those who perform them. They situate our bodies in a particular way and open up a space or moment for participants to enter in which they can imagine, experience, and live into fresh meaning. They also open to an inexhaustible well of meanings, widely diverse yet shareable, that can ground and orient participants' lives, individually and communally.

Ritual Is Intimately Connected to Imagination, Creativity, and Liminality

For me, ritual is the choreography of faith. You might call it *faith at play*, since, as Robert Bellah shows in *Religion in Human Evolution: From the Paleolithic to the Axial Age*, play and ritual are closely related in evolution. In his masterful summary of paleontology and neuroscience, Bellah includes this astonishing observation: "Other apes lack two skills that are important for humans: the ability to throw accurately, undoubtedly helpful for hunting with weapons, and *the ability to keep together in time, without which skillful dancing* [and other sequences of novel postures] *would be impossible.*"[10] Rituals are a kind of skillful dance we *homo sapiens* perform together. We, the dancing apes – the most liminal of apes? – move together in time, acting out a specific set of symbolic gestures intended to transform our relation to ourselves and our world, out of which something new may arise. The anthropologist Clifford Geertz's summary of ritual suggests how this happens: "In ritual, the world as lived and the world as imagined, fused under the agency of a single set of symbolic forms, turn out to be *the same world*,

---

[10.] Robert Bellah, *Religion in Human Evolution: From the Paleolithic to the Axial Age* (Cambridge, MA: Belknap, 2011), p. 86.

producing thus that idiosyncratic transformation in one's sense of reality," opening vistas and mysteries, creating, as George Santayana, says, another world to live in.[11]

Building on Bellah and Geertz, I understand ritual as an intentional sequence of symbolic actions that fuses together the world as lived and the *world as imagined* in such a way that it bumps us into a liminal space, betweenness, or what the philosopher-mystic Ibn 'Arabî (1165–1240 CE) calls the *barzakh* or isthmus. Ibn 'Arabî uses this term, William C. Chittick explains, to refer to anything that simultaneously divides and brings together two things, without itself having two sides, like the line that separates sunlight and shade.[12] Between the real and the impossible, for example, or between nondelimited being and articulated words, lies an intermediate world, the imaginal world, which is neither yet shares in both. "The imaginal – not imaginary – reality is one that dwells in an intermediate domain between two other realities and shares in the attributes of both sides."[13] This intermediate world, which Ibn 'Arabî often refers to as the "Breath of the All-Merciful," is the most hidden – like the imperceptible line between dusk and day or dusk and night – and "the vastest of presences," since it "combines the two worlds, the World of the Unseen and the World of the Visible."[14]

[11.] Cited in Bellah, *Religion in Human* Evolution, p. xvi.

[12.] William C. Chittick's entry, "Ibn 'Arabî," in *Stanford Encyclopedia of Philosophy* (Spring 2020 edn), https://plato.stanford.edu/entries/ibn -arabi/#Bar, is a clear and concise summary of Ibn 'Arabî's cosmology. For an in-depth presentation of the *barzakh*, the imaginal world, the cosmos, the soul, and the multiple different ways Ibn 'Arabî understands imagination, see Chittick's *Imaginal Worlds: Ibn al-'Arabî and the Problem of Religious Diversity* (Albany, NY: SUNY Press, 1994). *Barzakh* is also translated as *barrier* or *limit*, emphasizing that, though the two sides meet, they remain separate. For this essay I use the translation *isthmus* to focus on *barzakh* as a meeting place. I am not fool enough to think I understand the work of Ibn 'Arabî; I claim only to be captivated by his vision of life and his writing, including his poetry.

[13.] Chittick, *Imaginal Worlds*, p. 25.

[14.] Michel Chodkiewicz (ed.), *The Meccan Revelations*, trans. William C. Chittick and James W. Morris (New York: Pir Press, 2002), p. 172. This translation of parts of *al-Futûhât al-makkiyya*, focuses on the *barzakh* as the intermediate time between death and the final resurrection. Ibn 'Arabî speaks of the *barzakh* in both spatial and temporal terms, both as world

Ibn 'Arabî uses the term Supreme *Barzakh* (*al-barzakh al-a'lâ*) as a synonym for nondelimited imagination, by which he means the entire cosmos, which is the realm of possible things, things which in themselves are neither necessary nor impossible, neither infinite nor finite, neither visible nor invisible. In other words, for Ibn 'Arabî, the entire cosmos, or what we so blithely call "the creation," is a liminal state:

> The Real is sheer Light and the impossible is sheer darkness. Darkness never turns into Light, and Light never turns into darkness. The created realm is the *barzakh* between Light and darkness. In its essence it is qualified neither by darkness nor by Light, since it is the *barzakh* and the middle, having a property from each of its two sides. That is why He "appointed" for man "two eyes and guided him on the two highways" (Koran 90:8–10), for man exists between the two paths. Through one eye and one path he accepts Light and looks upon it in the measure of his preparedness. Through the other eye and the other path he looks upon darkness and turns toward it. (Ibn 'Arabî, *al-Futûhât*, 1911 edition, 3:274.28).[15]

Human beings, as microcosm, participate in all three worlds or presences. We are spirit, body, and soul, with soul or imagination the *barzakh*:

> Soul or imagination, then, refers to intermediate realm, neither luminous nor dark, neither alive nor dead, neither subtle nor dense, neither conscious nor unconscious, but always somewhere between the two extremes. Through imagination the high and low interpenetrate, the bright and dark unite. Imagination is neither high nor low, luminous nor dark, spirit nor body. It is defined by its in-betweenness.[16]

---

and a presence. This seems to me to point accurately to the complex reality experienced in liminal states, and why I choose to use both kinds of terms as well.

[15.] Chittick, "Ibn 'Arabî,".

[16.] Chittick, *Imaginal Worlds*, p. 25. For a full discussion, see ch. 7, "The In-Betweenness."

Like the image of oneself in a mirror, "imagination is neither existent nor nonexistent, neither known nor unknown, neither negated nor affirmed. And one who sees oneself in a mirror is neither a truth-teller nor a liar in [saying the] words, 'I saw my form, I did not see my form.'"[17]

Soul is where spirit and body meet. It is essential to note here that Ibn 'Arabî, like Merleau-Ponty, is not a dualist. For him, as Chittick points out, spirit and body are "qualitative distinctions not discrete entities"; one can speak of them as "dimensions of the microcosm."[18] Or, more to my liking, as powers that enable us to engage the world in different ways. Imagination, for example, is the power of the soul that "bridges the spiritual and the corporeal."[19] It is active, creative. As liminal beings, we are always moving back and forth between the invisible and the visible worlds or presences, bridging the two in fresh ways. Chittick quotes one of Ibn 'Arabî's disciples as saying, "The *barzakh* is a world where the outward becomes inward, and the inward outward."[20] This seems to me a handy definition for ritual as well. Perhaps ritual is one of the ways we remind ourselves we are liminal beings and intentionally open ourselves up to the power of transformation, creating new forms.

An ancient Yemenite midrash on Exodus from the fourteenth or fifteenth century CE offers an uncannily similar view of creation and liminality. It begins by quoting the Talmud, *Pirkei Avot* 5:6 : "Our rabbis taught, 'Ten things were created during twilight, and they are these: the mouth of the earth, the mouth of the ass, the mouth of the well, the rainbow, the *man*, the staff, the *shamir*, the writing, that which is written, and the tablets.'" Though *Pirkei Avot* specifies the twilight occurs on the eve of Shabbat, this is omitted in the Yemenite version, which continues:

> These happened "at twilight" because it was not necessary that these ten things should exist, nor was it necessary that they should not exist. Another item. These actions were associated with twilight because that is an [intermediate] state between two different states. From the aspect of His will (may He be exalted), it [each of the ten things] was possible, but from the aspect of the nature of things it was impossible.

[17.] Chittick, "*al-Futûhât al-makkiyya* I:304," quoted in *Imaginal Worlds*, p. 112.

[18.] Chittick, *Imaginal Worlds*, p. 25.

[19.] Ibid., pp. 71–72.

[20.] Ibid., p. 106.

Their existence was somewhere between the impossible and
the possible. Their possibility is due to His will (may He be
exalted) – which [will] created the whole world as He wanted
it to be created. That moment [twilight] is in supposed time,
not real time, for time is absolute.[21]

These ten were singled out, the midrash explains, because though
there are many miracles, the others, the "necessary miracles," were
created not at twilight but during the six days of creation. During
the days of creation the Creator placed within the breast the power
to give milk, within the seed the power to yield fruit, within the sun
the power to stand still, and within the nature of water the power to
split at the Red Sea. During the nights of creation, the Creator created
those things that it is necessary not to exist, of which it is better not
to speak. Only in twilight, the in-between, the realm of that which is
neither necessary nor impossible, the realm of the possible, do these
ten exist.

I was so taken by this imaginative rabbinic commentary that I wrote
a novel based on it, my own midrash on Exodus and the wonder-
working prophet-poet Miriam. In my view, these ten twilight creations
are openings – so many mouths! – that belong to the isthmus between
worlds. Each is an opening where the Creator and the earth creature
meet, on different ground than the ground of what is necessary or what
is impossible. They meet in the time and space of the possible, like hard
seed planted in soft ground, and, from their meeting, new life is created.
A way out of no way is born. From the womb of the possible, through
these openings, all the wonders of our world are brought forth. And the
way into that womb is ritual – drumming, singing, dancing. The body
leads the way.

Ontology and miracles aside – whether or not the entire cosmos is
a *barzakh* or the twilight creation exists and contains these ten non-
necessary miracles – I find the images of *barzakh* and twilight fruitful for
understanding ritual and creativity. I take *barzakh* or twilight to mean
that creative space between what is necessary and what is impossible –
in other words, the time of the possible, the realm between the world

---

[21.] Y. Tzvi Langermann (trans.), *Yemenite Midrash: Philosophical Commentaries on the Torah* (San Francisco: Harper San Francisco, 1996), p. 20.

that is, the world as we experience it normally, and the world that does not yet exist – the place where artists long to live and work, the field[22] where artists play.

Linking artists with "the realm of the possible" may summon up John Keats' famous concept of "negative capability" in art. Discussing artistic achievement in a letter to George and Tom Keats in 1817, Keats described "negative capability as when man is capable of being in uncertainties, Mysteries, doubts, without any irritable reaching after fact & reason."[23] This concept has been stimulating for many artists, with good reason. For me, however, the images of isthmus and twilight point more accurately to my experience of creative writing; and they do so without setting up an antagonism or mutual exclusion between art and reason. Knowing in art is not *against* fact and reason, the realm of the necessary. Nor is the intention of most artists to invade and conquer the realm of the impossible. No dualistic thinking, no adversarial relationship is needed for us to distinguish between these different ways of engaging the world. All it takes is stepping into a moment or a space *between*, to step onto ground that is neither the hard ground of fact nor the groundlessness of unbounded fantasy, but the soft fertile field of the possible, to discover what seeds will sprout and grow. Writing – whether fiction or nonfiction – is not expressing a preconceived idea or image. It is not a straight line speeding to a mapped destination. It is entering and exploring the unknown, which includes doubts and mysteries, but also much, much more – questions, an endless path, wordlessness, silence.

The question then is, how does one enter that *between*, the field of the possible between what exists and what does not yet exist, between what we know and what we cannot know, the realm of the unknown yet imaginable, the world of imagination, the imaginal presence – that

---

[22.] Being or what exists and the imaginary are not objects, Merleau-Ponty argues, but fields. I find this description of the imaginary as a field useful, though I still use the words *space* and *moment*. For me, time and space cannot be separated in these threshold experiences of the imagination; they are two ways of speaking about the same experience, like particle and wave, two sides of one reality, like body and mind, body and soul. Maurice Merleau-Ponty, *The Visible and the Invisible*, ed. Claude Lefort, trans. Alphonso Lingis (Evanston, IL: Northwestern University Press, 1968), p. 267.

[23.] John Keats, "On Negative Capability: Letter to George and Tom Keats, 21, ?27 December 1817," Selections from Keats's Letters, https://www.poetry foundation.org/articles/69384/selections-from-keatss-letters.

actively liminal space. For me, as for many artists, the body leads the way. It is ritual, an intentional sequence of bodily actions, that opens us up to or helps us to enter the field of the imagination, that faint, half-seen, half-heard, inchoate, space or moment when the world of forms we know softens and gives rise to new forms. It is when we intentionally enter that liminal space, step onto the soft ground of that isthmus, enter the twilight of the possible, move into the imaginal world or presence, that we can more easily envisage and create new forms, images, structures, events, ways of being that will transform ourselves and our world.

Role of Ritual in Creativity

Ritual gives rise to creativity. Far from being simply a repeatable sequence of events, the enemy, as it were, of novelty and originality, ritual is a discipline that makes room for freedom. Pitting habit or ritual, which works on our unconscious physical awareness, against freedom of the mind, is yet one more vestige of dualism plaguing art. In a phenomenology of the flesh such as Merleau-Ponty's, there is no contrast between these two; for both are actions performed out of habit and those out of a conscious choice are interactions of brains, world, bodies, and other bodies. The mind, he says, is "the other side of the body," and we have no idea of a mind that would not be doubled with a body.[24] It is the intentional repetition of a sequence of bodily motions that enables us to enter that isthmus or twilight, to stand in that place or moment dividing yet connecting that which is and that which is not – that blurred space with no hard lines of separation – and to give ourselves over to imagination and use its power to find new ways of thinking, acting, feeling, sensing, being in the world.

It is common for artists to talk about rituals of preparation. Writers are often asked about their creative "habits" by interviewers and fans or aspiring writers, a question I find moving, because it suggests a longing to find a key to unlock one's own creativity. Do you use a special pen or pencil when you write? They ask. Do you listen to music? Do you follow a certain routine? Twyla Tharp, in *The Creative Habit*, describes ritual

---

[24.] Merleau-Ponty, *The Visible and the Invisible*, p. 259. For a discussion of the complex relationship of freedom, will, imagination, and repetition in art, see Susan Stewart, *The Poet's Freedom: A Notebook on Making* (Chicago: University of Chicago Press, 2011).

as an "automatic decisive pattern of behavior" to help overcome those first steps into creativity, which are difficult because of our fears, doubts, and distractions. Because it is automatic, you do not think, you do not will, you do not decide, you just "step into it," she says. "Moving inside [the routine] gives you no choice but to do something; It's Pavlovian: follow the routine, get a creative payoff." Like Beethoven's morning walk and scribbles "limbered up his mind and transported him into his version of a trance during the walk."[25] Note Tharp's physical language, the language of motion – not unusual for a dancer and choreographer but also germane to ritual. More than anything, rituals of preparation "arm us with confidence and self-reliance,"[26] she says, as they did for primitive people, who appeased the universe with rituals out of fear, to gain control.

Not only for negative reasons – to overcome fears, blocks, distractions, or to appease the gods or our own demons – do artists practice rituals. Artists' rituals are not primitive acts. They are not superstition. They are intentional acts we perform to cross a threshold from ordinary reality to a space where the imagined world is fused with the real. Engaging in a familiar ritual helps us to step onto the isthmus, into the twilight, the field of the possible, that creative space where the real and imagined worlds are distinct from each other yet connected. That is the place I have to step into as a writer, that space between what has gone before and what might be, between what has happened and what might happen, what exists and what does not yet exist. I cannot write well if I am not in that space. This is as true for creative nonfiction as it is for fiction. An essay is not a logical argument; it is a trial, an attempt, a foray, a line of thought moving around an image or word or feeling or hunch. Whether I am writing a story, novel, or essay, I want – I need – to access what is beyond my reasoning, underneath ordinary logic, outside linear thinking. I want to let go of planning, what is necessary, banish limiting beliefs, what is impossible. *I want to lose control*, not gain control, as Tharp says, though the paradox is that by losing control one finds one's footing in the field of the imagination. I want my relationship to space and time – all ordinary reality, all that is profane – to be altered, as it

25. Twyla Tharp, *The Creative Habit: Learn It and Use It for Life* (New York: Simon & Schuster, 2003), pp. 18, 19.
26. Ibid., p. 20.

often is when I perform Jewish rituals, like lighting Shabbat candles at sunset on Friday, when I am buzzing from the six days of the week, and feeling peace and gratitude and joy wash over me.

All artists have their own ways of stepping onto the isthmus, into the twilight, and entering that plasticity of mind, that openness to seeing and hearing and experiencing and imagining new things. Marcel Proust wrote in bed. Susan Sontag did not answer the phone (a habit I swear by). Alice Munro walks three miles. Toni Morrison gets up before dawn, makes coffee, and watches the light come up. Haruki Murakami gets up at dawn and runs. "The repetition itself becomes the important thing," he says. "It's a form of mesmerism. I mesmerize myself to reach a deeper state of mind."[27] Tharp goes to the gym every morning. She *moves*, out of her apartment, into a taxi, out of the taxi, into the gym, in the gym, out of the gym, into a taxi, out of the taxi, into her apartment – crossing threshold after threshold.

To prepare myself for the hard work of writing (I know I am truly writing when I sweat), I often sit still and breathe, then pray or meditate – I move my spirit, or, more accurately, I feel my spirit moving, rushing-spirit hovering over the face of deep, dark, moving waters. To move my body, I do blind or free drawing, engage my hand and my brain in a different way. When I begin a story or essay, I write by hand on unlined paper, with a soft pencil, alone at my scarred cherry dining table – not my computer desk. I work in solitude. Silence. No music. I step onto the page, and I wait. I listen. Sometimes I have an image or idea or voice or structure I want to explore. Often, I sit with nothing. I stay still. And I wait. Wait until a voice or image or rhythm or word arises. When I am stuck, I get moving. I do the dishes, sweep the floor, throw in a load of laundry, take a walk, and my moving limbs stir up my imagination. There is nothing special about these physical acts. However, by engaging in them, I can often – not always, it is not guaranteed by any means – bump myself into that liminal state, a state of play, serious play, somewhere between consciousness and unconsciousness, where imagining flows (movement!) and something new emerges that I did not plan or anticipate, something that surprises me. When it comes to

---

[27] Quoted in John Wray, "Haruki Murakami: The Art of Fiction No. 182," *The Paris Review* 170 (Summer 2004), https://www.theparisreview.org/interviews/2/the-art-of-fiction-no-182-haruki-murakami.

editing, I work by ear. I stand in the middle of the room and read the words aloud, listening for the sounds, the rhythms, the meaning beyond and beneath the words on the page. The body leads the way.

Playing in the In-Between: A Writer's Vocation

As liminal creatures, we are constantly moving back and forth between different ways of being in the world, different powers of engaging the world, different ways of being present – between body and mind, body and spirit, word and idea, image and perception, heart and mind, sacred and profane. We move in both directions, any direction, all directions – each in our own way, our own rhythm. If we are lucky, we pause in the between and look around, listen; and in the movement of the outward becoming inward and the inward becoming outward, we discover something new. For me, however, it is most often the body that leads the way – into thought, into prayer, into the twilight of the possible, the isthmus between the seen and the unseen, the in-between, the imaginal world, where I become neither a truth-teller nor a liar when I say, "I saw and heard this form; I did not see and hear this form." Where I become a creative writer listening for a voice singing true, a voice between a shout and a whisper. Failing again and again to hear. Failing again and again to capture what I hear on the page. But trying.

> On the matter of spiritual realization mankind does not cease to err,
>   For God's secret is poised between the shout and the whisper.[28]

---

28. Ibn ʿArabī, Proem to *The Universal Tree and the Four Birds*, trans. Angela Jaffray (Oxford: Anqa, 2006), p. 25.

Extreme Liminalities that Shape Us

Timothy Carson

It should not have surprised any of us that at the outset of our most recent pandemic, Albert Camus' *The Plague* waltzed back onto the collective stage of our consciousness. The last time I read it was in college. Like many others I searched high and low until I found my dogeared copy. I discussed it with others in a book study. I noticed the novel making the rounds everywhere.

We read it, of course, looking for clues. How could Camus' rendering of the human condition *in extremis* assist us in our own understanding? Even considering the indifferent universe of his world view, was there some existential fortitude we might borrow, an inspiration to our resolve, endurance, even compassion? *The Plague* poses more questions than answers.

Among other material and philosophical concerns, Camus named the alienation, separation, and isolation that pandemic engenders this way: "The first thing that plague brought to our town was exile."[1]

Exile is a separated state of being, the experience of being unmoored from one's own sense of place. It represents the loss of home and meaning. When we are exiled by pandemic, we are exiled from the larger connections of community to the small world of our home or pod. Though electronic communication and media marks a significant difference between present-day pandemic and those of the past, we are still separated from natural human congress and freedom.

---

[1] Albert Camus, *The Plague* (New York: Vintage Books, 1991), p. 71.

Though Camus did not use the word, he was referring to what we now call *liminality.*

The word "liminal" derives from the Latin, *limen*, and refers to the threshold between two separate places. The liminal state is defined in its contrast to what preceded it, which was the ordinary structure of life. This experience of anti-structure is usually transitional, though in many cases can become indefinite or ongoing. It is marked by uncertainty and ambiguity. In the early anthropological research, the liminal state was ordinarily described in terms of developmental or cyclical transitions in agrarian pre-industrial societies.[2] In later applications, definitions of liminality expanded to include many of the modern experiences of in-betweenness, marginality, social disruption, and individual transformation. By sharing a common transitional experience, liminal people develop a special bond and camaraderie, a connection that transcends other distinctions and differences, which has been given its own coined name, *communitas.*[3]

When it comes to the reality of a pandemic, these liminal categories coalesce to provide a most helpful interpretive lens through which we may understand it.

During the Covid-19 pandemic, popular presentations of the liminal were ubiquitous; numerous websites and social media outlets became the platform for all things liminal. This popular appropriation of the term, liminality, included a loose definition: anything out of the ordinary, strange, abandoned, absent, or dystopian. They searched for a way to name an experience that defied naming.

A pandemic creates one of the most extreme forms of involuntary social liminality. It is joined by the other close relatives of natural disaster, war, and genocide. These are dramatic situations and events that push us over thresholds into a reality in which the old rules are suspended or absent and the way forward is entirely unknown.

A pandemic affects everyone with different degrees of intensity. For some the effects are disastrous. For others who are shielded or protected by distance, isolation or privilege, the experience may border on inconvenience. For anyone connected to the information stream of our society, the death tolls became unavoidable. Even when we averted our eyes, we could not help but look, count, and worry.

[2.] Gennep, *Rites of Passage.*

[3.] Turner, *The Ritual Process.*

As in the other pandemics of history, many clamored to assign the origins of disaster to some understandable cause; it must have been a plot, conceived by enemies to undo us. Likewise, all manner of fanciful talismans or folk remedies arose to supposedly protect us. Superstition and false narratives circumvented hard science, attempting to take vulnerable people hostage through social media, reeling them in through fear and false hopes. Ineffective and self-serving leaders engaged in public denial, conspiracy theories, and minimizing the danger.

On the most important fronts, however, people of good will and social conscience attempted to devise cures, to enact social policy to protect, and to communicate true empathy for the suffering. As in other similar circumstances, they became heroes for the rest of us.

Though people across the globe may not have named this common experience liminality, that is the state of being we entered, and many inhabit it still. It is a state of anti-structure in contrast to our former lives. Subjected to life-threatening, life-altering, and life-diminishing, people clamored to make sense of it, function in basic ways, and maintain some sense of humanity.

In the beginning of the pandemic, many people responded with creativity, which was a tribute to the human spirit. All manner of online engagements distracted us with Zoom meetings, games, culinary arts, and home photo contests. This huge compensation for social absence dominated the days of those who had the leisure to engage in it. It continued for many until they tired of it, wearied from weak substitutes for real interaction.

For others this represented a more existential threat. Not only could those who work and serve in the front lines of society become sick, infect their loved ones, and even die, but their source of income and employment often evaporated. The modest attempts of government to give emergency relief or protections helped. However, the already vulnerable were made more so; those on the edge often fell off.

As far as *Rites of Passage* go, extreme chaos events barely fit that model. They most certainly can become a pilgrimage of heart and soul, a shared experience that may reshape the physical and social world we know; but they are not culturally shaped passages that utilize and impart cultural wisdom: ritual, rites, prescriptions, community gatherings, liturgy, prayers, songs, symbolic dress, pilgrimage, designed deprivations. Many of those elements may arise spontaneously. Nevertheless, they are non-repeating and generally do not enjoy generations of cultural formation that assist people or groups in making the most universal transitions of life.

* * *

Daniel Defoe was just a child, perhaps five years old, when the plague hit London in 1665. His *A Journal of the Plague Year* was a retrospective in old age, written as though through the eyes of an adult in real time.[4] His descriptions are legendary for their conciseness and detail, reflecting the horrors of his childhood, and providing a view of plague and its effects in urban life. Along with *Robinson Crusoe*, this is his lingering literary legacy.

Bubonic plague was a recurring phenomenon, returning every twenty years or so. It was made worse by unseasonably warm temperatures and amplified by social conditions. It was often spread by fleas on rats. The wealthy classes escaped the city to the countryside. The poor had no choice but to stay, work, and get their meat from the super-spreader meat markets. Those who were sick were forcibly quarantined in their own dwellings, not for their own protection, but rather for the protection of the larger community. Their houses became family tombs.

What is difficult to comprehend today is how slowly news of plague spread; the forms of communication we take for granted did not yet exist. Newspapers and word of mouth via travelers were the most common forms of information distribution. Those delivery systems were ponderously slow. Plague seemed to hit suddenly and without warning. Civic leaders were mostly reactive; they devised plans to close the city, quarantine the afflicted, provide for removing the dead, bury the dead in mass graves in and outside the cemeteries, and post regular death counts. Except in the case of the most essential services, social life ended. Superstition reigned where science or religion could not bring deliverance. The liminal dimension of pandemic is well-described in Defoe's own words:

> But in the whole face of things, I say, was much altered; sorrow and sadness sat upon every face; and though some parts were not yet overwhelmed, yet all looked deeply concerned; and as we saw it apparently coming on, so every one looked on himself and his family as in the utmost danger.... London might well be said to be all in tears; the mourners did not go about the streets indeed, for nobody put on black or made a formal dress of mourning for their nearest friends; but the voice of mourning was truly heard in the streets. The shrieks of women and children at the windows and doors of their houses, where their dearest relations were perhaps dying,

---

4. Daniel Defoe, *A Journal of the Plague Year* (New York: Everyman, 1994).

or just dead, were so frequent to be heard as we passed the streets, that it was enough to pierce the stoutest heart in the world to hear them.[5]

In our own time of Covid-19 we experienced a parallel drama with families separated from their loved ones as they died in hospital sequestered behind plastic or glass. Temporary morgues were set up in refrigerator trucks behind hospitals. The death counts ran in scrolling banners at the bottom of our television screens. The accumulative impact of an entire society exposed to relatively rapid and numerous deaths is hard to measure, but like Defoe, the public internalized it. Shock, horror, and grief filled our actual and virtual communities. Face masks costumed our experience, providing a wardrobe for the cast of liminal characters acting in the precarious drama.

* * *

It was the summer of 1854 and London was a congested, and in some areas putrid, city of great extremes of wealth and poverty. Behind its respectable façade was a disaster in the making. The cholera bacilli had found a perfect outlet – one water pump that was a most central, frequented, and deadly source of the city's water. This was an invisible enemy. Only the diligent work of model-busting scientists would eventually identify the cause and treatment for the scourge. Nevertheless, it was too late for many Londoners.

At first, blame for the epidemic was laid at the feet of the poor. After all, citizens and leaders opined, they lived in the most squalid parts of the city. Surely their filth engendered the disease? The opinion was at least partially true: congestion and an inadequate sewage system were contributing factors; and the poor lived and worked where it was most dangerous.

Then people in middle-class and even upper-class households also fell sick. A pestilence was lurking at midday and it soon became apparent it was an equal opportunity infector. In time, the source was identified, the Broad Street pump, a pump enjoyed and used by many in adjoining areas. Cholera came to town through the favorite watering hole.[6]

---

5. Ibid., pp. 15–16.
6. Steven Johnson, *The Ghost Map: A Street, an Epidemic and the Hidden Power of Urban Networks* (New York: Penguin, 2006), p. 30.

One might assume that all of London crossed the threshold that plunged them into the liminality of epidemic with the first wave of cholera deaths, but that is not the case. It was only when the illness began to affect a much broader public beyond the outposts of the poor that the alarm arose. Only when the threat was understood to be universal, affecting all, especially the upper classes, did the city leadership understand itself to be in the throes of a deadly epidemic. Until that tipping point arrived, only some knew that some were getting sick somewhere in the city, and probably as the result of their own doing. With the deaths of a few prominent citizens, however, cholera suddenly became a grave public concern.

That pigeonholing of a threat is a familiar pattern in every time, of course, and it has been in the time of Covid-19. Much American discourse at the beginning of the pandemic focused on the elderly. It was true that seniors who were fragile and had pre-existing conditions were the most vulnerable segment of the population. Nursing homes were affected first and hardest. As commentators seized on the geriatric dimensions of the threat, the public created its own defense mechanism, an irrational solace. Surely, we asked ourselves, this does not concern everyone? In a relatively short period of time, however, we discovered that front-line workers and those in the service sector were falling ill. Soon it was revealed that younger adults were also afflicted. This was not, as we had imagined, a disease limited to the vulnerable elderly. Suddenly, as the circle of the threat expanded, when it was perceived to be as universal as the scientific community had warned, the pandemic became real. At that point, the whole society crossed a collective threshold, and we entered the universal state of involuntary social liminality.

* * *

The existence of liminality does not ensure progress or justice. In fact, it may create conditions that foster just the opposite. Authoritarian, fear-based movements prey upon the public's sense of insecurity and uncertainty. When people are afraid, they often clamor for security in whatever form it may come. Historically speaking, that has included the rise of tyrants and repression of human rights. At the same time, paradoxically, pandemics and disasters may also contribute to the *downfall* of demagogues and autocrats. Wild, unguided, decentering liminality can be a whirlpool that sucks people under in unpredictable ways. It also can be the earthquake that decenters what needs to shake loose.

During this recent pandemic we discovered how people who were on the emotional edge, those struggling with mental health issues, were adversely affected by this additional stress in their lives. Social isolation played an important part in the premature decline of seniors who were homebound already. Those for whom social interaction was essential to their identity and belonging, like adolescents, were more vulnerable to self-harm. With more people self-medicating with alcohol, alcohol itself became a presenting problem, especially amongst those who were already inclined to substance abuse. The dramatic rise in pet adoptions during this time was not only a testament to the way the pandemic often drove us back to home-centered living, but to our need for the emotional comfort that animal companions can provide.

Nevertheless, liminal chaos often dislodges that which has previously been intractable. It creates disruption and interruption, a shaking of the foundations in which opportunities arise to do deep emotional, cognitive, and spiritual work. The liminality of a pandemic makes some things more possible, provided people seize upon the opportunity for reform. Though liminality never guarantees growth, deeper insight into life, new vistas of faith, or personal and social transformation, it does hold *potential* for change. But the arc of that change depends on human agency and critically positioned liminal guides and leaders.

At its best, that work may unearth hidden treasure that was not apparent before. For example, if one's life has been cluttered with business and noise, the involuntary isolation can become a gift, a way to rediscover simplicity and silence. If we are reduced to a very limited social circle, we may rediscover one another, undistracted by frivolous pursuits. Families may press the reset button to right-size their way of life, abandoning the unnecessary. Frustrated workers may reassess their career paths, find different jobs, go back to school for more training, and get off the merry-go-round that has been the source of their discontent. Social issues like health care, wages and benefits, and ecological stewardship, which only a short time earlier seemed stalemated, suddenly shift, finding new openings.

Though liminality does not ensure permanent change, it does happen. When we adapt to new circumstances, the changes we make often awaken us to what needed to happen all along. In the world of work, for example, temporary home officing opened the world of commerce to a new way of work that is just as, if not more, effective, and protects personal and family life while doing so. As businesses and corporations had no choice but to experiment, they witnessed first-hand what can work in a new model of working. Our employment opportunities, workforce, and organizational structures will change because of all this. Business will not be business as usual.

For a time during the pandemic, the mental health collective of which I am a part provided services to clients exclusively online. Almost despite ourselves we discovered how effective we could be in a telehealth environment. As life opened back up, many of us retained our remote meetings alongside face-to-face care, a hybrid approach. I now see a full 50 percent of my clients online, and that has extended my reach far beyond my former geographic limitations. Left to ourselves, most of us would have resisted this shift; we viewed online counseling as a weak second-best option. Due to necessity, however, that method has now become another way to operate, another tool in the toolbox. Those changes will most likely endure.

What is to keep the liminal space created by pandemic from becoming permanent, indefinite, a protracted, unresolved condition? Nothing prevents that. Even so, we hope that the pandemic will rise and fall, that after all the damage and despair a resolution will finally come. We long to pass through this chapter into the next one but this requires more than hoping. The way in which people negotiate this liminal pandemic will determine not only its duration, but whether trauma will be eventually understood, healed, and even transcended. The way we write the ending to the story changes the story. What we need most in liminal time and space is the kind of human agency and leadership that escorts communities through tragedy to a new and transformed future.

* * *

Though we all lived through the same phenomenon, the same public health risk, it came to us in different degrees, with diverse impacts, at different times. As such, we did not actually experience one uniform state of liminality, but rather *many different liminalities, arising sequentially.* It was as though we were at the same amusement park, standing in different lines, taking different rides.

If we experienced different liminalities that were the result of contrasting exposure, intensity, effect, timing, and access to liminal guides and healers, then the experience of *communitas* was also different. A true *communitas* developed among those sharing the most similar experiences: health care workers working in a Covid ward; those who lost a dear one to the virus; parents attempting to make virtual learning for their children a success; the unemployed who were trying to make ends meet; failing businesses that could not stay afloat; the perpetually bored whose main concern was lack of social freedom. These pandemic sub-cultures became virtual or actual tribes.

In an over-arching way, the pandemic did pull many citizens together in common cause and a mutual need for survival. We often experienced a sense of solidarity with our neighbors. However, that was not always the case.

Because our society was already ideologically divided, the anxiety and uncertainty of the pandemic made us even more so. Instead of pulling together to face off a mutual threat, already entrenched tribes politicized science, public health, and social response. *Communitas* formed around different world-view flags: vaxers and anti-vaxers, wear-a-mask devotees and freedom-from-masks dissidents; shut-it-down protectors and open-it-up capitalists. The pandemic tore us apart, creating even more tribal resolve.

There is no guarantee whatsoever that the liminality of a pandemic or any other large-scale chaos event will result in some sense of progress. Rather, the outcome of a liminal event like this is determined by the quality of available liminal leadership and its ability to steer the society through turbulent waters.

Pandemics in every time have revealed the social inequities that preceded them. The poor are always with us and even poorer when times become hard. The lower socio-economic classes do not have access to the same resourses as, say, the wealthy in London who fled the plague by going to the country. Inequalities in health care become glaring when people become critically ill. Those working multiple low-tier, poor paying, no benefits jobs can lose everything more easily than those with a constant income stream and quality health insurance. If your job requires that you risk virus exposure, you go to work anyway. Pandemics are truth-tellers; they reveal the truth about the way things are and always have been.

* * *

Even though an entire society has plunged into a collective state of liminality due to a pandemic, that does not mean that it is exempt from additional events that precipitate other and different liminalities at the same time. As in individuals, complex conditions can also exist simultaneously in society. The causes, intensity, and duration may be quite different, but for a moment in time they intersect, creating even more confusion, disorientation, and anxiety. Many times, a shorter-term liminality nests inside a longer-term one, creating a kind of liminality within a liminality. The more recent and perhaps episodic liminality moves to the foreground, as the longer-term liminality hovers in the background.

In the United States on 6 January 2021, a massive insurrection laid siege to the U.S. Capitol building in an attempt to stop Congress from adopting the Electoral College results of the 2020 Presidential Election, results that the ideologically driven coup wanted to overturn. This seditious act had been preceded by a two-month-long, massive disinformation campaign, organized by radical fringe groups, and fruitless legal attempts to challenge the legitimacy of the general election. Investigations into the perpetrators and inside actors continue.

Citizens of the United States are not strangers to public demonstration, dissent, and even violent explosions in the public square. We are not shocked easily. Dramatic incidents of violence toward unarmed black people by law enforcement have frequently resulted not only in peaceful protest but have boiled over into expressions of rage. The violent repression of black people in protest has also been a part of the American story. We are sadly, chronically, accustomed to that.

Nevertheless, when George Floyd was publicly murdered in plain sight by a police officer, the whole world was watching. Citizen journalists had videoed the whole incident. There was no covering. The American public gasped. If this can happen in broad daylight, what else has taken place in the shadows? The answer was obvious: too much for too long. This contemporary lynching became a social threshold we crossed. It shook obscured racism into plain and reprehensible view; and within this liminal whirlpool not even the most incalcitrant white supremacy could hide.

For an American public numbed toward the specter of repeating racial violence, the public execution of George Floyd was compounded by the Capitol Insurrection, which was conducted almost exclusively by white males, many of whom were former military. It was another undeniable wake-up call. That threshold was also revealingly public. Insurgents had attacked a highly symbolic building of laws and attempted to subvert democracy itself. The public became aware of an old menace in a new way, a reality that had been present for centuries but had surfaced with impunity during the previous four years. Confidence in our democratic resilience was wounded. The very underpinnings of a free, democratic society were under assault. We had entered a sinister zone.

This, too, pushed us over a threshold into another state of involuntary social liminality. Whereas the Covid-19 virus was the agent of chaos in the pandemic, human ideology engendered another, lethal virus.

However, there was no vaccination for this social virus. It spread at the speed of the internet; and minds were twisted in its conspiratorial clutches.

Because the liminality of the pandemic and other liminalities, such as the murder of George Floyd and the Capitol Insurrection coincided, these liminalities overlap. Though our collective mind attempts to toggle back and forth between these simultaneous realities in order to address them, the sense of chaos and uncertainty multiplies, and people are inclined to freeze. Whereas it might seem possible to cope with one liminality at a time, the sheer scale of multiple liminalities seems too much to handle.

This does not even take into consideration very personal disruptions. One loses a spouse or a job, drops out of school, receives a diagnosis, or loses the family farm. These experiences layer into the palette of already existing liminalities. Multiple liminal loops intersect, coexist, and diverge. How does one negotiate such complexity?

* * *

It would be tempting to give simple, rational, orderly prescriptions for the way out of and through the extreme social liminality of a pandemic. However, liminality is not rational or orderly. As a form of anti-structure, it defies attempts to reduce matters to a formula. There is no return to what came before, only carrying forward some of the former elements.

Years ago, as I participated in an archaeological dig in Caesarea Maritima, Israel, I viewed a copy of the so-called Pilate Stone (the original is now in the Israel Museum in Jerusalem). It is a block of carved limestone with an inscription mentioning Pontius Pilate, the Roman prefect in Judea 26–36 CE. The stone was discovered in 1961 at Caesarea Maritima, the Roman administrative center that in 6 CE had replaced Jerusalem. The stone is particularly significant as it provides the earliest surviving historical record of Pilate, corroborating the extant literary evidence to his career provided by Josephus, Philo, Tacitus, and the New Testament Gospels. Pilate is the one who famously washed his hands of Jesus' death.

The interesting thing is that the Pilate Stone had been repurposed. As part of archeological excavation, the burgled stone was discovered serving as a step in a later-built colosseum. What had originally been an official marker of a prefect's rank and station was later used for feet to walk on.

Part of the structure that pre-exists any liminal period may survive, may be recognizable, but usually in altered form with changed purpose. Deconstructed physical, social, or personal realities are just that, deconstructed. In the same way, liminal leadership requires more than looking back to recreate the past. Liminal guides engage vision and imagination to recreate a transformed future. This is doubly true in the presence of multiple, complex liminalities.

Most usually, individuals, communities, and nations move through liminality best by depending on treasured values matched with (often changing) plans. It is the values that ultimately determine direction and priority. Lasting values, for instance, ensure that the most vulnerable are tended, the most important matters are prioritized first, and that the good of the many supersedes the good of the few. As people reconstruct life in and on the other side of the liminal domain, the ends do not determine the means, but rather the opposite; the means we choose determine the lasting ends. In fact, the way we address life in the liminal domain prepares us for what comes next.

A collaborative way forward provides an outcome that is qualitatively different from decision-making by a few. The many, however, depend upon wise guides and leaders who provide sage insight and foster true community. If *communitas* is created during liminal chaos events and their aftermath, it is often by liminal people giving themselves to great efforts of survival and reconstruction of a new world. Sharing that work of recreation creates a sense of camaraderie and solidarity.

Recreation also requires a spirit of improvisation. To borrow from the engine of jazz, themes are balanced with improvising over the themes. If the melody and chord structure of a classic tune are fixed, like values that are stated and restated, then the act of creativity moves the performer to create new lines and tonality around, over and within what is provided. Thus, the lasting is matched with the changeable in a creative tension. Liminal people and guides give themselves permission to improvise, experiment, and engage with the novel. Jesus in his role as wisdom teacher strikes a similar chord in his enigmatic parable of the householder: "Every scribe who has been trained for the kingdom of heaven is like the master of a household who brings out of his treasure what is new and what is old." (Matthew 13.52) Only the wise scribe knows which is which, and when which is called upon. Sometimes one plays the melody and other times improvises upon it. The best leaders hold shared values in one hand while they improvise with the other.

Since liminality is primarily a non-rational phenomenon, one that operates outside the realm of the predictable, manageable, and analytical, the landmarks by which we best navigate are also usually non-rational. The communities that are already equipped with traditions made for such transitions are a step ahead. They employ an array of rituals, symbols, liturgy, prayers, song, dance, drama, and story-telling, all meant to sustain individuals and communities during times of trial; and when such traditions are not already woven into the fabric of a culture or sub-culture, people often create their own.

* * *

I once was privileged to be close to a couple who share an interfaith marriage, one Christian and the other Muslim. During their life together, a tragedy befell them – their beloved young child died. We went through all the funeral rituals together and they struggled through the terrible loss.

After a year passed, I received a call. They were observing the one-year anniversary of the child's death and invited me to join them and others at the graveside. Though I was more than happy to do so, I had no idea what to expect. In Muslim practice, the one-year anniversary is of particular significance. The hardest and most important mourning often takes place in the dark interval of that first year. So, we gathered at the grave, the grieving parents in the center of our circle.

At a certain moment, everyone squatted down, took a rock from the surface of the ground, and began tapping on the grave. No words were spoken because words were unnecessary; they were tapping on the very place where their dear one reclined. They tapped and wept, wept and tapped. They tapped on the ground with their rocks until they could tap no longer. Then we rose, hugged one another, and left in silence. The ritual had done its work.

What I want to say is not entirely sensible or logical. These are not the kind of words you will find in a self-help manual and, of all the things you might expect to read in an essay about extreme liminalities, this is perhaps the most unlikely:

> We need to tap on the ground of liminality
> with the stones at our disposal
> until the past is placed where it belongs
> unavoidable truths arise
> and we step up and out
> into a new world.

Seven Practices for a Liminal Age

Justine Huxley

Before the Covid-19 pandemic, over three hundred thousand people worked in the square mile of the City of London. The pavements were bustling with a blur of anonymous, grey-suited people, at least half of them speaking into mobile phones, destined for investment banks and finance companies. The traffic noise was relentless: red double-decker buses and black cabs thundering past, with dozens of bicycles dodging in between. This speed, this urgency, this anonymity, and the relentless acquisitive mindset of materialism are what the City calls the "real world."

Counter to all my expectations about how my life should look, I am also one of those commuters and have been traveling into and out of the City for almost twenty years, even if at present the streets are more empty and half my working week is at home. My feet lead me down Bishopsgate on autopilot but, instead of through the shiny revolving doors of a corporation, they take me up a narrow alleyway flanked, on one side, by a 60-storey building of mirrored glass and, on the other, by the stone wall of a church built eight hundred years earlier. As is my habit, I run my fingers along the pale, irregular stone as I walk, and pass through the tall bronze-coloured gate into a tiny courtyard garden.

Those who stumble upon this garden are always taken by surprise. The sound of the traffic melts away, replaced by the sound of water flowing from a red stone fountain into a circular pond overhung by dark green foliage and a jungle of swaying purple flowers. The air smells different. The ground is paved with mosaics reflecting intricate patterns. The ornate wrought-iron grilles and pale green olive trees evoke the days of Andalucia – blending Mediterranean freedom with Islamic order. More surprising still is that through the stone arch and carved oak doors sits a circular Bedouin tent made of woven goat hair. Its windows are sand blasted with the phases of the moon and the words of peace in seven different languages, including Arabic, Sanskrit, Inuit and Chinese.

This is St. Ethelburga's Centre for Reconciliation and Peace. It has all the hallmarks of liminal space. On entering, one senses instinctively that here the rules that govern the City do not apply. The word that comes to many people's minds is "oasis." Others have called it a "thin space" where the boundaries with the inner world are more pervious.

The threads of my own destiny which brought me here began to unfold in 2001, in the moment of dislocation when the world was reeling from the shock of 9/11. I was working on the trading floor of an investment bank when it happened. The bank had offices in Manhattan. We watched the moment the plane hit the South Tower in real time, on the huge television screens positioned around the floor. The moment was burned into my memory by the knowledge that we had colleagues inside. At the time, I had strong connections in the Muslim community and in the strange weeks that followed, as the world revealed itself to be a different place, my heart stirred with a calling to build bridges, to play a part in exposing the hidden dynamics which lay beneath this dramatic rupture, to help weave back together the splintered fabric of our world. I held this feeling close in my heart, unvoiced, and waited to see if it was real. Three years later, I was still in derivative sales when Al Qaeda's violence came so much closer. One of the suicide bombers was in Aldgate, just one tube station away from Liverpool Street, where I had alighted less than five minutes earlier. Then something shifted and my feet took me to this diminutive medieval church that I had passed many times without ever noticing, just a few hundred meters from the trading floor.

The destiny of St. Ethelburga's, like my own, was also shaped by politically motivated violence. The church was collateral damage in an IRA bomb that destroyed swathes of the City in the 1990s. The incendiary device was hidden in a lorry parked outside its wooden doors. In the stunned days after that event, the Bishop of London, Richard Chartres, picked his way through the piles of rubble and shards of shattered glass, prayed for guidance, and saw how the church could be reborn as a place of reconciliation. Strangely, but as is often the case when one looks deeper, the seeds of this cross-cultural and inter-religious karma were visible a century before when John Meadows Rodwell, rector in the 1870s, published the first reliable English translation of the Qu'ran. Ethelburga herself, a seventh-century Benedictine abbess, also had a fortune which echoes contemporary themes and liminal experiences. Following a vision of an intensely bright light, she gained her sainthood as a healer in the midst of a pandemic.

St. Ethelburga's Centre is a sacred space, a liminal space, that aspires to play a role in the evolution of spirituality and human culture. Its smallness belies the magnitude of its mission – how it is connected to a global network of similarly destined places and people – one of the nodes in a vast web seeking to give birth to the new. It is also a place full of stories, and we have learned to read its stories like signs that point out a pathway towards reconciliation in an age of global crisis. The story of the devastating bomb and an ancient church reincarnated as a peace center invites visitors to recognize the opportunity that lies at the heart of every crisis. The story of our patron saint heroically putting faith into action in dark times leads us to ask whether, when the chips are down, we shall have the courage to risk our own lives serving those in need? Standing between the Christian church and the Bedouin tent, two iconic buildings from vastly different cultures, visitors hear the call to bridge divisions, to build community across differences of all kinds. The story of a tiny church that stayed true to its spiritual purpose for centuries, despite now being dwarfed by the shiny symbols of materialism, speaks of the need to protect what is sacred. It invites visitors to consider: How shall I protect what matters most when it is under threat? The act of walking up the alleyway, separating from the world of consumerism, invites the question: Where is my thinking caught in an extractive mindset? The woven designs depicted in the mosaic paving hint at the universal structures of being that are hidden beneath the surface of our divided world. They ask: With what and whom are you interdependent? Are you living true to that knowledge? As you leaf through the rector's Qu'ran, its faded pages whisper: Can you see how the seeds of change are planted long before the door to transformation opens? Look, the East window, made from fragments of stained glass collected after the bomb, is catching the early morning sun. The dance of light and colour calls us to ask whether you can trust in the potential for rebirth. Can you see how beautiful new patterns emerge from the rubble of utterly demolished things?

These stories, these questions shape what unfolds here and have grown deep roots into my heart. I have tried to make St. Ethelburga's like a lighthouse in a stormy sea, standing for 'the more beautiful world, our hearts know is possible'[1] keeping the light of hope burning as more and more is lost to us. These days, our core business can only be carried out in the full knowledge of climate breakdown. Reconciliation with Earth has to sit alongside reconciliation with each other, equal in priority. Climate is an accelerant in many of the world's conflicts. It is the silent story behind so many millions of displaced lives, already creating imbalances and resource pressures that drive our divisions deeper. Even the polarizing effect of Brexit in the United Kingdom was partly caused by fears about the long march of refugees, many fleeing wars inflamed by drought and famine. Like our understanding of the Covid-19 pandemic, we are still not good at joining up the dots, at recognizing how our destruction of Earth is feeding into every scenario, lying beneath so many things that no longer behave as they used to.

In this perilous landscape, our raison d'être is to call people towards bridging divisions and loving Earth and to recognize the links between these two desperately urgent tasks. In the words of the Lakota elder, Tiokasin Ghosthorse, there can be no peace on Earth unless there is also peace with Earth.

Finding myself a custodian of this place with its many stories has been a journey into curating and holding liminal spaces. My predecessor, Professor Simon Keyes, conceived the Bedouin Tent as a liminal space where one could step outside the bounds of everyday life, meet people one would not normally encounter, have conversations one would not normally have. The beauty and harmony of its design, drawn from principles of sacred geometry, and the surprise of finding such a structure in the back garden of a City church, all add to its power as a place of liminality. This is about gathering ourselves in a new way – and the art of gathering people and inviting transformation means to know how to weave together an experience which bears certain things in common with a tribal community's rites of passage – the arena in which the term liminality was first applied.

One must first know how to create liminal space for oneself. As a follower of the Sufi tradition, where retreat is an important practice, I have become familiar with this process – from time to time, when the heart prompts, to separate from one's everyday life and carve out the boundaries of a space in which one can sink deeply into emptiness. I delight in the various rituals involved in taking myself out of the

---

[1.] Charles Eisenstein, *The More Beautiful World Our Hearts Know Is Possible* (Berkeley, CA: North Atlantic Books, 2013).

stream of conventional thought and my own habitual patterns and creating a safe container in which the spirit can speak in ways that you cannot normally hear. Retreat often also involves weaving myself into the natural landscape and the more-than-human world, allowing the identities that hold my everyday urban persona together to fade into the background and allowing the silence of the wild to feed my soul. Afterwards, you learn how to hold the inner changes that come, gently, as you transition back into life, how to use symbols and archetypes to ground those changes inwardly so they do not evaporate under the avalanche of daily demands.

St. Ethelburga's programmes share a similar quality: a chance to come together with a diverse group of people, step out of the usual ways of thinking, grapple with both the uncomfortable truths of our time and the differences that emerge among us, immerse ourselves in new experiences, allow them to dismantle us and reshape us in a new configuration, then transition back to life, holding the seeds of something new, allowing the container of relationships, the bridges formed, to support you to plant those seeds in the world, catalyzing change, becoming the building blocks of relational, resilient communities capable of pulling together in times of crisis rather than fracturing and falling apart.

Otto Scharmer's Theory U[2] is an indispensable framework for this kind of group process. The shape of the letter reflects the arc of a journey, the bottom of the U depicting the 'messy middle' of this journey where often there is a dislocation, where we come up against blocks and barriers, and where there is a confrontation with not knowing. To accompany a group through any kind of transformational process means to become familiar with the bottom of the U, to model a sense of trust, holding the feelings of frustration, anguish or vulnerability, and being at ease with not knowing – in other words, how to hold the boundaries of a liminal space and enable the letting go, the dissolution of fixed patterns necessary if we are to open ourselves to something truly new.

On a global scale, humanity now sits at the bottom of the U. We are in the agony of a broken civilization, facing the possibility of an uninhabitable Earth. As is true with small groups in transition, being at the bottom of the U, *consciously*, changes things. It helps to have a roadmap – even one that is simply pointing out we are in a place where our old maps no longer make sense.

[2.] Otto Scharmer, *Theory U: Leading from the Future as It Emerges* (Oakland, CA: Berrett-Koehler, 2016).

In 2018 St. Ethelburga's focus shifted towards this need purposefully to face ecological breakdown. This was the year the Intergovernmental Panel on Climate Change report painted an alarming picture of a world dangerously close to irreversible climate tipping points. Extinction Rebellion burst onto the streets of Britain bearing images of skulls, calling for mass civil disobedience; and Professor Jem Bendell published his seminal paper, "Deep Adaptation: A Map for Navigating Climate Tragedy."[3] A taboo was smashed. Suddenly, there was permission to speak our worst fears: that it is not five to midnight, but rather five past, and some form of societal collapse is now inevitable. Initially using climate science and Bendell's paper as a framework, we began gathering people with the intention of going beyond naive optimism and deliberately looking into the abyss, asking: Do we need to prepare? And, if so, how?

What follows are some of the learnings from this work, which could also be seen as practices for living with resilience in a liminal age.

One: Face Reality

To be alive today, means to face truths and possibilities that are hard to take in. No one can know for sure what will unfold, but the bottom line is this: human extinction is a genuine possibility. It takes courage to be in relationship with that fact. To live with integrity, means to be willing to have our minds and hearts utterly crushed by that knowledge. Further, because of our tendency to revert to stasis, we have to be willing to go through the pain of that over and over again.

It is hard to do that in the midst of the collective lie that everything is going to be okay. It can also be mentally destabilizing to confront alone. We found that curating a retreat space, detached from mainstream reasoning, but also involving a container of peer relationships, can enable the tenacity to go through that shattering as a rite of passage.

To contemplate extinction means a confrontation not just with our own personal death, but with death on a much greater scale. Taking inspiration from ancient practices, from the dervishes who meditated in graveyards and mystics who dig their own graves and lie in them to contemplate impermanence, we designed retreats where this confrontation with

---

[3.] Jem Bendell, "Deep Adaptation: A Map for Navigating Climate Tragedy," IFLAS Occasional Paper 2, July 2018.

death was built in, and found that, rather than engendering despair or nihilism, it was empowering. As one participant said, "The monster you look in the eye, is less scary than the one you leave hiding behind the wardrobe." Meeting personal and collective death is an initiation into living authentically in these times. It grounds us in reality and keeps us rooted there.

On our retreats, sometimes we include silent night walks, navigating dark forests together, without torches, walking into darkness as a metaphor, meeting our worst imaginings of an apocalyptic future. The first time we tried this, my mind dwelled on a memory: volunteering in Moria, a massive, overcrowded refugee camp on the Greek island of Lesbos, in the time when thousands of Syrian and Afghan refugees attempted the treacherous crossing from Turkey every day. I watched a Syrian man whose face was etched with anxiety gather his family in the middle of the night – wife, brothers, sister-in-law, five young children, frail elderly father – and prepare to head down an unlit road on the three-hour walk to the port. He had tickets for the dawn ferry to Athens. We helped him get there safely, but I have no idea what became of him and his loved ones. As we walked through the safe English countryside – knowing we had the privilege of warm beds to return to and that, in the West, the worst is yet to come – it was his face that haunted me.

Two: Trust

Living in these times means to embrace profound uncertainty, to live in an intimate, daily dance with unknowing at the deepest level. However, perhaps we can trust this process. Perhaps we can know that the disruption and darkness are necessary and have their own transformative power. The instability of the liminal state is what allows entrenched ways of being to fall away and something new to emerge. Clearly humanity could have done this differently. There was surely a turning we missed which could have led us seamlessly towards a sustainable, just and spiritually meaningful way of life. Having missed that crossroads, we can only embrace the disintegration of our civilization as an opportunity, as a teacher, and trust it will clear away space for the deeper change we need.

Rebecca Solnit, in *A Paradise Built in Hell*, describes the way disasters such as Hurricane Katrina or the Japanese Tsunami can "topple old orders and open new possibilities." She documents how, in the aftermath of catastrophe, when societal structures have given way, new non-hierarchical ways of relating can emerge. People create new roles for themselves, resources are shared, prejudices bypassed, and, alongside the obvious pain and shock, there is also a freedom to reinvent what community means.[4]

On an individual level, our higher selves know what it takes to break deeply embedded patterns. Sometimes a car crash or some other unforeseen "calamity" is the best means to catapult ourselves into the liminal space we need. As the caterpillar dissolves in the chrysalis before reforming as a butterfly, sometimes only radical dissolution is enough.

As Llewellyn Vaughan-Lee writes in *A Handbook for Survivalists*,[5] we need the "unbinding power of chaos" to free us from the calcified story of consumerism, greed and exploitation that holds us in its grip. In our hubristic culture, we have not just lost the ability to welcome death, but we have forgotten the Divine has both light and dark aspects, not just Creator but also destroyer. It is not our place to judge the ways of the Divine, but rather to honour all His/Her faces. As we lean into the escalating frequency of socially and ecologically disruptive events, by bringing an attitude of trust and allowing, we are more able to align ourselves with the new ways of being waiting to emerge from the debris.

Three: Be Fluid with Identity

In the dualistic consciousness that pervades the Western world, often our sense of self is constructed through contrasts and opposites. We define ourselves by who we are not, as much as by who we are. We create "in groups" and "out groups." What creates the heat in a conflict is often threats to our identity. External threats (such as the resource pressure created by climate, migration or economic uncertainties) can in turn strengthen group identities in ways that increase the human propensity to blame those who are "not like us." However, at the heart of any rite of passage or any meaningful individual or collective transformation, there is the sacrifice of identity. In a tribal coming-of-age ritual, the identity of an adolescent is sacrificed in order to return to the tribe as an adult. Psychological integration or the spiritual journey can be seen as the repeated surrendering of ego-identities, all of which, whether

---

4. Rebecca Solnit, *A Paradise Built in Hell: The Extraordinary Communities That Arise in Disaster* (New York: Penguin, 2010) (Kindle).

5. Llewellyn Vaughan-Lee, *A Handbook for Survivalists: Caring for the Earth: A Series of Meditations* (Point Reyes, CA: Golden Sufi Center, 2020).

experienced as positive or negative, are barriers to wholeness and the direct experience of the Divine. In liminal space, our identities have the potential to be more fluid. There can be breathing space around who we think we are. In a world divided by identity issues, this possibility of fluidity is very much needed.

In a landscape already painfully polarized and suffering a profound crisis of meaning, the danger of violent ideologies, authoritarianism and cultural fragmentation is great. Holding our social fabric together is as essential as changing to a carbon neutral way of life. How we understand and hold identity is a key part of that. Joanna Macy has written about the "Greening of the Self"[6] to describe the process of expanding our identity to see ourselves as part of the wider web of the natural world. This expansion of our sense of self needs to include a recognition of how the exploitation of nature has only been made possible by the oppression of people, often along racial lines. We can no longer afford to separate these things.

Western materialism was built on colonization and the exploitation of both land and people. The wounds of that history remain deep and unhealed, and the injustice is very far from over. Whilst many Westerners wait for climate disruption to hit in a bigger way, countries like the Philippines, Malawi, Venezuela, and others in the global south are already immersed in that reality. Although this picture is changing, the countries responsible for emitting the most carbon are, for the most part, not the countries suffering its most devastating effects.

In this time of liminality, there is a need to expand our sense of identity in all directions so we can build much-needed bridges across these divides. This is often a painful process. It can mean to hold our own fears about a future of collapse together with the knowledge of our complicity in the causes of collapse elsewhere in the world. It can mean to wake up to the fact that our wealth and privilege could be built on the oppression of others. It can mean to reach outside our echo chamber and be willing to form relationships with people whose perspectives might seem abhorrent to us. It always confronts us with our own psychological shadow and the hidden shadows of our identity groups, whether they be religious, cultural, national, or political.

The dissolution of our civilization will continue to expose all these things. It will give us a choice: to retreat further into our identities and project our fears outward onto others; or to allow our sense of self to

---

6. Joanna Macy, *Greening of the Self* (Berkeley, CA: Parallax Press, 2013) (Kindle).

be melted and reshaped, revealing our shared humanity as well as our connection with the more than human world. Since our resilience lies in community, specifically, robust community across differences, a more flexible relationship with identity is now an imperative.

Four: Change Your Relationship with Suffering

In his autobiography, *From a Mountain in Tibet*,[7] Lama Yeshe describes how as a rebellious teenager he was placed in a monastery to serve his elder brother, the abbot, Akong Rinpoche. This made him miserable and resentful. It was not until the monks were forced to flee from the brutal Chinese invasion and experienced extreme cold, searing hunger and relentless fear, that he could see his suffering at the monastery had been caused by his own mind, and not by the situation itself. He recognized that, if he brought the same internal resistance to this new, truly harsh reality, it would only make things worse. What was needed was the quality of forbearance. For some privileged people, particularly in the West, we have not yet left that monastery. We may be fatigued from the Covid-19 pandemic but perhaps do not recognize that there is likely much greater suffering to come. Learning how to control our minds and endure with inner dignity the many things that will be outside our control will be a major element of our personal resilience.

Millions of people around the world are already experiencing different kinds of loss and trauma as a result of what we have done to Earth. Whether losing everything as a refugee, losing one's home in a flood or wildfire, losing one's livelihood due to lockdown, or simply feeling the deep grief of lost species – our capacity to process grief and trauma will become increasingly important in the years to come. This is already a much larger task than can be met by therapists and health workers. Our mental health may depend on tools and processes we can apply on a grand scale.

Necessary as it is for our health, more important than simply processing our grief is allowing it to change us. Grief for the world, both human and more than human, is part of the rite of passage we are journeying through. Grief has the power to open our hearts. In

---

[7] Lama Yeshe Losal Rinpoche, *From a Mountain in Tibet: A Monk's Journey* (New York: Penguin, 2020).

the liminality of these times, we shall be broken open again and again and again. Our hearts will be shaped in the fire of loss. As Joanna Macy says:

> We are capable of suffering **with** our world, and that is the true meaning of compassion. It enables us to recognize our profound interconnectedness with all beings. Don't ever apologize for crying for the trees burning in the Amazon or over the waters polluted from mines in the Rockies. Don't apologize for the sorrow, grief, and rage you feel. It is a measure of your humanity and your maturity. It is a measure of your open heart, and as your heart breaks open there will be room for the world to heal.[8]

Five: Hold on to Your Values

The Ancient Greek word for crisis contains a reference to the action of "sifting," pointing to how calamity helps us separate what is essential from what is an irrelevant distraction. As a society, we have drifted a long way from what matters most. Just as a life-threatening medical diagnosis can help individuals to remember what is most real or meaningful in their lives, we have the opportunity collectively to reconnect with our most fundamental human values.

At St. Ethelburga's, we use embodied exercises to make future scenarios fully real to ourselves. We invite participants to identify the different stages of possible ecological and social breakdown, and to walk those trajectories, using their imagination to prepare emotionally for what could be coming down the line. If I imagine walking into a future of increasing food insecurity, mass displacement, biodiversity failure, escalating conflict, and destabilized morals and mental health, it is quite frankly terrifying. If I imagine walking through that world with the value of service alive in my heart, it is a very different feeling. Rather than a battleground for my own survival, it can become a testing ground for the spirit. Knowing and living our values can be a huge source of resilience in a time of chaos.

I once met a young man from a South American country already in the throes of both social and ecological collapse, where increasingly authoritarian leaders had seized control. His advice to the world was

---

[8.] Macy, *Greening of the Self.*

this: look to your values now while you still can. Know what you stand for and embed it in your mind; otherwise, before you realize what is happening, your humanity could slowly be eroded and become irretrievable. A powerful warning!

Six: Protect What Is Sacred: Silence, Spiritual Practice, Nature

Carl Jung tells the story of the rainmaker who is summoned to help to end a drought. The people are expecting to see him perform some kind of ritual magic, but instead he retires to a hut in silent contemplation for three days. His withdrawal has the effect of bringing first himself and then the land back into balance, and soon after the rains return. As we traverse the chaos and confusion of this liminal age, contemplative practice is a powerful way not just to stay stable, but also to align ourselves inwardly with the new reality trying to be born. This is not the prayer of asking for our desires to be fulfilled, but rather the deeper wordless prayer of surrender. Spiritual practice can help us detach from the hypocrisies and absurdities of late-stage capitalism and a post-truth world. Through it, we withdraw our attention from what is false, and re-root ourselves in what is real. This is not just helpful for our personal resilience but, as the rainmaker shows us, it has a wider effect. It holds a place of stillness and sanity in the world around us. It brings life back into balance.

Prayer is at its most powerful in liminal space. If we can turn our hearts towards the Divine, we can energize what is in gestation and align it with its highest potential. To do this we must stay with the humility of not knowing, refrain from jumping to solutions or limiting the outcome with our preconceived ideas or desires. It is not easy to wait in the darkness, in a place of dissolution. It is here, however, that invisible magic can happen. It is here that love can penetrate the spaces that become available when things fall apart. It is here that we can plant seeds of light to nourish our rebirth. Life will not regenerate through technology or human cleverness. It can only regenerate from the place of the sacred. Our prayers, our silence, our longing, are needed to keep the world connected with the spiritual reality that our culture of materialism and separation has done so much to destroy.

Nature is cyclical and can also teach us to be at ease in liminal space. Everywhere you look there are natural cycles that move in and out of liminality. Dawn and dusk, when the light changes from day to night and back again. The seasons, moving through winter, when the seeds lie dormant underground, waiting for their time to stir. Our own breathing, bringing spirit to live by returning to its source. The rise and fall of civilizations, the evolution of life through crisis and extinction, these are not different, they just belong to a timescale which is harder for us to perceive.

If we do nothing else in this time, to come back into connection with the natural world and its sacred cycles is our primary need. I am always moved and inspired by the multitude of creative ways people are re-attuning to that relationship. I have learned so much and been changed forever by elders like Tiokasin Ghosthorse, Pat McCabe, Eleanor O'Hanlon, Charlotte du Cann, Llewellyn Vaughan-Lee. My own journey into that "great conversation" with the wild began to open up when six years ago I started a movement prayer that involves greeting the different kingdoms of the natural world. I love to do this outside, before I return indoors to meditate, in the borderland time as darkness turns into light, when my garden is still steeped in quiet and mystery. The combination of movement and breath and prayer for the more-than-human world opens something inside me and, after only a short time, I feel washed with peace. Over the years, I have got to know my garden in a new way, and my garden has got to know me. This brief fifteen minutes each morning, simple as it is, has helped to weave me back into the wider web of being in a way I could never have predicted. This is not just a resilience practice, but a daily reaffirmation of the inner shift Earth is calling out for us to make: back into the circle of life, where we all so deeply belong.

Seven: Keep the Fire of Vision Alive

A commitment to resilience and climate adaptation means a new relationship with vision – one that is designed for the long haul. No one who recognizes how serious the environmental catastrophe really is can be focused on their own lifetime. This is the task of many generations.

As this period of disintegration accelerates, holding a vision for regeneration that can survive through the decades until a new society can be established becomes of supreme importance. Vision is a great source of resilience. The difficulty is that the vision we need is of a "not-yet-imagined" reality. We must find a way to access a consciousness that is not reflected by the world around us. Although many people, especially young people, hold vital keys to that new way of life, there remains a need to hold faith in something that is beyond our imagining, the way a tiny acorn holds within it the as-yet-unknown reality of a mighty oak.

Perhaps there is a kind of magic needed to tap into a felt sense of this reality that we cannot yet fully know. We can learn much from indigenous wisdom-holders, but there is something our colonized minds cannot access via the usual routes. What lies on the other side of this transition might be more different than we know. In our retreats, we developed a method of "collective dreaming" that uses shamanic journeying into the future to draw on a different quality of consciousness, one that does not separate the physical and spiritual realms. It creates an experience that bypasses the mind, enabling each participant to catch a subtle scent or taste and return holding one small seed of that future.

Those who have the capacity to dream and imagine will be needed to keep the spark of vision alive, passing it like an Olympic flame down the generations until it can bear fruit. Symbols, archetypes, and myth-making have a role here: the seeds of the fire poppy, that lie dormant for decades only to germinate in the barren conditions after a wildfire; the painted lady butterflies, tiny, fragile insects who somehow manage to migrate thousands of miles across many generations, each generation completing its portion of a bigger map; or even the tiny church of St. Ethelburga with its many stories, showing how destruction can help us re-imagine spirituality for a new era.

As I sit here writing at my desk at St. Ethelburga's, in the quiet of a Sunday afternoon, the City seems empty of human life. Sunlight bounces off the mirrored windows of the towering corporate offices and illuminates the emerald foliage in the tiny courtyard garden outside my window. I can hear the water splashing from the fountain into the pool. It seems to me that liminality is everywhere I turn my gaze. It was in the bulbs waiting silently in the dark, hidden under the ivy I cut back this morning, each one putting forth tiny roots about to begin their downward mission. It is in every doorway I pass through. It is with me on this seventh day of the week, which I try to preserve as a day of rest and emptiness. It is in my breathing, which brings my spirit into my body and returns it to merge with the beyond. It is in the way my breath links me to the furthest reaches of creation and the vast cycles of time, where whole universes burst into being, expand, contract, and disappear.

Spirit has become associated with the liminal, something we find most easily in the spaces betwixt and between. Perhaps that is only because we put Her there. We banished Her from the rational center of our lives and confined Her to the edges, exiled in the borderlands.

Perhaps it is only our perspective that makes something liminal, that decides if where we are is the center or the edge, the transition or the established order. In truth, all is woven together, the inner and outer, the beginnings and endings, the everyday and the magical. Now, when the era of duality is past its sell-by date and rapidly turning toxic, Earth is calling out to us to weave the dimensions back together again and recognize the inseparable, interpenetrating Oneness of Being. Can we as a species surrender our need to control and dominate and come back into a humble relationship with the Infinite?

The Covid-19 pandemic gave us liminal time on a global level. Full of challenge and loss, but also full of potential for change. Without the willingness to enter consciously into that space, without the guides and shamans to hold us there and help us to plumb its depths, the experience will most likely be wasted on us. However, perhaps there will be a way for us to reclaim the shaman's knowledge that lies within each of us and grow in the wisdom of the liminal. We can never return to the safety of what came before, we can only surrender deeper into chaos and change. We can only learn to trust in the face of disruption, to resist the desire to define, to control, or to solve too quickly. Certainty is safe, but can imprison us in our collective conditioning, the mindset that got us into this mess. Uncertainty is scary – but it is wild and alive and can be a liberation. We do not know whether we shall make it through, or whether we shall drive ourselves to extinction, along with all the other species who call this place home, leaving a wrecked and unlivable Earth. Perhaps like the mystics who dig their own graves and lie in them, we can use the proximity to death to bring us closer to the mystery of life. By grounding ourselves in the most painful truths of our time, we can open a portal into a new experience of love.

Creation is a glorious symphony, in which everything is being born out of emptiness, flowering and passing away. Liminality teaches us to let go. It gives us a map, a means to recognize the place of confusion as a threshold of possibility. If we can welcome liminality and learn to live intentionally within it, perhaps it can lead us into a place of greater aliveness and, ultimately, show us the way back to balance and beauty.

As I write these last lines, the light is fading outside. In the absence of traffic noise, miraculously, I hear the notes of a solitary blackbird gracing the tiny garden with lucid evening song. By the time I walk to the window, he has gone. My heart hurts. I wonder how he survives in this barren, concrete world. Soon the sun will go down and stars will come out, only the brightest visible against the lights of the City. Day will lead us into night; and we shall wait once again for the dawn.

Unknownland, Blackness, and Liminality

Phil Allen, Jr.

Since the beginning of the transatlantic slave trade, people of African descent who were victims of a system of enslavement and death have had a unique existence in lands colonized and/or governed by white power structures. Historically, these power structures recognized enough of their humanity to exploit their bodies for white prosperity, but not enough to allow for equal treatment and full acceptance in society. The journey during the Middle Passage – the stage of the triangular trade between Africa and the Americas – lasted anywhere from one to six months with enslaved Africans surviving or dying in the belly of the slave ship.[1] A life of slavery was their intended destiny in perpetuity if white U.S. Southerners had their way. Once the importation of enslaved Africans was abolished, black women's bodies were then used to produce the "property" that would replace those brought in by the trade. Although treated as instruments, for the political gain of Southerners for the purpose of representation in Congress, they were counted as three fifths of a white person.[2] Slavery gave way to the short-lived liminal space of Reconstruction (1867–77). Following Reconstruction was ninety years of a Jim Crow, separate but *unequal*, structured society.

[1.] Thomas Lewis, "Transatlantic Slave Trade," *Encyclopedia Britannica*, 6 April 2020, https://www.britannica.com/topic/transatlantic-slave-trade (accessed 14 May 2021).

[2.] Joy DeGruy, *Post-Traumatic Slave Syndrome: America's Legacy of Enduring Injury and Healing* (Portland, OR: Joy DeGruy Publications, 2017), pp. 37–38.

Today, the residual of the racial history of the United States still produces disparate realities between white and African Americans from racial profiling, mass incarceration, media messaging and representation, hiring practices, punitive reactions in the workplace to hairstyles, dress, and other cultural expressions, and treatment of students in the school system, just to name a few examples. Blackness occupies the chasm between nothingness and "somebodiness."[3] The dominant ideology of white supremacy and the resulting social structure has imposed a perpetual liminal existence upon blackness that is the source of both the persisting lament and improvisational and creative tendencies of blackness; this liminality is traumatic but has redemptive potential.

It is critical first to establish working definitions for several terms – whiteness, white supremacy, and social structure – that make up the components of white power structures that render blackness a liminal reality in the United States. Although white power structures impact white people to various degrees, our primary focus is on the way white power structures affect the black community.

White power structures are the extension of the white ideology that casts its shadows across all of American society. In other words, these structures – or collective structure – allow whiteness to be felt, heard, experienced, and even seen in real ways. The structures are given life through laws, policies, and cultural attitudes. In *Can "White" People Be Saved?*, Love Sechrest, Johnny Ramirez-Johnson and Amos Young cite Willie Jennings in describing whiteness as "order[ing] global systems of dominance that favor Whites and that have in turn nurtured racism, white supremacy, and patriarchy ... an idolatrous way of being in the world."[4] White supremacy, in particular, "can be defined as the ideology that *centers whiteness*, and we can note how it creates and sustains institutions and practices that promote the social, political, and

---

3. Martin Luther King, Jr., "The Case Against Tokenism," in Martin Luther King, Jr., *A Testament of Hope: The Essential Writings and Speeches of Martin Luther King, Jr.*, ed. James M. Washington (New York: Harper One, 1986), p. 108. King uses the term "somebodiness" to refer to African Americans recapturing a sense of dignity and respect in spite of perpetuated anti-black racial injustice, inequities, and dehumanization at the hands of white Americans.

4. Love Sechrest, Johnny Ramirez-Johnson and Amos Young, "Introduction," in Love Sechrest, Johnny Ramirez-Johnson and Amos Young (eds), *Can "White" People Be Saved?: Triangulating Race, Theology, and Missions* (Downers Grove, IL: InterVarsity Press, 2018), pp. 12–13.

economic dominance of Whites and the oppression of people of color."[5] Andrew Draper defines whiteness as "a religious system of pagan idol worship."[6] This idolatry sits at the foundation of the U.S. American whiteness project that informs and infects its social structures. By social structure I mean the framework of society that we are born into which involves and influences inter- and intra-group patterns of relationship and guides individual and collective behavior. These social structures exist with built-in perpetual liminal spaces intentionally and unintentionally designed and reserved especially for blackness.

The following poem, "Unknownland," was originally written to evoke the imagination and create understanding around blackness as liminal existence or as embodied liminality. When I use the term "blackness", I am speaking of the entirety of the black experience in the United States. I am referring to what it means to be black. "Blackness," "the black experience," or "African American experience" are used interchangeably. Here I expound on the poetic stanzas and their ideas.

Unknownland

In-between humanity and nothing
Between visible and invisible
Threat and accepted
Is my black body
A body whose beauty is still a fetish
Whose intellect still questioned
Whose value is still measured against white bodies
The scar tissue from the tight grip of hundreds of years of
    physical economical
And intellectual chains that my black body has had to break
    through
Is immobilizing at best
Lethal at worst
Forty decades on this soil patiently waiting for the last

[5.] Ibid., p. 13 (my italics).

[6.] Andrew T. Draper, "The End of 'Mission': Christian Witness and the Decentering of White Identity," in Love Sechrest, Johnny Ramirez-Johnson and Amos Young (eds), *Can "White" People Be Saved?: Triangulating Race, Theology, and Missions* (Downers Grove, IL: InterVarsity Press, 2018), p. 177.

To be first
In the meantime my residence is Unknownland

In-between prophets and profits
Is my black body
Confronting social systems
That co-opt my limbs to generate revenue under the banner
Of the American dream
The ghost that dangles in front of me fortune and fame
I dwell in the Unknownland of not being familiar with all the
*   rules*
But having to forever play the game
The ladder for the success of my black body often ends
When the ball stops dribbling and my vertical leap diminishes
Because space in the C-suite for melanin is limited

In-between Egypt and Canaan
I've learned to thrive in spite of
I've learned to imagine my black self
Transcending artificial limitations like the Jericho wall in light of
Laws policies and cultural messaging that facilitates
The tyranny that attempts to dictate the plight of
My black body
This wilderness is not good for my dark skin
It leaves permanent marks when
The racist rhetoric the white gaze or silent complicity
Hits the center mass of my being by [racist] marksmen
Who simply claim they didn't mean to be bigots

The camera captures the violent in-between of Unknownland
The space between Gethsemane and Calvary
Between the cross and the tomb
Between death and life
In this purgatorial real estate
That black bodies inhabit
Dignity is stripped because blackness has been deemed invalid
The iPhone or the Android records the annihilation in real
*   time*
Paused by the invisible virus to be still and witness the
Manifestation of the visible one
Kneeling in full worship posture

Sacrificing black life once again to white ideological gods
What are the odds we are traumatized?

In-between the Unknownland of African and American
Is my black body
I cling to the dash that joins yet separates the identity in
*   my veins*
From the one imposed upon me
The identity that affirms me and the one that has abused my
*   selfhood*
Assimilation is its weapon
Amnesia is its weapon
But my body remembers the dance of my mothers and fathers
My body lives in-between the memory and amnesia
In-between assimilation and resistance
My body is insistent on being

Being in this in-between space full of life
Being seen in this space
Being heard in this space
Being beautiful in this space
Being creative in this space
Being black in this space
This is the space where Negro spirituals were born in the
*   invisible church*
Of the enslaved Africans appropriating the God that co-signed
*   their*
Servitude to become the God of their deliverance
This is the space where the improvisation of jazz was
*   conceived*
Where Hip Hop found its prophetic imagination
It's the space between when Rosa kept her seat
And 381 days on their feet
So not to feed the beast
Of oppression

In-between rhythm and blues
Is my black body
The space that makes beautiful music from the melody of my joy
And the lyrics scripted by my pain
Reconnecting my body and my soul

To once again be whole after being dismembered
By Euro-centric ideology that fragments what was meant
To not just be held but to behold
In-between free throw lines and hoops
Are the limbs of black and brown skinned bodies at play
Afros and cornrows 10 feet in the air on display
Image bearers from streetball to the NBA
In those spaces we find the sacred
The essence of creativity and power and grace
Intensity and focus and resilience
In the face
Of the beast plotting to capitalize on race

In-between the east and west wings
Were descendants of the enslaved
Filling the hallowed halls of the White House
Not the culmination of the dream
But the beginning of its reality
Where the Unknownland becomes known
The liminal space of black embodiment
Finds its home
And this space is attractive
It becomes the safe place
The space of the most promise
Where blackness
Emerges ex nihilo
Out of nothing became something
And it was good[7]

In-Between

Liminality, the threshold or the "point of entering"[8] (but not quite), is the in-between existence of Unknownland, also understood in this poem to be the black experience. It is a space of tension as the metaphors

---

[7.] The poem *Unknownland* is used with permission of its author, © 2021 Phillip Allen, Jr.

[8.] "Threshold," Etymonline.com, https://www.etymonline.com/search?q=thr eshold&ref=searchbar_searchhint.

explicitly and implicitly suggest. The in-between is the memory of the past, the uncertainty of the present, and the gradualism of progress toward a more just and equitable future. In-between is used as a refrain throughout the poem to reiterate the transcendence of blackness as liminality. The in-between transcends spheres of society, aspects of one's humanity as an African American, as well as the limitations that some place on what they believe is the extent that racism's tentacles reach and impact lives.

This space can be detrimental to black humanity and, simultaneously, it can be the space where black resiliency is evidenced. This is the space of lament because of trauma, but also hopefulness inspired by the opportunity – though forced – for improvisation and creativity: the former dehumanizing, the latter life-giving within this liminal reality. The trauma that produces lament has the potential to function in ways that produce the hopefulness of improvisation and creativity witnessed in black resiliency. So, we reflect on the lament and hopefulness inherent to blackness as liminality. These ideas of lament and hopefulness should not be fragmented or made into a sequence, but rather be understood as overlapping, occurring at the same time, and in many ways in tension with one another.

Lament and Trauma

To lament is counterintuitive to how most Americans have been disciplined to believe and this includes worshipers within the churches of the United States. In the foreword to Soong-Chan Rah's *Prophetic Lament*, Brenda Salter McNeil writes, "The church has lost its ability to lament!"[9] Questions to weigh, though not exhaustive, begin with "how" and "why." How did a faith community that recognizes the death of its Messiah weekly through worship liturgy, particularly through the sacrament of the Eucharist, not practice lament outside church services when injustice persists? Why is society fearful of or condemning towards lament? Because of the African American experience in the United

---

9. Brenda Salter McNeil, "Foreword," in Soong-Chan Rah, *Prophetic Lament: A Call for Justice in Troubled Times* (Downers Grove, IL: InterVarsity Press, 2015) (Kindle), p. 9.

States, African Americans have been disciplined to lament. To lament, according to Rah, "is a liturgical response to the reality of suffering and engages God in the context of pain and trouble."[10]

My understanding and use of the term "liturgical response" extends beyond the context of a corporate worship response, as Rah uses it, to include the personal liturgy of individuals and communities. Humans are, as J.K. Smith asserts, "[L]iturgical animals – embodied, practicing creatures whose love/desire is aimed at something ultimate."[11] In other words, the corporate liturgies in black churches and the personal liturgies of individuals and families in the African American community are shaped by and necessary for existing in the liminal space of blackness in the United States. These practices are imperative for defining and understanding our sense of self/identity and for the preservation of our bodies and community. The improvisation and creativity of hopefulness in the African American community are in and of themselves liturgical. The creation of this poem and others is part of my own personal liturgy as I metabolize my experience of blackness as liminality. The remaining sections of this chapter, consisting of interpretations of Unknownland, are my attempt at putting language to this reality.

In-between humanity and nothing

Between visible and invisible
Threat and accepted
Is my black body
A body whose beauty is still a fetish
Whose intellect still questioned

Whose value is still measured against white bodies

---

10. Soong-Chan Rah, *Prophetic Lament: A Call for Justice in Troubled Times* (Downers, Grove, IL: InterVarsity Press, 2015) (Kindle), p. 21.

11. James K.A. Smith, *Desiring the Kingdom: Worship, Worldview, and Cultural Formation: Cultural Liturgies Volume 1* (Grand Rapids, MI: Baker Academic, 2009) (Kindle), p. 40.

Blackness is a constant tug-of-war between humanity and nothing. By nothing, I mean what Calvin Warren, in *Ontological Terror*, claims about blackness as ~~being~~.[12] Nothingness stalks the very humanity of blackness daily, claiming blackness as its own possession. Nothingness, if personified, has been deputized and is seemingly aroused by the idolatrous ideology of whiteness. African Americans have had to hover in this shadowy space of uncertainty since the invention and the intensification of race, and thus racism, by the invention of the racial code "white." Why must blackness fight this particular fight – between humanity and nothing? I suggest, because blackness is too unorthodox (nonconforming) and frightening (terrorizing) an alternative to whiteness for humanity.

If blackness is on the brink of nothing, then not *seeing* blackness is justifiable. Not seeing the dead bodies that fell victim to the violence of over-policing or at the hands of racist white citizens while mining the video footage for details that may exonerate them is understandable if blackness is invisible. When blackness is in fact visible to white eyes, it is often because black bodies are viewed as threats, or for exploitative purposes. Ever since D.W. Griffith's 1915 film *The Birth of a Nation*, that depicted African American men as savages and, particularly, as threats to white women, the narrative has continued in explicit and implicit forms through media, education, and lack of white proximity to black people. Historically, black bodies have been symbols reminding all of white prosperity and white dominance, whether as free labor force during slavery, instruments of lynching as a show of white dominance during Jim Crow, and the combination of the two when black bodies are filed into money- and job-generating prisons across the country. The exploitation includes the tokenizing of black bodies (as entities, not persons) in white spaces, making use of their talents and skills (often of the body) that entertain and/or generate revenue. The liminal struggle between humanity and nothing is simply because African Americans are certain of their own humanity and yet know the reality of being treated as ~~being~~.

> *In-between prophets and profits*
> *Is my black body*
> *Confronting social systems*

---

12. Calvin L. Warren, *Ontological Terror: Blackness, Nihilism, and Emancipation* (Durham, NC: Duke University Press, 2018) (Kindle), Kindle Loc. 188.

That co-opt my limbs to generate revenue under the banner
Of the American dream
The ghost that dangles in front of me fortune and fame
I dwell in the Unknownland of not being familiar with all the
  rules
But having to forever play the game

The *prophet* is more than an oracle foretelling things to come or truth that disrupts both status quo and an unjust and inequitable society that dishonors God and marginalized groups. The prophet is the embodiment of disruption. The prophet's personal liturgy is disruptive to the dominant power structures. The prophet's scars are disruptive because often they are products of conflict with dominant power structures. The prophet's words are disruptive because they provoke analysis of dominant power structures. Blackness, as it enters and exits white-dominant spaces, is the embodiment of the prophetic, a community of prophets. Yet, to whiteness, as mentioned earlier, blackness is the means by which an America that has been formed by whiteness, generates *profits*.

Social systems, and the social structures they give life to, are intentionally and unintentionally designed to benefit the white community while, simultaneously, withholding resources from black communities. The game is rigged. The outcome has been fixed intergenerationally. African Americans have been chasing the aberration of the American Dream while existing in a perpetual nightmare. This ideal of happiness as a result of meritocracy, freedom, and capitalism does not account for (or does not wish to acknowledge) the anti-black oppressive nature built into the legal and cultural framework of the country.

Fortune and fame for the few are expected to nullify the experiences of injustice of the many as if to have medicinal qualities for the African American community because some have made it. Because some have made it, the rest of the community has been characterized as lazy, having a victim's mentality, or simply lacking the capacity to take advantage of the gift that the United States offers. However, those who invented the rules benefit from them the most, they know them the best, and have the power to change or bend them as deemed necessary to preserve their prosperity and power. Yet, somehow all are expected to win at a game that is ever elusive to those with less power and whose voices are silenced.

The camera captures the violent in-between of Unknownland
The space between Gethsemane and Calvary

> *Between the cross and the tomb*
> *Between death and life*
> *In this purgatorial real estate*
> *That black bodies inhabit*
> *Dignity is stripped because blackness has been deemed invalid*
> *The iPhone or the Android records the annihilation in real*
> *   time*

Jesus leads his disciples into the Garden of Gethsemane – literally the garden of "an oil press" – to pray as he knew the time was near when he would be arrested and eventually crucified. Considering the suffering he would soon have to endure, Gethsemane was the appropriate place to locate himself. This scene could be considered the location and dramatization of his greatest struggle, an emotional torture even greater than the physical suffering on the cross. Calvary was the location of the end of that suffering. It is the place where he takes his last breath but, ironically, where death would be turned on its head.

The time and space between the transparent, agonizing prayer of Gethsemane and the tragic injustice of Calvary is analogous to the Black experience – from the trauma of the initial capture of Africans who were shipped as cargo across the Atlantic to the criminalization and practice of shooting unarmed black people. Though centuries apart, both are indicative of a violent existence at the hands of white power structures and allied betrayers: the Romans (along with a rival Jewish leadership) and Europeans (along with rival African tribes). Jesus' experience becomes an analogous snapshot of the extended narrative of the episodic black experience.

The cross of Calvary is the unimaginable suffering leading to death. The tomb is real estate with death as its slumlord. The tomb is the place where expendable soulless bodies are discarded until further notice. It is dark. It is cold. It is an isolating ghetto owned and constructed by those in power that lacks adequate resources – in fact, it does not require many resources to house bodies, or ~~beings~~. It is the space where those cold bodies are silent, voiceless, and immobile. This is the historical description of too great a percentage of the African American community.

Blackness is a persistent struggle for the humanity of black people to be recognized and respected. Even the dismissal of African American accounts of history, personal experiences, and the legacy of white supremacy is a form of invalidation of the collective dignity of African Americans. In contemporary culture, particularly since the civil rights movement, the still and video images captured by the camera have served to broadcast the dehumanization of black humanity with the hopes of speaking to the conscience of the nation, especially white Americans. The annihilation of blackness is not just about black bodies but about black identity.

> *In-between the Unknownland of African and American*
> *Is my black body*
> *I cling to the dash that joins yet separates the identity in my*
> *   veins*
> *From the one imposed upon me*
> *The identity that affirms me and the one that has abused my*
> *   selfhood*
> *Assimilation is its weapon*
> *Amnesia is its weapon*

The space (or the dash) between African and American is a mystery. It is uncertainty. It is actually analogous to the body of Jesus; it is representative of the kingdom's "here and now, but not yet." The "African" in this identity marker gives a sense of rootedness to lineage and ancestry for black identity that "American" has attempted to erase. If the "African" is an "other" though, then so is the "American" an "other kind" of American. The African in African American from the non-black lens of whiteness/white supremacy might also say *this* kind of American is a lesser kind, a less valuable and more expendable and more exploitable kind of American. It says that *this* kind of American is a criminalized version. It is not quite as American as white people, by whom what it means to be American is measured. Yet, the irony is that the "American" part is what makes the "African" part acceptable at all.

African American as an identity marker consists of inherent tension for many black people. African is the identity of our ancestors and transports black people back to the land, languages, and culture from where they came. It is in our blood and DNA. American, on the other hand, was forced upon black people by way of the institution of slavery. In order to be fully American, the African had to, and still must, acquiesce to the violence of the white assimilation project. It is a prerequisite to become less of the African and more of the whiteness inherent to being American. Even history is presented to African Americans and other people of color in a way that lures them into remembering the greatness of the nation dating back to its slave-owning founding fathers while forgetting the uniqueness of the African American experience, culture, and contribution to the country's narrative. It is this coerced assimilation and incentivized amnesia that is the cause of much lament and despair. However, even in the midst of lamentations is hopefulness witnessed in the resiliency of African American people.

Hopefulness, Improvisation and Creativity

Blackness has built in "swag." Swag, initially made popular by Hip Hop culture, has become a pop culture slang, referring to a person's sense of style or "coolness."[13] Ironically, this swag has been shaped by the very struggle and suffering that the black community has experienced. It has been an invention born out of the quest to recapture the collective dignity of blackness stripped away by white power structures. It is the outward expression of hopefulness in spite of a traumatic reality.

The hopefulness of blackness is seen in its improvisation and creativity, its resiliency to produce. To improvise means "to make, provide, or arrange from whatever materials are readily available."[14] Improvisation for any marginalized or oppressed group is necessary for survival. However, to improvise could also be a means of subversive activism: to disagree with the narrative of the dominant group by utilizing the resources that can be gathered in order to create a counternarrative that uplifts, empowers, and validates the community. The improvisation and creativity of blackness is activism that fosters hope and passes that hope on to the next generation to build upon. The improvisation and creativity of blackness is post-colonial by its very nature. Emmanuel Y. Lartey writes that "postcolonializing activities are *counter-hegemonic*, insurgent, even subversive in nature and character."[15] The music, the artforms, the dance, the language, and so on, in the African American community are re-humanizing. They perform in ways that counter the colonializing, dehumanizing activities of whiteness that have been imposed upon blackness. Improvisation and creativity for African Americans is not merely *resistance* to accepting the conditions brought on by whiteness, but as Walter D. Mignolo and Catherine E. Walsh prefer,

---

[13]. "Swag," Slangit.com, https://slangit.com/meaning/swag.

[14]. "Improvise," Dictionary.com, https://www.dictionary.com/browse/improvise.

[15]. Emmanuel Y. Lartey, *Postcolonializing God: An African Practical Theology* (Norwich: SCM Press, 2013) (Kindle), Kindle Loc. 209.

re-existence – "the redefining and re-signifying of life in conditions of dignity."[16] Improvisation and creativity are cues that point to art. Blackness is the location of such art that is life-giving and life-affirming even in the shadows of oppression and death.

> *But my body remembers the dance of my mothers and fathers*
> *My body lives in-between the memory and amnesia*
> *In-between assimilation and resistance*
> *My body is insistent on being*
>
> *Being in this in-between space full of life*
> *Being seen in this space*
> *Being heard in this space*
> *Being beautiful in this space*
> *Being creative in this space*
> *Being black in this space*

Recent research on trauma is revealing how trauma is stored in the body and how socially or through epigenetics can be passed on intergenerationally.[17] Just as much trauma can be absorbed and passed on intergenerationally, so can the resiliency of our ancestors.[18] "*But my body remembers the dance of my mothers and fathers.*" When the body remembers resiliency, it remembers its life-giving, community-solidifying movements. Dance for African Americans is not merely a party activity. What once had religious purposes in the African homeland became a means of survival and expression of freedom, whether as a part of the invisible church during slavery or Friday and Saturday nights at juke joints. James Cone reminds us in *The Cross and the Lynching*

[16.] Adolo Albán Achinte, "Interculturalidad sin Decolonialidad? Colonialidades Circulantes y Practices de Re-Existencia," in Wilmer Villa and Arturo Grueso (eds), Diversidad, Interculturalidad y Construcción de Ciudad (Bogotá: Universidad Pedagógica Nacional/Alcaldía Mayor, 2008), pp. 85–86. Found in Walter D. Mignolo and Catherine E. Walsh, *On Decoloniality: Concepts, Analytics, and Praxis* (Durham, NC: Duke University Press, 2018) (Kindle), p. 3.

[17.] See Resmaa Menakem, *My Grandmother's Hands: Racialized Trauma and the Pathology to Mending Our Hearts and Bodies* (Las Vegas: Central Recovery Press, 2017).

[18.] Ibid. (Kindle), p. 10.

Tree that: "Blacks enjoyed Friday and Saturday nights so much that they nearly forgot, at least for a few hours, whatever humiliations they endured during the week."[19]

Africans danced before the gods in worship under spirit possession. African American Christians continued that practice and attributed that same possession to the Holy Spirit.[20] That same Spirit empowered "the slave to abandon his or her present condition, if only momentarily, through song and dance, where the sacred and the secular realms of reality embraced each other."[21] The dance of our mothers and fathers is the dance of both memory and forgetfulness. It is the dance of resistance to that which has confiscated black bodies for the violence of forced labor, forced imprisonment, and lynching. It is resistance to ~~being~~ and re-existence of black being.

> *In-between rhythm and blues*
> *Is my Black body*
> *The space that makes beautiful music from the melody*
> *   of my joy*
> *And the lyrics scripted by my pain*
> *Reconnecting my body and my soul*
> *To once again be whole after being dismembered*
> *By Euro-centric ideology that fragments what was meant*
> *To not just be held but to behold*

Rhythm and blues is more than a metaphor to provoke poetic imagination; it is also a reference to Rhythm and Blues (R&B) music, a genre of music born out of African American culture and one whose lineage gave birth to various genres of music like "country" music and "rock 'n' roll."[22] This soulful brand of music finds its roots in the soil of

---

19. James Cone, *The Cross and the Lynching Tree* (Maryknoll, NY: Orbis Books, 2011) (Kindle), p. 28.
20. Will Coleman, *Tribal Talk: Black Theology, Hermeneutics, and African/ American Ways of "Telling the Story"* (University Park, PA: Pennsylvania University Press, 2000), p. 51.
21. Ibid.
22. Mark Puryear, "Tell It Like It Is: A History of Rhythm and Blues," *Folklife Magazine* (Smithsonian Center for Folklife and Cultural Heritage) (20 September 2016), https://folklife.si.edu/magazine/freedom-sounds-tell -it-like-it-is-a-history-of-rhythm-and-blues (accessed 21 May 2021). Also

jazz, gospel, blues, and even African music. Mark Puryear frames the history of R&B in the context of African American migrations from the South to urban centers in the North and to the civil rights movement.[23] The development of R&B is traced to liminal movement, those eras of major transition for masses of African Americans.

Rhythm and blues has another reference that deserves recognition. The term "rhythm," according to Ruth Haley Barton, is *"regularity that the body and soul can count on,* but it also speaks of ebb and flow, creativity and beauty, music and dancing, joy and giving ourselves over to a force or a power that is beyond ourselves and is deeply good."[24] "Blues," on the other hand, is used to describe music that is "characterized by sad melodies, and even today the expression 'having the blues' means you are feeling gloomy.... The lyrics are raw and full of emotion, dwelling on love and loneliness. They tell of injustice and hopelessness, and the longing for a better life."[25] Blackness is the space in between a "regularity that one can count on" (rhythm) and sadness, emotions, gloom, and loneliness (blues).

This dichotomy of rhythm and blues parallels joy and pain. The joy of blackness and resiliency of the collective black soul clings to hopefulness, while black bodies still endure the mundane violence of the white gaze, the spectacular violence of white fingers pulling the triggers of firearms aimed at black bodies, and the often-undiscerned accumulative trauma of existing in white-created and white-dominant social structures and systems. Painfully, it is sometimes the "blues" that constitutes the "rhythm" for blackness. The rhythm of protest – sit-ins, marches, die-ins, music, poetry, etc., resistance, and lament – is what blackness has had to count on.

Ironically, giving space and purpose for the pain (as part of the "music" of the black experience) actually aids in making sense of it all. Black people appropriating black pain for meaning-making purposes prevents the suffering from completely annihilating blackness but, rather, can make it whole again. Martin Luther King, Jr., may call this

---

see "History of the Blues," BBC Bitesize, https://www.bbc.co.uk/bitesize /articles/zkbh2v4 (accessed 21 May 2021).

[23.] Puryear, "Tell It Like It Is."

[24.] Ruth Haley Barton, *Sacred Rhythms: Arranging Our Lives for Spiritual Formation* (Downers Grove, IL: InterVarsity Press, 2009) (Kindle), p. 147 (my italics).

[25.] "History of the Blues."

redemptive suffering: transforming and using the suffering as a creative [social] force for change.[26] This is African American men and women reclaiming control of their narrative after being subjected to a narrative that dismembers their identity and ultimately their humanity.

> *In-between the east and west wings*
> *Were descendants of the enslaved*
> *Filling the hallowed halls of the White House*
> *Not the culmination of the dream*
> *But the beginning of its reality*

The most powerful office on earth is the office of the President of the United States. Arguably, the most oppressed group of people in the history of the United States is that of the African American. One could also make the case for the experience of the indigenous people of this land. However, considering 246 years of enslavement, followed by ninety years of Jim Crow segregation, and the continued anti-black racism today, I believe a solid case can be made for 400 years of an anti-black agenda above all other groups of color. To see an African American family, the Obamas, occupy the White House for eight years – the same building built by their ancestors hundreds of years earlier – is to witness the potential of black resiliency and offer hope in the midst of perennial anti-black tragedy.

In November 2008, when Barak Obama was announced as the first African American president, and he along with Michelle Obama and their children graced the platform in Chicago in front of thousands, and millions more on television, tears across the country fell uncontrollably. Those were the tears that remembered and at the same time dared to forget for the sake of hopefulness.

> *The liminal space of black embodiment*
> *Finds its home*
> *And this space is attractive*
> *It becomes the safe place*
> *The space of the most promise*
> *Where Blackness*

[26.] Martin Luther King, Jr., "Suffering and Faith," in Martin Luther King, Jr., *A Testament of Hope: The Essential Writings and Speeches of Martin Luther King, Jr.*, ed. James M. Washington (New York: Harper One, 1986), p. 41.

Emerges ex nihilo
Out of nothing became something
And it was good

The ~~being~~ or the nothingness of blackness through white eyes has been evidenced by black people's status as property during slavery, the objects of the white gaze celebrating black terror lynchings during Jim Crow, and the systematic methods of filling prisons with black bodies in the twentieth century. Black being ultimately emerged from this nothingness (*ex nihilo*), the "waters" of terror, subjugation, and oppression, to take its true God-ordained form even in the wilderness of the in-between. God's re-creation of blackness in Unknownland is a good thing in the sense that God has done and is still doing a holy work; a work that is bringing blackness to wholeness after centuries of the literal dismemberment of bodies and the figurative, but no less traumatic, dismemberment of black bodies from black humanity. As God brings blackness to wholeness, white people (not whiteness) have the opportunity to be discipled into wholeness as well. This wholeness requires relationships characterized by solidarity, following the lead of the African American community, and being unafraid to look critically at the historically destructive work of whiteness upon the humanity of members of every ethnic background including those of European ancestry. Blackness is the liminal space that has been the context for black suffering and the context for its hopefulness. The reality is that blackness is not either/or, but both/and. Unfortunately, it is a space of lament, but it is an incomplete narrative to understand blackness without hopefulness embodied in black creativity, improvisation, and innovation. It is the mystery and the revelation of inhabiting Unknownland.

Liminal Dimensions of
Education Abroad

Gabrielle Malfatti

Whindia! The term, short for when-in-India, was coined quite
spontaneously by the 2014 cohort of students participating in the Teach
Abroad program I lead in Bangalore, India. Whindia encompassed
myriad "it-is-what-it-is" cultural situations that just had to be accepted,
as they seldom fit into their existing Western paradigms: everything
from impossible traffic, with cows sitting in the middle of a busy street,
that made an eight-kilometer trip take two hours; to lessons having to be
stopped on the spot because the chai was delivered to the classroom and
teachers simply needed a break. Whindia has since become part of our
orientation process in which I collaborate with Indian colleagues and past
participants to prepare U.S. college of education students for spending
six weeks fully immersed in Indian culture while completing a teaching
practicum at one of our partner schools – the caveat always being that
nothing really prepares you for India. As of late, Whindia has become a
way for me to see the inherent liminality in education abroad experiences.

Prior to my encounter with the concept of liminality, the experiences
I tailored for students abroad already focused on the transformative
nature of that in-between time and space offered by the period away from
home. The summer program in this sensory-stimulating environment
has the characteristics of a rite of passage, in that it involves a separation,
a stage of transition or liminality, and a stage of reincorporation,
whereby the individuals return to their own environment ready to
assume new roles, now wiser, more confident, and empowered. Yet,
because Western education focuses on measurable outcomes instead of

processes, international educators often complain about the challenge of conveying to others, beyond the anecdotal, exactly what it is that makes education abroad such a unique, high impact experience. I myself was asked during my job interview for the position I now hold how I intended to measure the impact of these experiences upon students. I simply replied, "How do you measure the etching of a soul?" I still stick to that non-answer. The type of soul-etching transformational program I seek to create for my students aligns philosophically with edusemiotics, which expands learning beyond the walls of the classroom and into the world of nature and social interactions in search of meaning: "Pedagogy in the spirit of edusemiotics is not reducible to teaching 'true' facts but aims to enrich experience with meaning and significance."[1] This type of involvement with new surroundings propels students to "question world realities, their own experiences, beliefs, and values, and helps them rethink the ways that they have come to see the world."[2] It invites them to question old assumptions, promotes experimenting with new strategies or approaches, and moves the learners to an enhanced self-understanding and understanding of the world around them.[3] Because transformational learning is often catalyzed by a disorienting dilemma,[4] what better means to disorient American pre-service teachers in a meaningful and significant way than to facilitate for them the separation, transition and reincorporation that characterizes transformative rites of passage in other cultures around the globe?

The liminal character of education abroad experiences and their transformative power is apparent in the reflective blogs of students I have accompanied to Bangalore, India, since 2013. Originally, the program was conceived as a cultural immersion opportunity to enhance the intercultural competence of future teachers at the University of Missouri, who, given the demographics of the state, have scant opportunities for

[1.] John Deely and Inna Semetsky, "Semiotics, Edusemiotics and the Culture of Education," *Educational Philosophy and Theory* 49, no. 3 (2017), pp. 207–19.

[2.] Omiunota N. Ukpokodu, "Teacher Preparation for Global Perspectives Pedagogy," in Binaya Subedi (ed.), *Critical Global Perspectives: Rethinking Knowledge about Global Societies* (Charlotte, NC: Information Age Publishing, 2010), pp. 121–42.

[3.] Kathleen P. King, *Handbook of the Evolving Research of Transformative Learning* (Charlotte, NC: Information Age Publishing, 2009).

[4.] Jack Mezirow, *Transformative Dimensions of Adult Learning* (San Francisco: Jossey-Bass, 1991).

rich intercultural interactions. As an added challenge, the teaching profession is notoriously homogenous, with most of its current and near-future practitioners being white, female, monolingual, Christian, and from middle to upper socio-economic strata. In contrast, PreK-12 student populations nationally are shifting to include increasing numbers of non-white and foreign-born or first-generation American pupils. The experience in India is one of the means we use to generate the cognitive dissonance and a liminoid state that brings about transformative learning and cultural adaptability. This transformative journey of the self begins with the decision to participate in the program and evolves through the physical journey, the immersion into the host schools and local cultures of India, the emotional tug-of-war as students prepare for their return, and the new ways of being upon their reincorporation to American society.

The Decision

In my experience as an international educator, I have encountered students who arrive at the University already planning to have an education abroad experience. Others make that decision following an information session or interaction with alumni from one of our programs. Still others I meet quite by chance; we start talking about what I do and, when asked if they have considered studying abroad, they often respond with an almost automatic, "There's no way." For this latter group, the notion of leaving everything they have known behind is inconceivable or deemed impossible due to finances, family, or job obligations, etc. Regardless of which group a student aligns with, the choice to participate in a program abroad carries with it the need to separate from all that is known, which can be anxiety provoking even for those early committed to the proposition.

The period between the decision-making moment and the journey is itself a betwixt-and-between state filled with mixed emotions. Many of our students are first-generation passport holders and having that document in their hands means they are about to cross thresholds no one in their family has dared yet to cross. The emotional rollercoaster sets in and the monkey mind goes into overdrive. Thus, the disorienting dilemma begins even before the moment of actual separation:

> I can't believe I will be on a plane for India in just a week! So much mental and actual preparation has led up to this much awaited experience. I am filled with feelings of excitement

mainly but also a bit of uneasiness because I don't really know what I've gotten myself into. There are always those small voices of doubt before leaving for an experience for this duration (6 weeks). What if I get sick while I'm there? What if I don't leave a lasting impact on the students and teachers I meet in Bangalore? What if I don't like the food? I've learned to quiet those voices because there is nothing I can do about it at this moment, at my home in St. Charles, Missouri. The only thing I can do is make the most of every experience I have in India by being the best I can be. – M.K. 2015

On some occasions, the intensity of the disorienting dilemma inherent in removing oneself from all that is known is aggravated by unavoidable hitches, such as the denial of a visa or the last-minute arrival of a passport with its visa on the night prior to the scheduled departure. Such events add conflicted emotions and even a sense of destiny fulfillment to the experience:

the road to get to here hasn't necessarily been easy and it sure hasn't been one filled with certainty. as of six pm yesterday, i didn't even think i would have my visa and wasn't sure i'd be flying out with the rest of my group. however, around 6:20, i received a call to pack my bags. everything had worked out. i was going to be on my way leaving my home the next morning. everything worked out. i can't help but believe this trip is happening for a reason and i cannot wait to see what that beautiful reason is.

i am excited and i am nervous. i am intrigued and i am anxious. i am curious and i am in awe. i have expectations but then again, i know that every single one will be shattered and blown away from me the second i step foot in bangalore.

i will try to breathe deeply. i will *really* taste the food. i will definitely enjoy rest. and more than anything, i want to be wholly alive. here goes nothing. – J.F. 2014

[Word capitalization was kept intentionally as it appears in the student's blog.]

Leaving the familial and the familiar also causes participants to reveal their vulnerability, the impostor syndrome often rears its ugly head, and a bewildered traveler talks him- or herself into excitement and finds solace in the knowledge that far from home he or she will be garnering something precious to share with loved ones left behind.

Now as I pause and write this post, I am overcome by thoughts and feelings about what lies ahead. I am worried that I am not going to be good enough. I am nervous about friends and strangers reading this blog. I am excited to write and reflect about what is happening. I look forward to my new adventure and sharing my experiences with those who are back home. – T.H. 2015

The time between acceptance into the program and actual separation customarily spans the whole spring semester. During that time students are often bombarded with questions about the journey they are about to start; well-meaning friends and family members may try to dissuade them from venturing into the unknown, while others cheer them vigorously along the way. It is during this time that as a group we begin to explore other ways of being in the world and challenge notions often associated with the privilege of U.S. birth, the blue passport, the supremacy of the Western episteme and problematic ideas of global citizenship. As with most young people, these students are often unaware of their own biases and driving values, and the light of their awareness rising beautifully begins to brighten as we compare, contrast, challenge and critically explore aspects of their identity and humanity that had been obscured until then. Transformation is at hand.

Cultural Immersion and the Liminoid State

Traveling over 8,000 miles to our destination, the students and I arrive exhausted, yet eager to take on the sites. For me, their threshold guide, joy comes from sharing with them linkages to people and places that have supported my own transformative experiences in India over the last eight years. The role is affirmed when year after year the students take to the sites and our local community with amazement, awe, and even poetic curiosity:

Bangalore is the barefoot walk through ornate worship temples that smell of the flowers the monk-like-men wave in front of statues. There are drums beating and music playing and chanting and fire burning. There are lines of devout beautifully dressed Indians. They pray with their hands folded before their closed eyes, their mouths moving in silent prayers. Watching them is watching true worship....

> It is the busy and sometimes scary traffic in Bangalore. The honks are constant and are used regularly instead of blinkers or checking blind spots. There is no such thing as a lane or as getting too close to another car in Bangalore. The driving makes you gasp but none of the cars have dents and there is not a wreck to be heard of. – T.H. 2015

Invariably, blogs from the first two weeks of the experience in India are filled with allusions to the pervasive sensory stimuli of Bangalore. Compared to our Midwestern university town, Bangalore is busy, loud, vibrant with color and sound. I often tell the students that my favorite aspect of being in India is that one cannot be "not present" there. India courts all your senses at once and rewards your attention with soul-touching allure. In that environment, students often find themselves awestruck and recognize that the culture shock and otherness they had been warned about can yield the amazing gift of "self-concept plasticity known as a liminoid state:"[5]

> It never occurred to me that I have never truly felt foreign in my 20 years on this Earth. However, these past couple of days have made me realize that feeling foreign is actually a gift. It is a gift for your character. To see this wonderful country through the eyes of a traveler is similar to opening your eyes for the first time as an infant. Your eyes have never been exposed to what you are viewing in this exact moment, and it can make you feel uncertain. But with uncertainty comes curiosity, and with curiosity can come awe. Bangalore thus far has left me in culture-awe. Everything in this city speaks to me, and I have never felt more in touch with the beauty of nature and the appreciation of good company. – A.N. 2015

Many rites of passage pull individuals alone into the wilderness for their transformative/liminal journey. When groupings of people share in a particular life-altering experience, as in the case of education abroad cohorts, Victor Turner suggests they bond into a circle of belonging, or *communitas*,[6] that emerges as shared expectations, aspects of the

---

[5.] John W. Schouten, "Personal Rites of Passage and the Reconstruction of Self," *Advances in Consumer Research* 18 (1991).

[6.] "Liminality and Communitas," in Turner, *The Ritual Process*, pp. 94,130.

journey, and the disorienting dilemma itself become part of a commonly held repertoire aiding in the development of all. At these moments it is "the appreciation of good company" that brings highest meaning and a sense of comfort to the experience:

> I am thankful to be experiencing this with my fellow education majors; each of them are [sic] empathetic, compassionate, hilarious, and nurturing. These qualities are important to have in the classroom, and they have made being so far away from home a lot easier.
>
> Some days have been hard for me; either I am desperately craving a cheeseburger, or I am homesick and remember that even if I had an internet connection, my family and friends at home would be asleep. My fellow tigers (and jayhawk) are what make this experience worthwhile, and I am happy to be with them every step of the way. – E.B. 2015

As days pass, the new surroundings become more familiar, and students begin to venture out. Yet, the crossing of a busy street during peak traffic may take you fifteen minutes and your very life may feel in peril. You may have to haggle with the rickshaw driver (over 20 U.S. cents) to ensure you only pay what the meter marks, or you may get lost returning home from the store just a couple of blocks away. All the same, the new environs are becoming known and a sense of belonging to them takes hold:

> After our first outing alone the other day to have dinner, our confidence to explore alone is at a whole new level. While Eugenia, Bethy and I may have gotten a little ripped off from the rickshaw driver, we made it in one piece and got to enjoy a nice Indian microbrewery. Knowing we can make it around town helped us feel more comfortable to plan our first day alone. – J.G. 2015

Comfort and ease open the doors of the heart, and those who once were strangers now feel that a home away from home is not only accessible to them but earned through the power of surrender to the experience:

> Home is where you are comfortable. Home is the people you love. Home is the memories from the past and the memories to come. I am starting to learn what a blessing it is to know

that I have more than one home. Here in India, I have found a piece of home in my new friends and experiences.... I have found a home in the people here: the students on my teach abroad trip, my professors, my host teachers, my principal, and all the people I meet here in India. – E.N. 2015

One of the rites of passage often associated with the creation of a liminoid state is that of the pilgrimage marked by the rapturous joy that overrides the physical pain of walking a new path. The sense of union to others on that path, and oneness with the overall experience, can be read in this entry that both acknowledges the exertion and pleasure of playing full out in the liminal space:

Wow! What a week. My first week at Magnolia has left me with swollen achy feet, a scratchy throat, and a raspy voice. In other words, ... I couldn't be more pleased. I have never been so involved in a classroom and school community and am beyond grateful I get to gain this sort of experience in enchanting India! – A.N. 2015

Sometimes playing full out can leave the participant vulnerable and exhausted, yet in reflection that too is a gain:

Standing in front of the class failing to get their attention was not the worst part. To make matters worse I was non-stop sweating. All I was thinking was how none of these students will take me seriously as I am dripping sweat and squealing to get their attention. My sweating and squeals may not have [been] the only source for their side talking, but it was enough to have the classroom teacher come and take over. Reflecting on this class, I would not consider it a fail because I lasted 40 minutes in front of the class and a student in the front (who I have formed a nice relationship with) made sure to let me know she understood the lesson very clearly. – J.G. 2015

Overall, fully immersed in the cacophony that is Bangalore, students surrender themselves to a passage of being and becoming that later in the trip makes it hard to even think about the conclusion of the stay and the imminent departure from the place that has grown to feel like home and the people who have become their liminal family.

Emotional Tug-of-War

I do not personally believe in the old adage that all good things must come to an end but, by its very nature, study abroad does. These programs designed to offer students an opportunity temporarily to be foreign, to engage with unknown parts of the world, to step into new ways of being and explore other world views, are always a parenthesis within the larger liminal parenthesis of the college years. College attendance is perhaps the most common rite of passage among youth in our society. In 2019, 66.2 percent of high school graduates enrolled in college the fall after graduation.[7] For traditional students, the time spent attending college, whether as a resident or commuter, places them in that in-between zone where childhood and adulthood are at once linked and differentiated. During this four- to six-year liminal span, students have an opportunity to learn about themselves, their chosen academic subjects, and the world around them. A very small percentage, 1.6 percent[8] of them, take this idea of getting to know the world around them to mean surmounting geographic and cultural boundaries around the globe, thus engaging in threshold-crossing, destiny-bending and box-smashing practices that forever alter their sense of self and how they view and experience the world.

For those in our college who have chosen to go beyond national borders to teach abroad, the final weeks of the journey are always a tug-of-war of heightened emotions. A sense of being at home in two vastly different cultures and geographic spaces adds to the sequence of disorienting dilemmas forming the transformative experience in the liminal space that is education abroad and problematizing the final stage of reincorporation:

> The last few days have been full of so much love and appreciation for my time here in Bengaluru. It has truly become a second home to me and each of the goodbyes here have reminded [me] of how special the relationships I've stumbled across

---

[7.] *TED: The Economics Daily*, 22 May 2020, https://www.bls.gov/opub/ted/2020/66-point-2-percent-of-2019-high-school-graduates-enrolled-in-college-in-october-2019.htm.

[8.] NAFSA: Association of International Educators, "Trends in U.S. Study Abroad," 2018–19, https://www.nafsa.org/policy-and-advocacy/policy-resources/trends-us-study-abroad.

All students' blogs may be accessed at https://education.missouri.edu/global-engagement/student-experiences/. Each quote has the student's initials and year of participation as reference.

have been. No words can describe how thankful I am for the warm welcome this city and its people have provided or how much I will miss it all until next time! – M.M. 2018

The emotional tug-of-war is further linked to the relationships the student has at home and the ones built during their time abroad:

> Man, time flies. I can't believe this is our fifth week in Bangalore. I can't even think about saying goodbye to these kids – I can take them all with me, right? No? Oh …
>
> As much as I am in love with India, I do miss home. I miss my bed, I miss my family, I miss my friends. But luckily every time an adorable third grader smiles at me and says hi to me, I forget all of that for a little bit. I have a week left here and I am going to soak up every minute of it. – J.F. 2014

There is an inner conflict between wanting to return home, and also wanting to stay. Knowing all along that a definite choice was made to return, even before the departure for the trip, does not ease the bittersweet feelings of the imminent end:

> Just when you create strong relationships with your teachers, students, and peers, you realize you have less than two weeks left. Am I missing home? Sure. Has India become my home? In many aspects, yes. I have expressed my feelings for leaving my school in previous blogs, but as the days I have left in the school become less and less, I find myself very conflicted. I know there's no possible way to stay in the school any longer, but when I think about having only 3 school days left, I can't help but try to maximize the rest of my time there. However, there just isn't [sic] enough school hours to suffice in a day. – S.B. 2018

So, the long-awaited journey ends and, after over 25 hours of travel, the students return to their old surroundings for the reincorporation into their home and college communities.

Return and Reincorporation

The return to one's community following a liminal experience such as study abroad ought to be as celebrated as the more traditional rites of passage. Customarily in those, individuals returning are recognized for their efforts and vested with different status and/or role befitting their victorious selves. Void of said celebration and intentional reincorporation, the disorienting dilemma associated with transformational learning can continue to affect those who experience it with lingering questioning and disbelief:

> As I sit in home in my bed – very jet-lagged, if I may add – everything from the last six weeks rushes into my mind. This summer went by so fast it honestly feels like a dream. Was I really just in India? – J.C. 2018

To reincorporate, students grab on to recognizable people and landmarks that at once confirm the return and allow for the unpacking of lived experiences while away:

> I have to remind myself sometimes! Yes, Marianna, you did go to India. Even driving home from the Columbia airport, talking with my family, and observing familiar highways and cornfields and gas stations and Taco Bells on the side of the road, I felt as if I had never left. Every day, though, the truth settles in more and I'm slowly remembering every piece of India that has resonated into my words, outlook, early mornings, and (probably most importantly) breakfasts. – M.M. 2018

Because normally we do not do a very good job with the reincorporation phase, students are left to figure out what the experience means for their sense of self and purpose:

> Overall, this trip taught me more than I could ever imagine – both about what it means to be an educator and what *I* mean as an educator. I will never forget the people I've interacted with here. The students have showed me immense amounts of love, admiration and affection and I reciprocate that 100% to them. – J.F. 2014

As I reread the students' blogs and plug their experiences into the frameworks of liminality, I see the need for a ceremonial reincorporation and a public recognition of who they have become and are becoming by virtue of having had the experience of teaching in India for those six weeks. In their final reflections, students often talk about changes they see in the ways they go about their days:

Another change that I have noticed in the way that I conduct myself is presence. Before the trip, I found my life to be stuck in a monotonous routine. I was doing the same things day after day with very distant ambitions that seemed so far away. After achieving something as drastic as traveling across the globe, I have found so much zest and excitement for each and every day. Rather than wearing the same shirts every day, I dress in clothes that remind me of the vibrant colors of India. Rather than sleeping in until I absolutely have to wake up, I am finding myself waking up with the sun ready for whatever the day might bring (thanks to my Coorg coffee). Errands no longer feel like a chore, but a mini adventure to see how my town has transformed in two months. I no longer avoid small talk with strangers, but see each individual as they are, yearning to make connections with those around me. In short, I am mentally a lot more cognizant of the present moment. – A.M. 2018

Reflections of how the experience has heightened one's existing gifts serve as further evidence of the power that education abroad has as a rite of passage in a young person's life:

I have always held on to hope, even in difficult situations; now I feel that I am living not merely as a bystander, but a champion of hope. The people of India that I was blessed to meet showed me what it looks like to believe in others, to fight for the good of others, to never back down. Their passion has translated into my life – in different ways, of course, but I find that I seek conversation to truly know another soul. I am not concerned with what I am gaining, or taking, from others, but rather, I want them to know they have found a home, too. Just as I was welcomed, accepted, and greeted warmly by my school community at Vidyashilp, I want to extend that generosity to those I meet as I am back in the States. – M.M. 2018

Looking into the experiences of education abroad participants through the frame of liminality highlights the ways in which these worldly outbound and personally inbound journeys function as rites of passage by demanding a period of separation, creating a space for transition/transformation, and requiring meaningful reincorporation to maximize the effects of the experience, the lessons learned by the participants, and their contributions to the community. Reflectively, I see that as an education abroad professional, it is of the utmost importance that as much attention be paid to the separation and reincorporating phases as to the transitional phase.

Appreciating education abroad experiences as liminal processes can add to their richness by intentionally and adequately preparing students for their separation, supporting them through the disorienting dilemmas of the transition phase abroad, and celebrating the reincorporation of their enhanced selves into the sending community upon their return. This will not only be advantageous to the students who participate, but will undoubtedly enrich the understanding that others in their home and college communities have of the world and the humans who inhabit it. Education abroad professionals seeking to create programming that mimics transformative rites of passage would benefit from exploring the literature on liminality and how it has been applied to other learning, especially experiential learning.

Unending Liminality

J.D. Bowers

Easter (28 April 2019), Northwest Horn of Cyprus

Kormakitis is the last significant village of the Cypriot Maronites. Nestled in the northwest forests of Pedelia, Agia Eirini, and Diorios, and sheltered by the western fringes of the Pentadaktylos Mountains, while also overlooking the Mediterranean Sea, the village is home to fewer than 150 full-time residents.

The Maronites are Eastern Rite Catholics who have lived on the island of Cyprus amidst the numerically greater Greeks and Turks for well over 1,500 years. Once a thriving people of nearly 160,000, they now number around 7,000 and, with each passing year, that number continues to decline. Kormakitis is virtually all that remains.

The central square is easily spotted. The graceful, yellow stone twin towers of the Cathedral of St. George, so unique within these lands, is easily the most distinguished structure. Nearby stands a small convent and the parish rectory, both attached to a small chapel, the predecessor of the Cathedral and still in use today for daily services.

There are also several cafes and restaurants on the square, one adjacent to the Cathedral, and three just across the road. Given that this is the part of Cyprus that is occupied by the Turkish military and has been declared the Kuzey Kıbrıs Türk Cumhuriyeti (KKTC, the Turkish Republic of Northern Cyprus), one of the latter is proudly Turkish, its interior decorated with Turkish flags and images of Atatürk, and a menu to match.

Finally, but most significantly, there is the village fountain – a spigot drawing on a flow of water that has streamed, underground, to this spot for over 1,100 years – the reason for the location of the village.

Normally it is a fairly quiet village, where the drift of the sea breeze and the rustle of leaves is punctuated by the noise of passing cars, farm equipment working the distant fields, and the bleating of the occasional flock of sheep making their way across the land.

However, on this, the holiest of weekends, the village is crowded and lively. I have come to visit friends and celebrate with their family, and experience Kormakitis in all of its splendor.

On this weekend, it lives up to its historic and communal reputation. It bustles with up to a thousand people and the cafes are inundated, the religious services and celebrations are thronged with worshipers, and there is a hum to the village. Long shuttered homes are opened, extended families gather and roast lamb or goat on the backyard spit, old friends reminisce about days gone by, and neighbors gather to talk about contemporary issues while playing cards and drinking coffee or tea. The Maronites have gathered to sustain the ties that bind them.

Looking back from the road out of town leading to Cape Kormakitis or from a more sweeping view up in the foothills, seeing the village in its fullness (both literal and metaphorically), one sees a serene, small village surrounded by granite-topped mountains, fertile fields and forests filled with Cyprus cedars and prickly pear cacti, farmed plots of grains and hay, groves of olive and carob trees, and a beautiful azure blue sky and sea. It is easy to imagine the village of old, as seen in sepia-toned photos, and reflected in the conversations of the village elders.

There are three other, historically Maronite villages, all within a thirty-kilometer stretch. Karpasha, Asomatos, and Agia Marina are all passed on the road to Kormakitis. Of the three, only Karpasha has any Maronite residents, perhaps as many as ten families, but certainly no more. Each equally represents the former status and stature of the Maronites.

Upon a closer and more thorough look, however, the idyllic appearance belies a harsh underlying reality: the Maronites are dying out.

Stemming from decades of unresolved conflict in Cyprus, marginalization by both the Greek and Turkish communities, and being cut off from their villages by the geopolitical dynamics, they are a people swiftly losing their heritage and their identity.

Kormakitis itself is not whole. While many of the houses and businesses in the village are modern and well-kept, others, interspersed along the narrow roads, are destroyed or dilapidated, shells of once solid and prosperous homes, now a vivid reminder of the post-colonial collapse and subsequent violence that took place throughout Cyprus from 1963 to well into the 1990s, and continued to plague the villages of the Maronites, who were cut off and remained enclaved until 2003.

In fact, two of the other villages are under Turkish military control, serving as bases. Agia Marina is not accessible at all, while Asomatos is only open for limited church services at the Church of St. Michael the Archangel on Sundays and religious holidays by advanced reservation and special permission.

Today, for most Maronites to get to the villages and the religious services, they must travel from their homes located in the south, the Republic of Cyprus, where many of them fled in 1974 or 1975 after the Turkish invasion and continued occupation of the northern third of the island. Depending upon who you ask, there is one Cyprus, with a third under foreign military occupation, or there are two, one for the Turkish and one for the Greek communities. Maronites, along with the Latin Community of Cyprus, a Roman Catholic religious group, and Armenians, are rarely even mentioned.

They can use a couple of the seven crossing points, five of which can be crossed by the public in vehicles, but all are a stark reminder of the island's division and failed attempts at reconciliation since 2003. Cyprus and Nicosia, the last divided capital city in Europe, have been cut in two by a UN-patrolled zone since 1964. For the Maronites, the crossings are physical representations of their never-ending liminality. Those who wish to go "home" must cross both physical and emotional borders, reminding them, each time, of the ways in which they have been restricted and disregarded, and of their hastening decline.

Taken together, this is all that remains of a community of people that only a century ago numbered well over 160,000 people living in 60 villages. Coming in at just around 7,000 Maronites, today, it is easy to see that the community is dying out.

Summer (July 2018), Bosnia (Republic of Srpska)

Every year, between 8 and 10 July, Bosnian survivors and those who wish to pay witness alongside them take part in the *Marš Mira*, a 56-kilometer, three-day pilgrimage tracing the steps of the men who escaped the clutches of the Serbs during the genocide of Srebrenica in 1995.

The trail, going in reverse from the original flight of the Bosnians, goes from Nezuk to Potočari, and is marked by blazes of the Bosnia and Herzegovina (BiH) flag. By the time I set off with my group, thousands of others have already walked ahead of us, with thousands more yet to follow.

While the path is nothing like it was in 1995, it is still very difficult, both physically and mentally. It winds through unswept minefields, passes alongside unexcavated mass graves, and is, at points, little more than a foot-wide ledge on steep mountainsides or seemingly endless and deep ruts filled with mud when it rains, as it so often does. It is a challenge to undertake this trek; but it is also a privilege to walk alongside survivors, hear their stories, understand their decades-old plight, and participate in their remembrance of things that many wish had never happened.

Though the hike is a deeply personal experience, geopolitical issues permeate the entire experience. Today, as it was in 1995, the trail passes through territory that is controlled by Bosnian Serbs. As a result of the Dayton Accords, Srebrenica, though once a "safe area" that was given promises of perpetual protection, now lies in the Republic of Srpska (RS), a semi-autonomous entity within the boundaries of BiH, controlled by those who perpetrated the genocide.

Srebrenica, named for its silver mines and known for its thermal springs, is situated in a deep ravine among the mountains and forests in eastern Bosnia, not far from the River Drina. One passes through several other smaller villages, including Potočari, on the way into the town, which rises up, somewhat suddenly, around a forested bend in the road.

The road into town, the Maršala Tita, takes its name from an old Yugoslav anthem celebrating Josip Broz Tito, the beloved ruler who held together the separate peoples of different faiths and ethnicities. While seemingly inoffensive to all, it is a stark reminder of the tenuous and fleeting nature of his efforts, as marked by the collapse and accompanying ethnic violence that took place here.

Crossing into the town, Maršala Tita runs past the bus station, the local school, and partially empty high rises, before splitting as it enters the commercial district which consists of a scattered assortment of restaurants, a grocery store that sits at the central roundabout, a bank, and a few small shops selling clothing and various other goods.

Far lengthier than wide, the town itself is only three streets or a dozen homes across, hemmed in by the mountains. At one point along its southern reach, a swift-running stream runs down the middle giving a bucolic feeling to the European mountain village. At its far southern end, the road suddenly veers right into a tight turn and doubles back on itself, marking the start of a series of switchbacks taking it over the ridge and toward even more remote villages.

Once prosperous and vibrant, Srebrenica and its greater municipality have yet truly to recover from the war. With a present-day population roughly one third of its prewar total, many of the town's structures and homes still lie in ruins, pock-marked with bullet holes, and collapsing. Those that are shuttered and noticeably empty give entire stretches of the town an eerie feeling, especially when blanketed with the morning mists endemic to mountain passes and valleys.

Mostly, however, the village is marked by silence. The legacy of what happened in and around the municipality, and in forever having the name of the town attached to those atrocities, hangs heavy over the people, the landscape, the memories, and the very reason that people come here at all. For every poster advertising a commemorative event there is a counter example.

Bosnian Muslims, sometimes called Bosniaks, who survived the genocide and who want to return to Srebrenica, either as a resident or for such commemorative events as the *Marš Mira*, are reminded constantly that, despite the world's condemnation of the genocide and the atrocities of the war in Bosnia, they remain subject to the will of the perpetrators. Srebrenica will forever be marked by genocide.

The Liminality of Genocides and Atrocities

Over the course of a single year, I passed over or through four different boundaries that were the result (or cause of) some of the modern world's most ignoble atrocities.

The Green Line in Cyprus divides south from north and separates hundreds of thousands of Greeks, Turks, Maronites, Armenians, and Latins from their ancestral villages and homes. The Berlin Wall, once a dividing line between East and West, is discernable today by street-level markers, contrasting architecture, and occasional remnants of the actual wall, and underlying ideological and political issues that continue to divide Germany. The gates and walls of the Falls Road and the Shankhill Road that still mark areas and boundaries of dominant residency in Belfast, Northern Ireland, a legacy of "The Troubles" separating Catholic from Protestant which seems to have no real end. The Federation of Bosnia and Herzegovina and the Republic of Srpska, two entities, both within the state of Bosnia, but separated by an internal, distinctive, and increasingly visible boundary as one passes from one side to the other, a reminder that the war might be over, but the divisions remain very real.

Each conflict is distinct, yet shares similar causes and effects, so much so that at times they seem universal or part of a trope of atrocity studies. Collectively, they bear witness to the reality that what happens after the violence ends is just as traumatic and destructive as the atrocity itself.

I have spent over two decades studying such events and it is clear to me that the illusion, generally held by the public, that a genocide or mass atrocity ever truly ends is just that, an illusion.[1] Both the causes and actions continue to play out in any number of ways, for any number of reasons, and almost always perpetuate victimization. The killing may have stopped, the territorial expansion may have been halted, the world may have intervened and pronounced an end to the event, but so much continues, unabated.

The victims, thrust into what the world considers a liminal stage, are, in fact, impacted much more deeply. Both temporally and situationally, they enter a liminal loop from which they may never escape, as individuals or as a community. As others have written in this volume, they are stuck.[2]

The Liminal Permanency of Victims and Survivors

Today, there is no Kormakitis and there is no Srebrenica, at least not in the sense that either the Maronite or Bosniak peoples, and their supporters or chroniclers, imagine them. A recent Maronite social media post pined for the "Cyprus we could have, the Cyprus we should have, and unfortunately we don't have."[3]

Both are "imagined communities" relying on the stories and history of their origins and evolution, of a prior group consciousness, culture, and community, forever changed by the atrocities, and continuously sought after through vague notions of restoration and restitution. Shrunken and limited, not by choice, but by external forces that have ended, forever, their coterminous existence with both their past and

---

[1.] Roger W. Smith, "American Self-Interest and the Response to Genocide," in *The Review: The Chronicle of Higher Education*, 30 July 2004, https://www.chronicle.com/article/american-self-interest-and-the-response-to-genocide/. Smith writes: "Genocides don't ever really end; their consequences play out through the ages."

[2.] Lisa Withrow, "Wayfinding to Freedom," in this volume. Withrow discusses how people can become "stuck" in a "closed system."

[3.] Κύπρος βάθρο Μαρωνίτη (Cyprus Maronite Podium), Pavlos Nacouzi, administrator and post author (accessed 21 June 2021 [4:33 p.m. CDT]).

present communities, they both suffer, deeply, from the disconnections.[4] Unlike Berlin and Belfast, which continue to thrive and engage with the broad issues, Kormakitis and Srebrenica are literally and figuratively closed off and in decline.

Lacking, also, true transitional justice and any semblance of sustainable reconciliation, the peoples of these two villages are caught in a seemingly endless loop of imagining their communities. The very structure of the societies in which Maronites and the Muslims of Srebrenica exist, both internally and externally, are devoid of the capacity to build peace, to support the dynamics of a transformation, to create a structure and system from substantial and meaningful resources, to allow them to evolve beyond the narrow confines of the historical atrocities and circumstances that currently define them.[5]

There is no escaping the fact that both are physically isolated, situated in lands that are, as a consequence of the conflicts, controlled by (former?) perpetrators and governed by laws and regulations over which the Maronites and Bosnians have no say.

These geopolitical realities seem unlikely to change, and the consequences of the past cannot easily be undone. Both peoples and both places are left to navigate through the cracks in an effort to recover what they can and make the best of the modern-day realities.

In a twist, when taken all together and applied to various communities as they experience the post-genocide or post-atrocity eras, we find that liminality, the supposed state of transition, becomes a permanent, structural reality, in very real as well as emotional ways that survivors cannot seem to escape.

---

4. Benedict Anderson, *Imagined Communities: Reflections on the Origins and Spread of Nationalism*, rev. edn (New York and London: Verso, 1991), pp. 3, 5–7, 204. Anderson notes that every social-political community is conceived and invented, by its own members, as a limited, sovereign, fraternal, and cultural entity, in opposition to all others, and according to its own conceptions of the past, present, and future. In the end, its biography (or "identity") is based on a selective and self-serving (not always negatively) pursuit of a future based on an equally selective and self-serving conception of the past.

5. John Paul Lederach, *Building Peace: Sustainable Reconciliation in Divided Societies*, 10th edn (Washington, DC: US Institute of Peace Press, 2013), pp. 149–52.

Although most interpretations of liminality examine how people experience and undergo transitional periods of their cultural lives and achieve new customs and institutions, mass atrocities result in disruptions that often do not allow for a transition and casts them upon an endless journey shaped by both the unobtainable future they had once envisaged, a past to which they are always bound, and the present that they now endure.[6]

The Limitations of Liminality in Everyday Maronite and Bosniak Life

Over the course of my time spent in both communities (nearly two full months over a period of years within the Maronite community and over thirty interviews, and a period of fifteen days and ten interviews in Srebrenica and Sarejevo) it has become evident that, while Maronites and Bosniaks of Srebrenica are making some changes and new developments in the wake of their experiences, there remain significant impediments and intentional roadblocks to their ability to transform themselves – and, in fact, save themselves.

For Cypriot Maronites, the problems and impediments are a result of the fact that they are forced to straddle three different realities – life as a religious group within the dominant Greek Orthodox Republic of Cyprus, their marginalization as citizens of the Republic (Greek Orthodoxy is both a political as well as a religious force in Cyprus), and their life as a religious minority within the TRNC and its dominant Muslim culture. Each status comes with limitations and has collectively contributed to their impending demise.

Pick up virtually any history of modern Cyprus and scan the index for even the merest mention of the Maronites; with rare exceptions, they are absent. Within the larger framework of the Cyprus conflict, it is as if the Maronites (and the Armenians and Latin Cypriots) have no place

---

[6.] For discussions of the potential and limits established by scholarship on liminality, see both Arpad Szakolczai, "Liminality and Experience: Structuring Transitory Situations and Transformative Events," *International Political Anthropology* 2, no. 1 (2009), pp. 141–72, and Thomassen, "The Uses and Meanings of Liminality", pp. 5–27.

in the modern state; in many ways, they seem not even to exist.[7] The story of Cyprus for the past 50 years is the Greek and Turkish divide. The needs and issues of the minorities are left to be addressed internally, without any regard from the international community.[8]

For their part, the Bosniaks of Srebrenica, who were widely acknowledged as a major presence and political force within the region, are experiencing an increasingly hostile response and reaction to their very presence in the Republic of Srpska.

Bosnia, like Cyprus, was once widely integrated with interspersed populations of different ethnicities. Nonetheless, the settlement of the war and the end of the genocide arrived at in Dayton drew internal boundaries delimiting the Republic and giving Bosnian Serbs control of a substantial amount of territory within the state, including control of all the former "safe areas", except for Gorazde.

The Serbians have made the most of it. They have erected monuments to Serbian war heroes, are consistently making political efforts to rescind recognition of the genocide, to vandalize and attempt to erase mention of the genocide from memorials to the Bosniak victims, and to elect politicians who openly deny genocide.

As a result, like the Jews who attempted to return to Poland post-WWII, Bosniaks who had hopes to return to their homes and reclaim their property in the newly declared RS find themselves unwelcome, repulsed, and unsupported. "Srebrenica is my home, but why would I

[7.] One exception to this is the edited volume focused on these groups by Andrekos Varnava *et al.* (eds), *The Minorities of Cyprus: Development Patterns and the Identity of the Internal-Exclusion* (Newcastle upon Tyne: Cambridge Scholars, 2009). The political limitations placed upon the Armenians, Latin Cypriots, and Maronites relegate their concerns and status to near irrelevancy, especially when it comes to addressing the "future" resolution of the state and the island, and any territorial and minority rights for non-Greeks or non-Turks.

[8.] Maronites, Armenians, and Latins were not mentioned as independent minorities or peoples at all within the Annan Plan of 2004, the proposed UN plan for settlement of the Cyprus problem. Only the Maronites received one mention, and that was regarding resettlement of their villages, as an exception to all the other rules. See Annan Plan (formally known as "Comprehensive Settlement of the Cyprus Problem"), final version, 31 March 2004, http://www.hri.org/docs/annan/Annan_Plan_Text.html. For the Maronite exception, see Annex VII, Art. 16, s. 8, p. 101.

want to live here, where I am not welcome and would be a victim all over again," noted one survivor on the march, who asked not to be identified.[9] As a result, few have returned and, as one former diplomat and scholar notes, the prospects are "grim" for both them and others who may wish to follow.[10]

Bosniaks and Maronites find their political input and future to be extremely limited, both in their traditional villages as well as in their civic homelands. While Maronites are not specifically mentioned in the Cypriot Constitution (stemming from 1960 and the independent emergence of the Republic), they are acknowledged as a religious minority. Importantly, they are not considered as a minority people, which gave them only a nonvoting "observer" representative to the Cypriot House of Representatives and required them to make a declaration of membership within and underneath one of the two majorities. They opted, as a collective, to take refuge under the Greek Cypriots, a decision which, over the past 50 years, has taken an assimilationist toll.[11]

Most of the Bosniaks of Srebrenica[12] who have chosen to live elsewhere within Bosnia, almost always outside of RS-designated territory, find that, while they are clearly a part of the majority within BiH, their interests and concerns regarding repatriation, reparations, and repair, have been marginalized. Meanwhile, within the RS numerous structural barriers are being enhanced and created to drive a wedge further between the Serbs and Bosniaks. From language – the RS has adopted the Cyrillic

---

[9.] For the situation on the Jews in post-war Poland, see Jan T. Gross, *Fear: Anti-Semitism in Poland after Auschwitz* (New York: Random House, 2007). Interview, Ahmed (assigned name), 6 July 2019, no. BiH.4.2.18, personal files.

[10.] Christopher Bennett, *Bosnia's Paralysed Peace* (Oxford: Oxford University Press, 2016), p. 232; for a full assessment, see all of ch. 8, pp. 184–240. See also Peter Lippman, *Surviving the Peace: The Struggle for Postwar Recovery in Bosnia-Herzegovina* (Nashville, TN: Vanderbilt University Press, 2019).

[11.] See Republic of Cyprus, Constitution, August 1960, https://www.consti tuteproject.org/constitution/Cyprus_2013.pdf?lang=en.

[12.] Many of the Bosniaks who were present at Srebrenica and Potočari in 1994 were not actually from there but were from throughout the region and had gathered there because of the designated "safe area" and the presence of UN troops holding the area secure from Serbian incursion. For the purposes of this study their original villages may or may not be relevant and will be noted if essential to the narrative.

alphabet for daily and official uses, thus creating a barrier for those who only use or know the Latin alphabet and establishing another marker of the nationalist impulses that divide the two peoples – to recent efforts to erase any mention, teaching, awareness, and public memorialization of the genocide, the RS has adopted and condoned numerous behaviors to scapegoat and ostracize Bosniaks.[13]

The Maronites also find themselves challenged at the core of their culture and history. Alone among the island's villages, the residents of Kormakitis have spoken their own language, Sanna, for centuries. Also known as Cypriot Maronite Arabic, Sanna is a compilation of Arabic, Aramaic, Syrian, Greek (modern) and Turkish. Owing to the long separation of Maronites from the village between 1974 and 2003, few today speak the language and, of these, almost no one aged under 50. While there have been some efforts to introduce the language to the younger generation through classes and cultural events, for all intents and purposes, the language is in decline. Such a cultural loss equates with a loss of knowledge and the very "center" of their identity.[14]

Even movement across these internal borders constitutes a liminal act, forced to be repeated time and time again, as Maronites and Bosniaks seek to return to their villages either for commemorations and celebrations, or more permanently.

Kormakitis consists of four distinct population groups – the enclaved, the non-enclaved or remaining villagers, Turks and Turkish Cypriots, and South East Asian home health care aides. The enclaved make up about three quarters of the village's permanent population and are considered the heroes of the village, having remained behind, endured the decades of separation and siege, and sustained the Maronite claims to the village and its history. Unfortunately, they are all elderly and steadily declining in number.

However, the remaining villagers, those who fled the violence and separation of the island in 1974 so that they would not be enclaved, must pass through check points to visit and spend time in the village. They must cross into a land that is not internationally recognized, save by Turkey, and which the United Nations considers to be territory under occupation and for which the laws and rights of individuals are in

---

[13.] Somdeep Sen, "Cyrillization of Republika Srpska," *Perspectives on Global Development and Technology* 8, no. 2-3 (April 2009), pp. 509–30.

[14.] Sarah G. Thomason, *Endangered Languages: An Introduction* (Cambridge: Cambridge University Press, 2015), pp. 73–93.

suspension. Global assertions to the contrary, the reality on the ground is that the TRNC (with the military and political backing of Turkey) controls the territory and their village, so, however repugnant it may be, the Maronites must produce additional insurance (vehicle insurance is not valid once you have crossed the line, so those driving must hold two separate policies and present proof of insurance as they cross) and other documentation to be able to travel to the village. This, along with differences in banking and loan practices, permitting for construction, cell phone service, and many other routine facets of life, means that the Maronites must contend with constant marginalization. "We live in two worlds and we must have two of everything. It is twice as expensive for us. This is a problem," noted one of my sources.[15]

Those who survived the Bosnian genocide face a different set of affronts. Getting into Srebrenica requires driving in from the north, past various sites of the genocide in 1994, especially those in Potočari, including the former UN base, the battery factory where many Bosnians were detained and killed, the "white house" (scene of interrogations, torture, and killings), and the memorial to and cemetery of the dead, all stark reminders of what they went through, often evoking memories of the pain and injustice.

While many of the sites are becoming a part of a larger memorial complex (the UN base and battery factory are now museums and a learning center), many others have been neglected, are in the hands of Serbs, or are still in disrepair. Further, the very act of having to pass by can trigger a range of emotions. Ann Petrila and Hasan Hasanovič, himself a survivor of the death march, write about the "complicated grief" and maladaptive beliefs, behaviors, and expectations that plague the survivors of war and genocide. Constant reflection and unavoidable confrontations with the causational elements have forced Bosnians to experience their victimization again and again.[16]

There are constant reminders in Srebrenica of how deeply the Serbs sought to destroy the Bosnians. All 23 mosques within the Srebrenica district were destroyed, demolished to their very foundations, with the materials and land repurposed. It has taken years to rebuild some of

---

[15.] Interview with Napoleon Hadjiandreou, 12 January 2019, no. CMK.1.6.32, personal files.

[16.] Ann Petrila and Hasan Hasanovič, *Voices from Srebrenica: Survivor Narratives of the Bosnian Genocide* (Jefferson, NC: McFarland Press, 2021). See especially ch. 7, "Ramifications," pp. 193–202.

them and reestablish one of the most important facets of Bosniak identity and life. Even then, only four have been reopened within the village itself, and those that have been rebuilt, such as the Sehidska Dzamija along the southern end of the main thoroughfare, have been vandalized and targeted with threats and graffiti. The religious dimensions of the genocide have not gone away, despite the passage of 25 or more years.[17]

Both groups are the object of significant resentment, which they are forced to confront nearly every day. This resentment is directly linked to the causes of the initial atrocity and, rather than dissipating over the past 50 or 25 years, it has resurgently resurfaced.

In Srebrenica many Bosniaks were forcibly dispossessed of their homes and property, some of which occurred in the wake of the killing of entire families. Local authorities, Serbs, issued titles to the new occupants and effectively intended to repopulate the entire village and district with their own brethren. Such efforts were met with resistance by the Office of the High Representative (OHR) who pressed for legislation to overturn the newly issued titles and restore prewar ownership. His efforts have met with some success, backed by aid given through agencies such as the UN Development Programme, the U.S. Agency for International Development, and Britain's Department for International Development and Foreign and Commonwealth Office, among others.[18] However, the aid and legislation only go so far, and are often thwarted by more local efforts to control permits, access to building materials, and infrastructure development, all controlled and often manipulated by local Serb politicians.

[17.] Albina Sorguc, "Bosnian Mosques Threatened by Vandalism, Srebrenica Threats," in *Balkan Insight / Balkan Transitional Justice*, 14 June 2019 at https://balkaninsight.com/2019/06/14/bosnian-mosques-targeted-by-vand alism-srebrenica-threats/ (accessed 04 October 2021); and Organization for Security and Cooperation in Europe Mission to Bosnia and Herzegovina, "Hate Monitor," https://www.osce.org/hatemonitorbih (accessed 23 June 2021).

[18.] See the Office of the High Representative, "Decisions in the Field of Property Laws, Return of Displaced Persons and Refugees and Reconciliation," http://www.ohr.int/cat/hrs-decisions/decisions-in-the-field-of-property-laws -return-of-displaced-persons-and-refugees-and-reconciliation/. See also interview, Muhamed Duraković, 6 July 2019, no. BiH.1.18.9, and 29 June 2021, no. BiH.1.47.1, personal files.

Moreover, while Bosnians still attempt to return (the town today is roughly 40 percent Bosniaks, 60 percent Serb), the town's Serbian leaders have fought against any restoration of the pre-war and pre-genocide status by excluding Bosniaks from the town council and by electing a Serbian mayor, for the first time, in 2016, who is an avowed genocide denier. Mladen Grujicic, who won re-election in 2020 and again in 2021 during a rerun of the prior elections which were so plagued with fraud and manipulation that the Bosniaks boycotted them, has always denied the genocide. Each year during *Marš Mira* he appears on local television, acknowledging that Bosnians died, but recontextualizing those deaths: "It is an imposed story, and it will fall sometime. No Serb and most Bosniaks living here believe in the Hague farce."[19] Thus he leads the far right toward their final aim, which is to have a region devoid of Bosnians. The caustic "politics of national homogeneity" have come to dominate the region once more.[20]

Maronites also face resentment even though they were never really combatants (nearly a dozen Maronites fought in the coup and invasion in 1974 and one is still among the unaccounted-for "missing" in Cyprus). Because Maronites held onto Kormakitis, the lone village in the northern third of the island not to directly fall into the hands of the Turks, the Greek Cypriot government has bestowed upon them, specifically the enclaved, monthly payments and shipments of provisions, hoping to sustain at least some link to their perpetual right of return claims for individual and state property.

This assistance, which most recently has included the shipment of Covid-19 vaccines, has, in turn, engendered resentment from both Turkish Cypriots and Greek Cypriots. The Greeks, who have been denied similar right of return by the prolonged division of the island and territorial occupation, resent such privilege given to a group that stands in contrast to so many facets of the Greek and Greek Orthodox experience and life. Meantime, while the Turkish government has assured the Maronites of their practical right of return, and allows it to be carried out in practice, their legality and presence remains tentative, heavily circumscribed, and incomplete. For their part, the Maronites

---

[19.] Miloš Mitrović, "Mladen Grujičić: Dete Srebrenice," *Dnevni list Danas*, 5 October 2016 (accessed 23 June 2021).

[20.] Ivo Banac, "The Politics of National Homogeneity," in B. Blitz (ed.), *War and Change in the Balkans: Nationalism, Conflict and Cooperation* (Cambridge: Cambridge University Press, 2006), pp. 30–32.

see both sides as failing to sustain their pledges – the years of division without crossings have contributed heavily to their diasporic decline, two of their villages remain occupied, and the Republic of Cyprus has done little to help secure their status.[21]

The assimilation and slow burn of cultural destruction – the erasure of social, historical, and linguistic characteristics – that has resulted from such circumstances is called to task in the principles of the Declaration of Human Rights (1948), the Charter of the European Union (2000), and the Council of Europe's Framework Convention for the Protection of National Minorities (1998). The latter obliges states "to promote the conditions necessary for persons belonging to national minorities to maintain and develop their culture, and to preserve the essential elements of their identity, namely their religion, language, traditions and cultural heritage."[22]

There have been several cases using this line of reasoning brought before the European Court of Human Rights, including the Maronite case for being declared a national minority rather than a religious minority (as enshrined in the Constitution of the Republic of Cyprus).[23] Coinciding with the independence of the island in 1960 and according to the terms of the Constitution of the Republic of Cyprus, the three minority groups, including the Maronites, were regarded not as minority peoples, but rather as "a religious group" whose members were asked to choose to belong to either the Greek Cypriot or the Turkish Cypriot community. They were therefore "deemed to be members of" the chosen community and to "belong" to said community:

[21.] "Resentment" of victims has long been a reality in post-atrocity societies. Once the morality of the victimization is cast aside, survivors are often viewed through economic, memorialization, international, and political lenses as favored. This resets the cycle of resentment and recriminations. Such emotions and calculated responses were verified and solidified through numerous interviews: Maria (assigned name), 13 January 2019, no. CMK.3.6.1; Prime Minister Kudret Ozersay, 16 January 2019, no. CMK.9.8.1-16; Yiannakis Moussas, 15 January 2019, no. CMK.15.5.1-19, personal files.

[22.] Council of Europe, *Framework Convention for the Protection of National Minorities*, European Treaty Series No. 157, Strasbourg, 1995 (in effect 1998), Section II, Art. 5, https://rm.coe.int/168007cdac.

[23.] Republic of Cyprus, Constitution, August 1960, Art. 2, s. 3, https://www .constituteproject.org/constitution/Cyprus_2013.pdf?lang=en.

The communities in Cyprus were divided according to their religious beliefs and not according to their ethnic origin, for reasons only known to the joint committee established with the duty to complete a draft constitution for the independent Republic of Cyprus, incorporating the Basic Structure agreed at the Zurich Conference. It may be true that what distinguishes the communities may not only be the factor of religion but also their ethnic origin. Whatever the description of the community may be, the fact is that we cannot change the description given by the drafters of the Constitution. Nevertheless, the gist of the difference is not how the groups are described but whether their rights are safeguarded.[24]

Today, Greek Cypriots claim that they cannot possibly amend the Constitution to reorder or affirm a different recognition. In reality, to change the Constitution would be to formalize a history and reality they would rather not recognize.

A Liminal Future?

Much more could be written about both Bosniaks and Maronites and their respective liminal cycles. Both groups are circumscribed in numerous additional ways that this chapter does not have space to explore – deeply particular matters of faith, internal communal dynamics and politics that leave them divided against themselves, and administrative and civic affairs. What has been covered, however, is sufficient to document clearly the ways in which both are uniquely being pushed to the brink.

Nearly two thirds of my Maronite interviewees independently noted, with resignation, that they fear the end of their community is near. One put it succinctly: "We are but a small community trying to survive, but we face the risk of extinction."[25] For his part, the current Maronite

---

[24.] Report Submitted by the Republic of Cyprus to the UN International Convention on the Elimination of All Forms of Racial Discrimination, CERD/C/299/Add.19, 15 October 1997, para. 68, http://www.bayefsky.com/reports/cyprus_cerd_c_299_add.19_1997.php.
[25.] Interview with Michael Hadjiroussos, 18 January 2019, no. CMK.24.1.1, personal files.

Representative, Yiannakis Moussas, is a man of great optimism: "with a solution will come our survival." Yet, he acknowledges the complicated past and present and notes, as did so many other Maronites, that, without a solution, the future of the Maronite community is in grave danger. In that case, he shared with me, it is "an existential problem" that will cede to the "inevitable" forces of assimilation, indifference, and domination.[26]

Bosniaks, like Maronites, have had moments of progress and promise, but also, increasingly, a series of setbacks, including the rise of denialism, prejudice, and resistance. With the simultaneous end of the international tribunal attempting to bring the perpetrators to justice and the rise of a stronger and more assertive Serbian republic, they find themselves more adrift, both geopolitically and locally, than ever before. Their victimization has been compounded. Nothing made this clearer to me than the Republic of Srpska policeman, monitoring the *Marš Mira* as we crossed a highway on the second day, while casually yet conspicuously flicking the safety of his service revolver on and off and sharing pejorative phrases about Bosnians with his partner. He saved his use of English expletives for us, so that we were sure of what he thinks about the entire affair.

People across the world rarely think about the Maronites or Bosniaks today. The world has moved on, presuming that the end of any active violence or atrocities, accompanied by peace treaties and territorial agreements, means that the problem and underlying issues have been solved. However, the truth is starkly different and, as such, both peoples are rapidly approaching the brink of communal extermination.

* * *

Though a broader public, removed as it is from the actual locales of atrocities and genocides, often holds the view that when violence ends, when the end of an event is pronounced, it is resolved and over, such is rarely the case. Mass atrocities often result in disruptions that do not allow for transition. When combined with the later absence of truth-telling, transitional justice, reconciliation, or reparations, victims enter and remain in a revolving and endless liminal loop that has no exit, no

---

[26.] Interview with Representative Yiannakis Moussas, 15 January 2019, no. CMK.15.1.7, personal files.

escape. They are constantly reminded of the unimaginable in the very geography they traverse and inhabit. They are left with a haunted past, unresolved present, and unobtainable future.

When what is most usually understood to be transitional becomes permanent, then the liminal space itself is changed. In that case, liminality takes on the character of another structural reality, taking the place of what might have been transformation on the other side of transitional liminality. This is the endless journey of the permanent liminality created by a genocide or mass atrocity.

Hope in such situations is always in short supply. We are left with an open question as to how anything redemptive may emerge out of such tragedy. To those who have borne such unimaginable suffering, I dedicate this question and our attempts to address it.

Liminal Pathways to Healing

Elizabeth Coombes and Kate Weir

Informed by rites of passage, David Epston and Michael White forged a dynamic counseling model that included passage through liminal time and space toward an unknown but transformed future.[1] From their work and the work of others, the rite-of-passage metaphor has been employed in the interest of navigating critical transitions. The three stages of passage – separation, liminality, and reaggregation – provide a framework for both assessment and treatment. The model includes an understanding that a liminal guide and contained space is essential to the process and that new knowledge and wisdom will be discovered as a result. Mindful rituals of reincorporation into the social world rehearse the pathway and learnings of the journey.

Various therapeutic practices of recent times have provided a contemporary equivalent to pre-modern rites of passage. Lévi-Strauss went so far as to equate the present-day therapist to a type of the shaman.[2] In the same way, Jan and Murray Stein claimed that psychotherapy is the modern instrument of transition that replaces earlier liminal

---

[1.] Michael White and David Epston, *Narrative Means to Therapeutic Ends* (New York: W.W. Norton & Co., 1990), p. 8.

[2.] Claude Lévi-Strauss, *Structural Anthropology* (New York: Anchor Books, 1967), p. 200.

rituals.[3] Robert Moore reconceptualized the role of the therapist in anthropological terms; the therapist is a ritual leader within a rites-of-passage process.[4]

Following are two present-day therapeutic practices which borrow from the rites of passage model – music therapy and child-centered play therapy. They draw on liminal concepts in the construction of therapeutic time and space and embody the role of ritual leader and guide. With transformation as the end goal, they dare enter enchanted space with their clients and accompany them with unconditional love.

Music Therapy with Young People on the Autistic Spectrum

Elizabeth Coombes

I came late to the concepts of liminality and rites of passage in music therapy, my chosen profession for over twenty years. My attention was drawn to these ideas while I was supporting a student undertaking an MA. Nick Wilsdon (d. 2017) had studied medical anthropology before coming to music therapy. He used liminal concepts to explore the idea of our profession as a healing ritual, with the therapist as witness to and gatekeeper of the experience. He collected narratives from music therapists about their understanding of these terms as applicable to music therapy. He began to develop a theory that could be of use to them in terms of opening a discourse on the subject and underpinning music therapy practice. Sadly, Nick died just as his work was completed and was therefore unable to develop his thinking further. It seems that in his stead I have taken up these ideas and moved to the next level, applying the tenets of liminality and rites of passage with certain client groups transitioning between life stages. It is also possible that these ideas may find a useful role in the wider practice of music therapy.

[3.] Jan and Murray Stein, "Psychotherapy, Initiation and the Midlife Transition," in Louise Carus Mahdi (ed.), *Betwixt and Between: Patterns of Masculine and Feminine Initiation* (La Salle, IL: Open Court Pub. Co., 1987), p. 289.

[4.] Robert Moore, "Contemporary Psychotherapy as Ritual Process: An Initial Reconnaissance," *Zygon* 18 (September 1983), pp. 283–94.

One of the key tools used in music therapy is improvisation, an approach that helps to form a therapeutic relationship and support client self-actualization. Here, client and therapist enter into a musical partnership. Co-created music becomes a tool that facilitates connection, communication, and co-produced explorations. These are linked with supporting the clients in order that they become their true selves. Client and therapist may use accessible instruments and voice to compose bespoke musical interactions that have meaning within the relationship. The therapist might also improvise music for the client empathetically, reflecting the feelings in the room or the client's ways of being. This enables clients to connect with themselves as whole persons in music, as well as gaining insight into how they themselves are experienced intersubjectively by others. Typically, music therapists work with a range of clients of all ages with a variety of challenges. Though some clients are non-verbal, others can use words but find communicating through the medium of music more comfortable. Music therapy enables a move away from established and sometimes confining patterns of communication and may provide opportunities to develop new relational skills.

Musicologists often appeal to liminality when discussing jazz, referring to the freer forms of this genre of music-making as liminal. Within this music, structures that exist, such as one musical line having dominance, or one person in an ensemble being a leader, melt away. An equality of engagement arises, a *communitas* forms as fixed roles are no longer present and ebb and flow exists between those engaged in the music. The musical experiences enable other spaces to be entered, spaces that are rich in spiritual and transformative potential. These liminal spaces present a variety of opportunities for therapeutic work. It is the stepping into another way of being, in this case "musicking," the act of making music, that brings the encounter and experience alive and permits the creation of a potential space where many possibilities co-exist.

My own thinking about liminal spaces and rites of passage was further stimulated as I worked with non-verbal clients on the autistic spectrum and their special educational needs. They were at the point of transitioning to adult services by virtue of age. All were around eighteen years old, with but a short time left in the supportive environment in which they were living. They were soon to be catapulted into a different world, with fewer curated opportunities for education and experiences, reliant on advocates to ensure they could still lead full lives, exploring their identity and continuing to develop as human beings. The period when one moves from adolescence to adulthood is rightly considered a critical point in the lifespan for identity formation. Typical teenagers with fewer challenges than those described above have a range of experiences that could be considered rites of passage, experiences that mark the movement between different stages of life. Bar- or batmitzvahs, religious confirmations, *quinceaneras*, and other coming-of-age rituals all encompass ways that young people move into adulthood. Anthropologists may pay less attention to the actual rites themselves, ascribing more significance to the impact on the individual's life in which they occur. In music therapy, however, the musical rituals that become part of the therapeutic experience assume a far greater importance.

Through my research in liminality and rites of passage with children and young people, I discovered much that I had already known; music may become a very important part of maturing and moving through life stages. How many of us recall the excitement of attending a gig, perhaps one that was disapproved of by parents, or belonging to a peer group comprising like-minded fans of a genre such as Heavy Metal or Emo? We can describe our attendance at concerts or forming bands with peers as ritualistic behavior that provides an opportunity for the unknown to be experienced with others and processed within the group. However, how might young people with learning disabilities access such experiences? Moving into adolescence entails growing independence and the developing of personality; was there a way that these theories could be incorporated in music therapy to provide an experience of liminal space for those who might struggle to access experiences such as these? My setting-specific clinical work led me to understand that the interrelated stages identified in rites-of-passage theory – severance, thresholding, and incorporation – can in fact be linked to music therapy work. To further illustrate, the following composite description of clinical work with young autistic people describes the evolution of my thinking.

Liminal work, while requiring a psychic space to be uncovered, is also impacted by the physical surroundings in which it takes place. In music therapy, the location of a suitable therapeutic space is often a challenge. Practical matters such as locating a sound-proofed room, situated in such a way that music created in sessions cannot be overhead or disturb others, become very important. I remember one such problem of space, a residential setting for young people on the spectrum. I was initially offered a therapeutic space that had a dual purpose; it also served as a meeting room and was equipped for this purpose. Each time music therapy took place, instruments had to be brought into the room, and the furniture moved as best we could to infuse a sense of therapeutic purpose to the space. It felt as if the very fabric of the room, with its white walls, hard furniture and formica-topped tables, resisted our work. In addition, the key for the room sometimes could not be located. It seemed as though my attempts to work therapeutically with clients were doomed to failure.

The Music Therapy Cabin. Photo by Elizabeth Coombes.

One day, I decided to take a stroll around the grounds of the building. As I wandered across the playing fields, my eye was caught by a door in an old wall that I had not noticed before. The sun shone brightly, and as I moved further away from the college and its car parks, the sound environment began to change. I began to be aware of bird song filling my ears, and the gentle breeze made the trees and shrubs rustle. I stepped through the door and across the stone slabs that marked the threshold into a small woodland area. Almost immediately I felt the space to be more intimate and private. It was secluded, and offered a place of in-betweenness, where there was a sense of moving from one world into another. Through the trees I spied a small building, rather like a cabin, made of wood. It had been intended as a star-gazing space where the roof could be accessed to look at the night skies. Inside, the wooden floors and floor-to-ceiling windows created a space where there was the potential for ritual time to be created in musicking. I had found the space!

Following on from this experience, I was able to arrange for music therapy sessions to take place in this cabin. A new ritual was then created in music therapy sessions. I would greet clients in the reception area of the college. They were encouraged to carry some of the instruments with them as they traversed the field and entered the woodland through the door. As they walked through the woods, I noticed a change in their ways of being. Their body posture became both more alert and relaxed as their senses became accustomed to a change of rhythm in this secret, sacred space. They were more connected with a range of sensory experiences: sounds, scents, the breeze on their faces. Experiences were offered that provided opportunities for empowerment and discovery, bringing with them the chance of moving into a new phase of life. By severing themselves from the college environment, the first stage of rites of passage could be entered.

Once in the space, we established music rituals that equated to the idea of thresholding, where new skills are acquired and new beginnings offer a way forward to a different life. While some of the elements of the music therapy sessions were the same as those that had been offered in the old therapy space, here they came alive. Sessions would begin with a simple greeting song. Some clients would take a while to settle in the room, so this song, either played with guitar or percussion accompaniment by the therapist, oriented the client to the here and now. This could be adapted as needed to suit each client's preferences. Rhian needed to experience firm hand-touching of arms and shoulders during the music for her to engage fully in the therapy. This became a part of the music therapy ritual. Others simply needed a short welcoming song that clearly identified the space as a setting for music therapy.

When the greeting song was completed, I found a strong shift in dynamics from previous work. Clients were able to be more autonomous in the musicking; Robert would make express choices as to the instruments he wanted to play. In this therapy room, he selected instruments predominantly made of wood. In previous spaces there had been a marked lack of interest in using any equipment. Whereas he used to be passive and reactive, now his agency had been aroused. The instruments Robert selected had a variety of textures, such as ribbed or highly polished surfaces. It was almost as if he was feeling himself more closely connected with the nature-filled setting of the log cabin in which we were working. On another occasion, we were treated to the arrival of a squirrel near our room. Jamie, another client, focused intently on the experience, and we sat in silence, observing the animal as it moved in that stop-go rhythm that squirrels favor, darting here and there, then pausing and looking around. Patches of sunlight in the woodland floor would also sometimes appear and cause clients to pause in the musicking. I saw these moments as magical places where imaginative thinking was given free rein, allowing clients space to find their own rhythms and sounds.

The sessions ended with a specific piece of music tailored to and developed with the client. This could be a song with words, or an improvised piece of music reflecting the session mood and preparing the client for the journey back to the everyday routine of the educational center. Aggregation, or incorporation, could then take place during the rest of the day and the times in between music therapy sessions. While working with the music therapist, clients explored new ways of interacting and experiencing themselves with others. The staff who worked with clients began to notice that changes were taking place. Robert showed new communicativeness in asking for specific music to be played during his daily routines; he became more purposeful in his general demeanor and physical movements. Whereas before he had carried himself with very lax body posture, he now showed more embodied confidence in his movements. These observed changes also impacted interactions between staff and clients: they discovered new opportunities for relationships to develop and potential to be recognized, both essential aspects of rites-of-passage experiences.

The transformation that is realized when liminal space and musicking combine is life-changing; removed from the stark realities and routines of everyday life, clients find new safe spaces to explore and grow. Providing permission to play music without rules or established roles gives the chance to explore new ways of being. It facilitates increased self-awareness and relational capacity and, in this particular instance of clinical work, it provided a pathway for those with no language. Allowing the music to develop afresh with each client results in a new language being created. In this way, we can establish musical rituals; chordal structures or short melodic phrases, unique to the relationship between each client and therapist, can be established. These can be developed and extended in the moment, liberating clients from established structures enforced by educational or residential settings. Victor Turner describes these moments as "instant(s) of pure potentiality, when everything trembles in the balance."[5] When this happens, musicking offers a variety of ways using rhythm, dynamics, tempo, timbre and genres in which human capacity can be extended in the liminal space. The regular occurrence of these experiences through music therapy offers the chance for these micro-moments to be re-experienced on a regular basis. Embedding these moments in the rhythm of being for our clients means that these instances in time can be fully embodied and used as transformative tools in other rites of passage that occur during our lifetimes.

Passing through the Land of Play

Kate Weir

> Welcome to the playroom. This is your special time to be you. You can do almost anything you want with almost everything that you see. If it's not O.K. with me, I will let you know.

---

[5] Victor Turner, "The Center out There: Pilgrim's Goal," *History of Religions* 12, no. 3 (1973), pp. 191–230.

The above words are those with which I greet a child when he or she comes to the therapeutic playroom for child-centered play therapy. The children are not greeted with rules, lessons, or plans. They are not given instructions, ideas, or solutions. Rather, they are given an invitation to explore the room in ways that feel good to them.

In the playroom, the children lead. They decide what to play with, how to play with it, and whether to include the therapist. The child comes up with the plans, the ideas, the solutions, and the magic.

> Abigail appeared curious and delighted as she explored the playroom. She was animated and talkative and curious, asking questions about everything she saw in the room. She bounced around the room, exploring one toy after another.
>
> Like most children who visit the playroom, Abigail lives in an adult-focused, adult-directed, adult-led world. Like most children she is told what to do, how to do it, and is celebrated and rewarded when she acts, does, and performs the way that adults want her to. Abigail is no stranger to behavior charts, rewards, and punishments.
>
> Abigail was described by her teachers and her parents as intense and strong-willed. Her parents initiated therapy because Abigail was becoming aggressive, more hyper-active and her behavior was escalating at school. Abigail was often in trouble for misbehaving and almost always seemed anxious. Her parents were at a breaking point. They were exhausted and desperately hoping for a change in her behavior.
>
> Children's impressions of themselves, their worth, and their gifts are formed in large part by the way that their attachment figures perceive them. Thus, when we first began play therapy, like most children new to it, Abigail was not sure of herself, her abilities, and her preferences. Children are often not in touch with their essence, their true desires, or their emotions when they are away from their attachment figures. In other words: who are they when no one is telling them who and how they should be?
>
> While in the playroom, children's feelings are welcomed. Abigail was uncertain if her authentic feelings would be allowed in the playroom. She immediately told me: "I'm not scared of anything." It was as though she was saying: *Some*

grown-up might have told you that sometimes I am anxious, but I am here to tell you that's not true. And, even if it were, why would I let you see that?

We do not do for children what they can developmentally do for themselves. We do not ascribe praise or criticism to personality characteristics, efforts, successes, or failures. It simply is what it is; and they simply are what they are in all their raw, unedited glory.

We serve as an accepting, non-judgmental observer. A companion. One who observes, with warmth and acceptance, what the child is experiencing and learning about themselves. Feelings are embraced and not fixed. Resiliency is noticed, not prescribed. Boundaries are verbalized consistently and calmly by the therapist when they are needed.

Crossing the Threshold

The playroom is a place in-between. Outside the playroom is the child's ordinary life, the routine interactions with peers, authority figures, and family members. The child is often defined by his/her symptom, his/her challenge, or his/her problem. Outside the playroom the child is one of many.

Inside the playroom, the child is the only. The child is prized, delighted in, and afforded the deepest respect and non-judgmental presence by the therapist. Inside the playroom, the child slowly discovers or remembers who he or she is. Inside the room children experience a liminal space apart from their tribe, outside the structure of daily life.

Outside the playroom, the child is back to ordinary life. However, it is not the same child who first came into the session. On the other side of the play session, the child is changed. Sometimes minutely. Sometimes colossally. Nonetheless, the child has learned something, unlearned something, gained something, or lost something that no longer serves him or her. The child has perhaps grown a layer of self-respect and shed a layer of guilt or shame.

Creating the Liminal Container

In the liminal domain of the playroom, the child is between worlds, between identities. This is sometimes thrilling; the child revels in the freedom and safely within a container of predictable boundaries. With the invitation to be creative and free, the child often flourishes immediately. Many times, the child soaks up the therapist's undivided attention and presence and unconditional acceptance, like a sunflower turning its face to the sun.

Sometimes, however, this liminal womb seems frightening. In the beginning, the child may flounder without adult-led structure. He does know what or how to play, but he may not know how to choose, and it feels intimidating or anxiety producing to try. It seems strange that the adult will not solve or fix the child's problems. Children are often overwhelmed by the acceptance of their feelings. Will the feelings eventually be punished? What are these feelings that they are not used to feeling? It can be terribly uncomfortable to be seen, to be known. In these ways, the playroom can initially feel daunting.

Curated by a Liminal Guide

The Play Room. Photo by Kate Weir.

It is the presence of the therapist – grounded, accepting, and confident in lovingly keeping predictable boundaries – that helps the child to navigate this terrain. In a way, the playroom provides an opportunity for a young child to set out on a quest to find, claim, and take ownership of him- or herself. To remember his/her true essence. To hear the whispers of his/her own, unique, divine calling. For humans of any age, a quest like this can be daunting at best and terrifying at worst.

As the child embarks toward a landscape in which *he* is responsible for his solutions and his decisions, where he is encouraged to look into the alligator eye of his emotions, he does not travel alone. The child is accompanied by a wise, compassionate partner. His liminal guide. His play therapist.

The guide is one who will nudge when needed, but never push. One who will collaboratively assist, but never take over. One who will protect the child always. Protect him from harming himself, his therapist, or his sacred shared space of the playroom.

The child's guide is one who will treasure him no matter how ugly and raw things become. Because ugly and raw is part of the beauty. Ugly and raw are the deep shadows in the pockets that we all have.

The guide is one who *will* allow the child to fail but will *not* allow danger to befall him. One who will witness the tears, the fury, and the frustration *without* wishing that the child or the feelings were different. One who will not wipe away the tears, but rather honor them deeply and witness all that they communicate.

The guide is one who will witness, slowly over time; the most remarkable triumphs that from the outside might look like play. However, in the interior life, the child is conquering fears and claiming all of their aspects. Dragons are slayed and hope is reclaimed. As the child gains mastery, the therapist will have a front row seat. Cheering. Celebrating. Applauding. But not praising. Rather, the liminal guide will point out what the child has achieved. How he/she got here. What the child overcame to accomplish such victories.

Physics and logic make this truth plain: *in order to move to a new place, it is necessary to leave.* It is that simple; but it is also incredibly frightening. It is frightening even if we really want to be in the other place, even if we know we shall feel better and enjoy life more. Leaving the comfort of what we know is frightening even if staying is worse.

Children who are perpetually frightened or angry or sad do not want to feel that way. However, to get to a place of more emotional peace and regulation, the child must take a trip. A journey always begins with a process of leaving; and leaving what you know is much easier with a companion. Though children in the playroom are not changing physical locations, they are leaving their current self-understanding of who they are in the world. They are headed toward a greater knowledge of themselves as authentic beings who have feelings, skills, and capacity. They are headed home to themselves.

How do we make the liminal, journeying part less scary? We create a container that is predictable. We maintain predictable and healthy boundaries that the children can count on. We bridge the child's guardians into the process by communicating with them and teaching them how to support their children on the journey outside the playroom; and we honor the process with the greatest of care and respect.

One of the most difficult boundaries that child-centered play therapists honor is the boundary of anchoring the session to reality. We cannot encourage or support children's fantasies about the playroom or the play therapist or the process of therapy that are not real. This would be a betrayal of the great trust a child develops with his play therapist. For example, children need to understand that other children use the playroom, too. The play therapist works with other children. The play therapist cannot be the child's parent or teacher. Play therapy will not last forever.

This boundary is difficult to keep, especially for novice play therapists because we do not want to hurt or disappoint the children that we work with. The difficult reality is that nothing lasts forever. No relationship lasts forever. No process goes on without end. Grappling with those truths is hard and painful for children. It is also necessary and empowering for them. They learn that they can live with hard truths and painful realities. They have the inner resources to cope with the hardest of the hard.

In the most painful moments, in the most frightening of times, we ultimately draw on inner resources. Almost every terrifying thing I have personally faced I faced alone. Yet, I was not alone. I had a deep well of inner resources and an incredible connection to my spiritual source. This is the greatest gift that we may impart within the play therapy liminal domain, within this wide-open space where children fight their alligators, slay their dragons, and discover their magic. Independently, but not alone.

Crossing Over to a New World

How do we know when it is time to leave the playroom for good? Beautifully, it is almost always the child who decides. He no longer needs this magical island, this oasis. He has tapped into inner resources that he brings to his daily live. He has spread his wings and touched his inner beauty, resiliency, and capacity. The child's tribe has learned to empower him outside the playroom and to celebrate the beauty of this human creature. The child becomes an empowered individual in touch with his own capabilities.

Will the child return? Well, don't we all need to return, at various times, to a home-base? A sanctuary? A healing relationship? Most certainly we do. We hope that these precious human beings never stop progressing, never stop journeying. That dynamic kind of change will always require leaving the comfort of the known and, during those times, we shall need liminal guides. The form of that may not be a playroom and a play therapist. The next liminal sanctuary might look quite different. However, the previous experience of a safe and nurturing liminal space will make it easier and more desirable to seek that kind of transformative space again.

As always, the fear will be in taking the leap. It is true, as they say, that this is a leap of faith. The leap is out of normalcy into a sacred and uncertain time. It is during the leap that we adjust our sails and take flight to the next good place.

> Abigail delighted in making choices and structuring her time in the playroom. During an early session, she exclaimed: "Let's just stop playing this game and spend the rest of our time talking about stuff!" Initially her self-worth seems to hinge on her ability to be successful at tasks, including winning games. Abigail seemed frightened that I would not value her if she did not prove her competency to me. Thus, early on, Abigail structured games so that she would win.
>
> After we built trust in our relationship, Abigail arrived at a session in a very dark mood. She seemed discouraged, pessimistic, and detached. When she walked into the playroom, she immediately wrote one word on the dry-erase board: "NO." She then picked up a piece of paper and methodically started ripping it to shreds. I did not try to cheer her up. I did not ask questions to try to determine what was bothering her. I simply allowed her to be and do that which she was and needed. After several minutes, Abigail stopped ripping paper, stood up, and silently chose a board game. She put it on the table, and we started playing. In that moment she learned that all of her was welcome in our playroom – all of her moods and all of her feelings.
>
> Throughout our sessions, Abigail played in the sand, played with band-aids, and had dance parties. Abigail tested limits and boundaries, frequently at first – seldom near the end of our time together – and she always redirected or chose a more adaptive behavior upon the first limit set. She had learned through our journey that the boundaries would always be the same. This built trust. She learned that she was capable of making adaptive choices.
>
> Slowly, Abigail began to see herself as inventive, capable and a problem-solver. She learned to recover from failed attempts and, importantly, that my perception of her as

a delightful and valuable human being did not change. I remained constant even when she failed at something and even when limits needed to be enforced. She glowed when I reflected what I saw her doing: "jumping high," or "trying a different way" or "using her strength." She learned that she could do hard things and that her body and brain knew how to relax and focus. Over time, she no longer felt the need to impress me with skills or success; rather she experienced the most important thing in the liminal domain of the playroom: being fully accepted for being herself.

Radical Uncertainty in
a Time of Transition

Llewellyn Vaughan-Lee

Walking early along the beach, the winter sun breaking through the fog, I love to watch the birds at the water's edge, the little sanderlings scurrying back and forth with each wave, often accompanied by larger curlews whose long beaks search for insects. When I come close, they wait until the last minute and then take flight, the tiny white birds forming a murmuration for a few minutes until alighting further along the shoreline. This magical beauty beside the waves reminds me of the simple rhythms of nature, a life governed by the seasons and the movement of the waves. Here by my feet is a world of primal patterns, so close and yet so distant from our human world, whose stories today seem so divisive, far removed from the seasons and the tides.

* * *

Yet I also wonder at the movement of our human stories, their hidden patterns. Last summer an unseasonable dry lightning storm set fire to this coastal land and for weeks the air was dense with smoke, the sun rising red, ashes falling. After sheltering in place for months from fear of the pandemic, we sheltered from fire and smoke, hardly daring to open a window. Our bags were packed – a few possessions, change of clothes, the necessary documents – should our home burn. Our small community here on the coast was so grateful to the firefighters holding the line, risking their lives.

Elsewhere in the country, cities were burning as peaceful protests against racial injustice, police brutality and killings turned violent, with armed vigilantes on the streets; all further signs of a divisive world.

Moreover, the miasma of fake news and social media distortions ensured a dystopian vision of our future. Later in the year, the election brought an even more toxic flood of disinformation, lies as poisonous as the air of the pandemic. It is as if the very fabric of our consciousness became distorted, creating not a fairground hall of mirrors, but a dark web of conspiracy and deceit that sees truth as a primal adversary.

Shared truth used to support us as a community, a shared sense of reality. However, in our present collective consciousness, we appear to have crossed over into a country where simple truths do not reach us, whether in daily dramas of fake news, stories of stolen elections, the dangers of vaccines, or other conspiracies. Social media has created a world of alternative facts, stories that seem to arise out of some field of disinformation, trying to catch our attention, wanting to be shared, re-tweeted, until, lacking real substance, they often dissolve back into our dark collective imagination. They have even created their own mythology, calling themselves "Kraken," a tentacled creature of Norse mythology that arises from the deep, swallowing ships.

The Threshold of Unraveling

Is this what it means to live at the end of an era, when conspiracy theories and lies begin to pull at the threads of our civilization? When nature becomes more and more unbalanced? This is not a revolution, imagining a better future, but part of a great unraveling – what happens when a civilization begins to die, when its egocentric values of greed and exploitation reach a tipping point, the web of life stretched to breaking. We do not know how it will unfold; our computer models cannot predict this future. All we know is the radical uncertainty of this moment in time.

We are living in the dying days of an industrial civilization founded upon conquest and oppression of both human beings and the natural world, whether in the slaves who formed the basis of the American economy, or the raw materials extracted from the developing world to feed our factories. If we look closely, one of the most primal lies of our present way of life is the very myth of materialism: that more "stuff" will make us happy. In order to embody this myth, humans have become "consumers" whose lives are dedicated to the profit of corporations, even as these corporations are pathologically destroying the very ecosystem that supports us all. Moreover, while some politicians and corporations now speak encouragingly about "green growth," they do not dare to confront the fallacy of endless economic growth independent of ecological sustainability. As Christopher Ketchem simply states, "The idea that economic growth can continue forever on a finite planet is the unifying faith of industrial civilization. That it is nonsensical in the extreme, a deluded fantasy, doesn't appear to bother us."[1] Our present way of life and its core beliefs are simply not sustainable, even as we continue to support them.

This is the story we celebrate, one of progress and prosperity, even as we are now witnessing increasing poverty and hunger, injustice and inequality. According to the World Bank, the poverty rate has worsened dramatically since 1981, from 3.2 billion people to 4.2 billion.[2] Also, global hunger is now increasing, even in the United States where one in four children faced hunger in 2020. There are almost 60 million more undernourished people now in the world than in 2014.[3] Economic inequality is increasing, with the world's richest 26 people owning as much as the poorest 50 percent. The carbon emissions attributable to the richest one percent of the global population account for more than double those of the poorest 50 percent. This data invalidates our image of global progress, even as we are still being sold its story of increasing prosperity.

---

[1] Christopher Ketcham, "The Fallacy of Endless Economic Growth: What Economists Around the World Get Wrong about the Future," *Pacific Standard*, 22 September 2018. The seminal best-selling book, *The Limits to Growth*, by Donella H. Meadows, Dennis L. Meadows, Jørgen Randers and William W. Behrens III (Falls Church, VA: Potomac Associates, 1972), began the work of describing this danger, even more important today as the planet is facing a deeper and longer-term crisis, rooted in a number of interconnected global challenges, such as rising socio-economic inequalities, growing social malaise, climate change, massive biodiversity loss and environmental degradation. However, although many of its forecasts have proved correct, it was widely criticized at the time.

[2] Poverty is defined here as living on under US$7.40 a day. Jason Hickel, "A Letter to Steven Pinker (and Bill Gates, for that Matter) about Global Poverty", 4 February 2019, https://www.jasonhickel.org/blog/2019/2/3/pinker -and-global-poverty.

[3] Harry Kretchmer, "Global Hunger Fell for Decades, But It's Rising Again," 23 July 2020, https://www.weforum.org/agenda/2020/07/global-hunger-rising -food-agriculture-organization-report/.

The Covid-19 pandemic forced us to confront our vulnerability, our own physical health and the fragility of an economic system so easily threatened by the breath of a virus. The fear of those who confronted this illness was real, as was the anxiety of those living paycheck to paycheck, having to choose between paying the rent or buying groceries, with people of color being the most adversely affected. Moreover, in the world's most impoverished communities, the danger was amplified – the poor even more destitute, the rickshaw driver without customers having nothing to feed his family.

This pandemic also triggered a collective anxiety, one that can be felt even out here on the coast, where my only companions are the waves and the birds. This is the anxiety that comes from the deep wisdom of the collective psyche that knows our civilization is coming to an end, that it has passed its sell-by date, and has no understanding of what comes next.

* * *

Just as a forest is connected by an underground fungal network, enabling individual trees to communicate with each other and warn each other of danger by releasing chemicals into the air, so are we all connected together deep within, sharing the wisdom and knowing of the Earth, our common home. This network is sending us warning signs that our present way of life is not only unsustainable, but over. Sadly, much of the response in North America has been to become even more divided, seeking refuge in tribalism, making the simple precaution of wearing a mask against Covid a political, ideological statement. However, for how long shall we be able to cover this primal anxiety with divisiveness and denial? What will it take for us to face the facts of our shared existence with the Earth, that we are all a part of one living system that we are dangerously damaging?

The pandemic gave us pause, a chance to breathe air that is not polluted. As the air quality improved, the peaks of the Himalayas became visible from parts of India for the first time in thirty years, wild goats were seen wandering a Welsh town, and fish became visible in the quiet canals of Venice. However, with the promise of a vaccine, we could return to "normal," even if normal was what caused this pandemic, with the loss of habitat and wild places. Already our carbon emissions are again increasing; we are razing to the ground more pristine forests for palm oil; more plastic trash is flowing into the seas. Loss of biodiversity continues. We appear addicted to our own self-destruction, even as young people cry out for climate justice and the living Earth.

Emerging from Ashes

Unless the present ecocide is so extreme that humanity cannot survive, a new civilization will emerge from the ashes, from the devastation of our present time. Some people envisage a technological, clean energy future, a new world, greener and more sustainable, "fueled by smart innovation-led economic growth."[4] However, those who have looked closely through the cracks in our present culture know that this is just a figment of science fiction. We can no longer afford the fairy tale of eternal economic growth; and, if sustainability only refers to humanity and does not include the whole more-than-human world, we are just recreating a dying image. If we do not take the foundational step of returning our consciousness to the living Earth, reconnecting to the ground under our feet, the future will not come alive. Rebirth requires an end to the story of separation and an awakening to the story of a living oneness, recognizing our place in the interconnected web of life to which we belong. We need to return to a respectful and reverential relationship with the Earth, rather than that of conquest and domination.[5] These are primal values we need for a future to come alive in the ruins of our industrial world.

Any vision of transition into a new civilization, however, needs to include the very real possibility of social collapse. As our society has become more and more enthralled with materialism and consumerism, this addiction appears to form the basis of our collective way of life – our consciousness manipulated by increasingly targeted advertising. We can see the power of this addiction in our present denial and inaction on climate change, despite its disastrous consequences. In the words of Kathleen Dean Moore:

> It isn't easy to change. Our choices are all tangled up in nets of profit and entrenched patterns of environmental destruction. But if we understand exactly how skillfully we are manipulated, we'll get angry, and that will motivate us

---

4. The economist, Mariana Mazzucato, quoted in the New York Times, 19 November 2020.

5. It can be argued that the biblical idea that man should have "dominion" over nature (Genesis 1:26) has fostered much of our Western attitude of subduing and exploiting nature.

to make changes. We are at a critical point. We have a very narrow window of opportunity to get it right, and to get it right, we first have to imagine a new world, story by story.[6]

We may imagine a new world, a new story, but is social breakdown the only way we can be forced to change, that primal pain the catalyst we need? The pandemic brought both increasing food lines and more social divisiveness. What will happen when we confront the looming disaster of climate collapse, flooding and unbearable heat, fires, and vast numbers of refugees fleeing failing crops and hunger?

The theory of collapsology describes the collapse of our industrial society caused by climate crisis and unsustainable economic growth. This theory emerged in France and was popularized with the publication of *How Everything Can Collapse: A Manual for Our Times* by Pablo Servigne and Raphaël Stevens. Today 71 percent of Italians and 65 percent of French people agree with the statement that "civilization as we know it will collapse in the years to come."[7] It is echoed in the young activist Greta Thunberg's simple refrain, "Our house is on fire."

Seeing young people protest for a future that they may never know – for wildflower meadows they may never see, colorful coral reefs turning white skeleton dead – touches a deep chord. How many generations will be lost until we turn back to the Earth? Until we awake to what is always around us, visible in the simple beauty of a leaf turning golden in autumn, or a bud breaking open in spring? Or most simply, how long will it take before we return to values that support life, that recognize that all life, all creation, is sacred? How much will we have to suffer as we walk through the burned landscape of possible social and economic collapse?

Shall we have to wait centuries before a new civilization is born from the ashes, one that is not built upon violence against nature, extraction and pollution, but once again recognizes the Earth as an organic,

---

6. Kathleen Dean Moore, quoted in Mary Democker, "If Your House Is on Fire: On the Moral Urgency of Climate Change," *Sun Magazine*, December 2012.

7. In a recent letter to the *Guardian*, Professor Gesa Weyhenmeyer, Professor Will Steffen and 256 climate scientists and academics gave "A Warning on Climate and the Risk of Societal Collapse," stating that: "researchers in many areas consider societal collapse a credible scenario this century;" https://www.theguardian.com/environment/2020/dec/06/a-warning-on-climate-and-the-risk-of-societal-collapse.

interdependent living being to which we belong; one that returns us to the wisdom of our ancestors who knew how to listen to the Earth, respect its patterns of biodiversity?

Attending to the Signs

We can already see signs emerging of a different way to live and care for the Earth. One example is the transition network that began in the small rural British town of Totnes, Devon, and has spread to over 50 countries, focusing on creating a caring culture, encouraging communities to come together to imagine a sustainable future, a future we would want to inhabit, in which we feel connected to each other and to the Earth. This is what I experienced during the wildfire: feeling connected to the land that was burning as well as to our threatened community. Something so simple, known to our ancestors who lived in villages or smallholdings, working the land, aware of all the plants and the trees, before progress came and drew them into cities and factories.

Another image comes from the Indigenous activists of Latin America who have returned to the Quecha concept of *sumak kawsay*, which translates to "living in harmony and balance." *Sumak kawsay* recognizes that our human wellbeing is inextricable from that of our ecosystem, and also acknowledges the rights of nature, rather than regarding nature as property.[8] Indigenous wisdom offers us many tools for transition, an inherited knowing that teaches kinship with the Earth, reconnecting us with a story of creation in which we are not exiles, but once again alive in the garden, where the land and the soul are bonded together.

Yet I am concerned that, if we dream too early of a sustainable future, we shall miss the importance of this moment with all of its radical uncertainty. The moment between death and rebirth – as in the space between the in-breath and the out-breath – is when the worlds come together, where magic is born. The Earth has a magical nature, hidden, buried by rational consciousness, but long known to shamans, wisdom keepers and any who have felt its uncensored numinosity. Magic does not make plans, but offers us unexpected opportunities, comes alive in unforeseen ways. Magic belongs to the world we have forgotten, where

---

8. *Sumak kawsay* also means "good living" and was incorporated into Ecuador's 2008 Constitution, which was the first country to legally acknowledge rights of nature.

our dreaming self becomes part of our outer life. Belonging to mystery, wonder, and the real nature of creation, it weaves stories into existence without following the rules of our rational self. Without this hidden magic, there is the danger we shall just repeat the patterns, the images of the past, and be unable to grasp the significance and opportunity of this moment. We shall pass by an open doorway without noticing.

We belong to a culture that looks to plans and problem solving, rather than being fully attentive to the moment. What is the Earth telling us at this moment of time, how can we first attune ourselves to its ancient wisdom before we decide how the future should unfold? This present mass extinction of species is the sixth in its history. The previous mass extinction, most likely caused by an asteroid impact, killed off the dinosaurs along with 70 percent of species, but gave space to the rise of mammals and flowering plants, and eventually humans. The Earth Herself has an innate understanding of these deeper rhythms of death and rebirth, these times of transition. However, our culture has forgotten how to speak or listen to this living being. It can be helpful to regain this awareness that belonged to our ancestors, through a Cherokee practice, "the sound of the green forest humming," that is similar to mindfulness, but different because it is grounded in the earth: "the awareness of the sound of the forest, the sound of the water and our breath. When people are very well attuned, they hear a certain sound and are mindful of that sound. When they don't hear it, they realize they have stepped into a place where their thoughts have become imbalanced."[9]

When I walk on the beach in the mornings, I am attentive not just to the breakers and the shoreline birds, but to the whole texture of life that is woven around me. I try to still my mind and sense the moment that is fully alive, not with my own thoughts and its patterns, but with an awareness that connects the skyline with the sand dunes, the spray of the waves with the clouds or the fog. I am returning my consciousness to the rhythms of the Earth, which is also what is most every-day and ordinary.

Staying true to this moment means also hearing the cry of the Earth, the grief for a beauty and wonder being lost. Often, I wake in the morning with my heart and soul heavy for this beautiful suffering being who has given us life and continues to nourish us with endless generosity, even as we continue to poison Her air, soil, and seas. For over half a century we have known the increasing effects of carbon emissions and the "limits

---

[9.] Cherokee peacemaker Dhyani Ywahoo, quoted in "Maintaining the Fire," by J.M. White, *Parabola* (Winter 2020–2021).

to growth," even as we have continued to destroy Her biodiversity, burn Her ancient forests, and cover the land with monocultures. We seem unable to see further than short-term profits, to care for a future "seven generations and more" as expressed in an ancient Iroquois way of life that the decisions we make today should result in a sustainable world seven generations into the future.

Now our very future hangs in the balance. As Greta Thunberg poignantly stated: "Our civilization is being sacrificed so a very small number of people can continue making enormous amounts of money. Our biosphere is being sacrificed so rich people in countries like mine can live in luxury." We belong to a civilization that has lost its way. For so long we have treated the Earth as a resource to be exploited to fulfill our materialistic fantasies that we seem unable to awaken from this nightmare, even as we become more and more aware of its disastrous consequences. Even when the pandemic showed us that we could stop – pause in our relentless "progress," stop flying and driving – we still seem unable or unwilling to face the facts and make real change.

Radical Uncertainty and the Seeds of the Future

Learning to live in the radical uncertainty of the present moment is absolutely essential. If the year of the pandemic is going teach us anything, it is how unpredictable, how insecure is our present way of life. When you are in a wildfire evacuation warning, you have to choose what to pack, what to carry with you. Now we need to choose what belongs to the next stage of our collective journey, the values that can support us as one civilization dies and before another is born from the ashes. Rather than plan for a future that may never happen, we need to return to what is essential.

Walking on the winter beach I can feel this change in the seasons of the Earth, this shift. What does it mean to live in the winter of our world, at the end of an era? How can the patterns of nature and its cycles of transition help us to connect with the teaching within this present moment, to see what life and the Earth are telling us? Only from this understanding can we gain access to the tools, the spiritual and moral values, that can help the Earth and humanity in this darkening season, and then in the transition from winter to spring, to what is waiting to be born.

Winter is a season that draws us back to what is essential, to the roots that sustain us. As we move into this time of great dying and the unknown future of climate catastrophe, it is crucial that we return to the values that are essential to our human nature – we may find that generosity is more important than stockpiling food, kindness more potent than force. While the simple values of connection, values that place cooperation above competition, community above commodity, can support us during the bleakness of winter, and take us into a new era, belonging as they do to a shared future with the Earth – a future that can only come from a radical shift in our collective consciousness. If we are finally to step into spring, it will be as a diverse and socially supportive community in which we belong to each other and to the Earth. These seeds – of interdependence and living oneness – are already present, along with a deepening sense of the mystery of life and its wonder that is within and all around us.

This is why an awareness of this moment in our shared journey together with the Earth is so essential, an opportunity to step outside these patterns that are driving us into the abyss. It is a liminal moment when we can move between stories, when we need to find a pathway that can return us to wholeness, to the simplicity of what *is* – a landscape where we can live in balance and all things can be known according to their true nature, when we can return to the qualities of love and care for the Earth, our common home. What is more essential than our love for the Earth, what every gardener can feel when they nurture their plants, when they feel the soil in their fingers?[10]

Staying true to this moment means holding both grief and love. This is the real resilience required. Like any moment of real initiation, it is a descent into darkness that is also the womb of rebirth. Rebirth always comes from the darkness, like seeds underground, or the initiation chambers of the ancient mysteries. However, this darkness can be full of the nutrients needed for rebirth, and soil that looks barren can still be tended with love and attention.

Here, waiting in the darkness, are the seeds of the future. Which seeds will grow into green shoots depends in many ways upon our attitude at this moment in time. What values do we live? Is love for the Earth central to our consciousness, because as Mary Oliver writes so poignantly in her poem, "Spring," "There is only one question: how to love this world." Love does not plan for the future but lives in the intense vulnerability of the moment, with each heartbeat. Love is life's greatest

---

[10.] To quote the Buddhist monk, Thich Nhat Hanh, "Only when we've truly fallen back in love with the Earth will our actions spring from reverence and the insight of our interconnectedness."

gift and our greatest gift back to life. We can help the world remember what our culture has forgotten – how the soil, the seeds, the rivers, and the stars all carry a central message of love. In all its diverse forms, its different ways of being and breathing, the living Earth is a celebration of love. Now it is calling out to us, crying to us to remember its sacred nature.

Day after day we watch the divisiveness in this world, the distortions of social media, a certain insanity that has entered our collective consciousness. We watch our Earth dying and our hearts grieving. We cannot escape this darkening. Have we even fully recognized that our human destiny and the destiny of the Earth are part of a single tapestry, woven with all the threads of the natural world as well as the patterns of our civilization?

Nonetheless, if we listen closely, under this chaos we may hear a song that is so ancient that it goes back to the beginning and also belongs to the future. I have heard this music at times over the past decades – and when I empty my mind, it is present in the fox found curled asleep in my garden, or the chipmunk searching for seeds under the birdfeeder. It is the song of the world coming alive, being sung into existence, not just in some distant past, but as in the Aboriginal Dreamtime, "everywhen." Even though we have long forgotten this song – no longer include it in our stories, rarely live it through prayers, ceremonies, or other practices – it is always present in the moment that is fully alive. It can be heard in the joyous laughter of a child, or the night-time screech of the owl. It is life speaking to us as it spoke to our ancestors, who knew that everything they saw and touched, felt and heard, was sacred. It is a fully animate world where we really belong.

This primal awareness is for me like a lodestone, keeping me aligned with what is real amidst the swirling chaos of our world. Here there is no fake news, but what is most simple – the joys of baking bread and cooking soup, smelling herbs, gardening, or walking and watching in nature, the sound of the wind, the rain falling. In this time of transition when we walk between stories, I need to feel the ground under my feet and remember what is true.

I also sense that this connection to what is most simple is an essential note in what is waiting to be born, in a new story. It is as if we have wandered so far from the source that we need to return to the first day, when the water of life ran pure and our consciousness had yet to experience any knowing of separation. Here, in this direct experience of life *as it is*, there is no experience of time rushing forward; each moment is for itself, complete – our original mind woven into the landscape, into rivers and mountains and patterns of kinship. In this deep ecology of consciousness, spirit and matter are one – there is no division. The soul and the seasons of nature move together; they speak the same mystery, the beauty that is within and around us. It is all as natural as breathing, not needing to be remembered because it has never been forgotten. How can you forget the wind on your face or the songs of birds? How can you forget the rise and fall of the tide? These are not stories written in books, but lived from morning until dusk, until dreamtime weaves another texture into the firelight.

This living story is not something static or easily defined. It belongs to the wonder of life and its deepest meaning. It is also part of life's flow, its constant change. Yet, it has cycles, patterns of meaning. Both creation and our human stories have their seasons, their times of light and dark, times of birth, blossoming and abundance, times of fruition, decay and apparent barrenness. It can be helpful to recognize these changing seasons and how the deeper patterns within our own lives follow these rhythms – how we are part of this ever-evolving mystery. Then, even in this present time of transition, we can be fully present in the wonder of what *is*, rather than waiting for something to unfold; we can be a part of its happening. So, we are able to participate fully, co-create the future as it comes into being. Amidst this present dying world, we can help dream a new story into existence, be the seed and the bud and the plant.

* * *

Real wisdom belongs to understanding the patterns of change, just as sailors need to know the shifts in the wind and the weather. At this present moment, we cannot afford to be caught in the destructive patterns of the past, but neither can we be caught in an imagined future. Rather, we need to be present in the radical insecurity that surrounds us, attentive to what life and the Earth are trying to teach us. For too long our civilization has been based upon lies, until so little is true. However, if we are fully awake to the truth of this moment, we can reconnect to an innate wisdom, a knowing that reaches deep into the earth even as it stretches seven generations into the future. Then we shall find ourselves in a place of belonging, no longer alienated, but back in the garden where we began.

The Art of Liminality

Júlia Coelho, Louise Fago-Ruskin, Mary Farrell,
Jenny McGee, and Katie Potapoff

One does not expect a Nobel Prize-winning physicist to name beauty as one of the keys to understanding reality, but that is exactly what Frank Wilczek does.[1] He asks whether the world embodies beautiful ideas or, more closely put, if the world itself is a work of art. Many of the great scientists of the world found that the beauty of the physical world inspired their work and guided the direction of their inquiry. Beauty, says Wilczek, is at the heart of the world, and its many varieties reflect the deep and beautiful structures of the universe.

Artists also create out of beautiful ideas, observations of beauty in the world, and their personal experience of it. They embody this beauty in their work, and it becomes a pathway to better understanding the deep structures of life. If this is true of art and existence in general, it is also true of liminality in particular; artists often create representations of the liminal that help us to understand it. Through their renditions we come to know liminality in ways we could not without them. In this sense, art is revelatory.

The following creators and teachers all work at the liminal thresholds. Their work embodies or points to the deep structures of liminality. Just as there are many varieties of beauty, so there are many varieties of liminality. By experiencing their interpretations of liminal reality, we are escorted even more deeply into its mysterious inner courts.

---

[1] Frank Wilczek, *A Beautiful Question: Finding Nature's Deep Design* (New York: Penguin Books, 2015).

Painting: Courage, Telling the Truth, and Video Tape

Jenny McGee

I once created an entire series of monochromatic black, white, pearl, and metallic works that all focused on the theme of courage. In fact, each piece was dedicated to the story of one person's courage. I spent months interviewing people across the United States, from coast to coast, and asked them to share their stories of courage. The participants took videos of themselves telling their stories and those stories became the raw material which I translated into art. After receiving a story, I created an abstract acrylic painting which was inspired by the subject's experience. The entire series was exhibited at a large gallery in the arts district of Kansas City. It was a huge space and would be dedicated solely to my series.

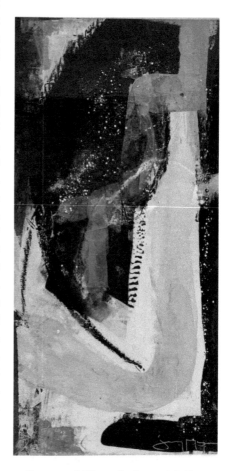

Of all these moving stories, one stands out, especially considering what materialized as a result. It arose as an inspirited moment, full of sacred power. Many years ago, I was acquainted with a young woman named Crystal and she shared her story of adoption with me. She had never met her birth mother and it was for her the source of no little struggle. Years passed and we later connected on Facebook. When she saw the announcement of my project, it coincided with efforts to find and then correspond with her birth mother for the very first time. At the age of 40, Crystal reached out to her mother in what became a string of letters.

This was a closed adoption from the start, so letters were the only option for connecting. It

Courage 6. Photo by Jenny McGee.

required great courage on both of their parts to reach across the divide of circumstance and time in this way. Crystal had been kept a secret at the time because, if the birth mother's family had discovered her pregnancy in college, she would not have been accepted.

As the letters continued, their bond strengthened. The letters began to transform a sensitive secret of the past into a longing; Crystal hoped that one day she and her mother would have the opportunity to meet face to face. After Crystal shared her courage story, I began to create a painting that was inspired by her incredible journey. Upon completion, it joined the entire *Courage* series in the Kansas City exhibit. The location of that gallery is not incidental; it is integral to this larger liminal story.

Crystal's birth mother lived only a few miles from the gallery and Crystal invited her to the show's opening. When her mother arrived at the show, she sought out where her daughter's video autobiography was playing and my artistic representation was displayed. It was the first time she saw her first-born child and heard Crystal tell her story in her own voice, a story that included a newly found relationship with her birth mother.

This revelatory moment took place in the liminal space of art. The liminal spaces of art include the liminal aspects of art itself: the edges, boundaries, openings, contrasts, and negative space. However, the liminality of artistic expression also includes the back liminal stories, the place in the world where the art is presented and, indeed, the intersections where one thing meets another, like a mother and daughter, long separated from one another. This third space was the divine ecotone where past and present converged, space bent, and what was hidden became revealed.

A few months later, Crystal and her mother emerged from the decades-long liminal space and met in person.

Sculpture: Liminality, Thin Places, and Sculptural Installation

Katie Potapoff

Thin places are locations where the barrier between our everyday perception and another world is thinner, allowing access to marginal, liminal realms.[2] In considering how one might interact with the idea

---

[2.] Ciara Healy, *Thin Place: An Alternative Approach to Curatorial Practice* (Bristol: University of the West of England, 2016), p. 6, http://eprints.uwe.ac.uk/26057/68/Ciara%20Healy%20Thin%20Place%20PhD%20Thesis%20for%20Repository%20%281%29.pdf (accessed 20 April 2021).

of a thin place, the feeling of *sinking* comes from my own experience of becoming immersed in a bog, on the Isle of Iona.

Iona, a tiny island off the west coast of Scotland, has a long-documented history of being a spiritual, surreal, perhaps even magical place. I was skeptical of what I might find in this thin place and how visiting would change me. What was I looking for and, more importantly, how would I know when I had found it? However, as soon as I stepped off the ferry onto the island, I felt a visceral and embodied response to the place:

> *a shift in my ribcage suggests*
> *a distinct disengagement from this realm*
> *they said this was a thin place, and yet*
> *I feel thick with time*

For an island so small, Iona offers numerous points of interest to explore; on the morning I chose to make the short pilgrimage to St. Columba's Bay, the island was shrouded in a grey mist. My journey began simply enough but, as I picked my way past the sheep and swans, I came to a point where the path split in two. I turned to the right, as the path looked wider and more heavily trodden upon, but it quickly disappeared, leaving me up to my knees in boggy ground.

Walking, or rather schlepping, one's way through a bog feels very much like losing a limb when your foot sinks in deep up to the knee. As the water pooled into my boots, there was a distinct sense of being swallowed or enveloped by the landscape. I continued, carefully pulling my foot up with a loud squelch. The ground, if you could call it that, seemed unable to decide whether it wanted to be fully formed or remain an in-between state.

When looking later for the Scottish Gaelic spelling and pronunciation for "sinking," I came upon the phrase:

> *eadar dà lionn (edər da: LʲũːN), which means*

> *Semi-submerged, half submerged*
> *Between wind and water, sinking and swimming*
> *Undecided, in two minds, unable to make up one's mind*[3]

---

3. "Sinking: eadar dà lionn," Am Faclair Beag online Gaelic-English Dictionary, https://www.faclair.com/ViewEntry.aspx?ID=EB40E2CF8150C F510DC818B7BDBC98E9 (accessed 30 April 2021).

Looking upon St. Columba's Bay. Photo by Katie Hart Potapoff, 2019.

This colloquial phrasing resonates with how I visualise existing in a liminal space. Part of the mysterious nature of a thin place is the journey that one takes, not only to get to the geographical location, but into a state of in-betweenness. A journey situated in both the physical and the metaphysical realm.

Trying not to panic, as any sense of time began to stretch, my feet worked hard to find stable ground. I slowly made my way towards the highest point in the landscape, hoping at least to empty my boots of water. As I crested the hill, I noticed the mist had lifted and there, glittering in the distance, were the silvery grey pebbles of St. Columba's Bay, and I knew I had found my way.

Not all thin places will physically sink you into a state of in-betweenness like my experience with a bog. The Scottish writer Nan Shephard wrote at length, in her book, *The Living Mountain*, of her liminal experiences in the Cairngorms, a mountain range in the eastern highlands of Scotland.[4] In the chapter aptly titled, "Being," Shepherd wrote:

> It is therefore when the body is keyed to its highest potential and controlled to a profound harmony deepening into something that resembles trance, that I discover most nearly what it is *to be*. I have walked out of the body and into the mountain. I am a manifestation of its total life, as is the starry saxifrage or the white-winged ptarmigan.[5]

[4.] Nan Shepherd, *The Living Mountain* (Edinburgh: Canongate, 2011).
[5.] Ibid., p. 106.

The sense of liminality appears in stark contrast to our current state of ever-accelerating movement, a need to rush from one destination to another because terminus has an element of stability or specificity.[6] This can be seen manifested in the way contemporary travel methods have removed the opportunity for exploration and self-awareness, instead people apply barriers like headphones to remain separate from the present moment. This creates an increasing anxiety linked with the acceleration or "whizzing" from one place to another.[7] It was in a thin place that I slowed the feeling of acceleration and let go of that accompanying anxiety:

> *the wind whips over the land and my body with it*
> *I embed myself into the ground and remain*
> *at a precipice*

> *it is deafening and electric*
> *I speak the words louder*
> *yet, once past my lips they are erased*
> *I hear silence for the first time*

I set out on another journey, one which sought to explore the initial question I had on Iona, how could a place change me? Now that I knew it was possible, could I create this sense of a liminal thin place for a viewer in a gallery setting?

There were three components developed concurrently to create the immersive mixed-media sculptural installation *Eadar dà Lionn | Sinking into Thin Places*, an exploration of my own embodied experience with thin places. Undulating around the space was a 2.5 meter by 20 meter black-and-white drawing, an abstracted image reminiscent of the solidity of a landscape juxtaposed with impermanence as the visual weight dissipates into the atmosphere.

Inhabiting the center of the space was a sculpture made with materials evoking fragility; covered with screen-printed translucent paper, the white ink and the skeletal structure was illuminated from

---

6. Byung-Chul Han, *The Scent of Time: A Philosophical Essay on the Art of Lingering*, trans. Daniel Steuer (Cambridge: Polity, 2017), p. 22.
7. Ibid., p. 31.

Eadar dà Lionn | Sinking into Thin Places, Katie
Hart Potapoff, 2019, immersive mixed-media
installation. Photo credit: Agata Urbanska, 2019.

within by randomized light patterns. These patterns were triggered
when one unknowingly interacted with the form and the space it
inhabited.

Finally, a looped soundscape, which was not accumulative or narrative,
provided the viewer the opportunity to decide how long he or she wanted
to engage with the space, and encouraged the viewer to return again and
again, to experience the work anew.

While I hoped the viewer would become immersed in the installation,
to be enveloped in a liminal space is not to be overwhelmed by what
surrounds you; instead, I believe it is deeply tied to the concept of
interconnectedness. It was not about feeling small and insignificant
but, rather, feeling a deep and boundless connection to the space
itself.

The response from visitors was intriguing, almost immediately
they brought a sense of tentativeness, of paying attention to the
surroundings and the physical space between the form, the drawing,
and their own bodies. The main intention of the installation was
appreciated and a little bit of liminality found its way into the
gallery space. This interpretation of a thin place created a moment of
duration: to linger, reflect, meditate, to catch one's breath in this age of
accelerated existence.[8]

---

8. Ibid., p. 30.

Photography: Exile Outside the Camp

Louise Fago-Ruskin

Creed. Louise Fago-Ruskin, 2021.

"It is the unhealable rift forced between a human being and a native place, between the self and its true home: it's essential sadness can never be surmounted."

– Edward Said

"Being inside is knowing where you are."

– Edward Relph

Where are you from? Asked the man
at the border.
From the world.
Where are you going?
Home.
But where is home?
I don't know.
— Januz Korczak, *Little King Matty and the Desert Island*

Exiled souls do not have a hope in hell – at least as far as Edward Said is concerned. In his famous essay *Reflections on Exile*, he describes the soul of the exile as "perpetually haunted," marked for always by an "unhealable rift."[9] He warns poets and dreamers: do not romanticize the outsider, for they are nomads forever marked by an exposed wound.

[9.] Edward W. Said, "Reflections on Exile," in *Reflections on Exile and Other Literary and Cultural Essays* (London: Granta Books, 2000), pp. 180 and 173.

Living within the liminal space of banishment is a very different experience from the wanderings of the nomad. Whether voluntary or not, the experience of longing for the homeland is accompanied by the sheer horror of displacement. Yet might it be possible there are two sides to this most distressing of traumas? Whilst imbued with feelings of estrangement that we would be better off without, is there something that happens to the inner drive of the individual seeking to exist within such unfamiliar territory? Could it be that amidst the frantic searching over one's shoulder and desperate longing for a reappearance of the lost familiar, there lies the potential to force out and birth newness in ways never anticipated? For this I am grateful. For the exercise of the creative spirit and for the relationship I have with my camera.

At fourteen years old I joined a close-knit evangelical community in the United Kingdom. This community was to grow into a worldwide global movement and affected every aspect of my growth from vulnerable teenager to young woman, mother, and wife. Raised by non-religious maternal grandparents, my entry into this fundamentalist family was an independent one and my commitment to its ideology whole-hearted and long-standing. When I reached 37 my role within the denomination was clearly defined. I was pastor's wife, mother, and homemaker – and exercised all with an unwavering, if feverish, allegiance. It is worth remembering: some are exiled through the experience of a collective shunning, some jettisoned by choice. I was both.

It was and is my relationship with my camera that has been my saving, but it has been a strange coupling. Photography ruptured everything. It opened wounds and unearthed secrets, leading me out beyond the borderlands whether I wanted it to or not. As the camera's shutter was activated, image after image became an undoer of my life and of the life of my family. Coming like a thief in the night, it also undid my faith. The writer Susan Sontag likens the camera to a gun. To photograph the subject, she believed, was to engage in "soft murder." Strong stuff. Yet looking back on those early days with my camera, it is not such a far-fetched idea after all. Photography has led me into places of deep psychological conflict, and it continues to do so. The careful containment I had built and preserved for my life was forever breached. Would I have taken the journey I took without my camera? Would I have seen what I did without the darkened viewfinder clarifying uncomfortable truths? It is difficult to know. I think my entry into the battlefield was an unwilling one – I just barreled out of control and straight into shrapnel. When I began my own journey with photography, my own life was set within its carefully constructed boundaries. The demarcation borders of home, family, faith, and identity resolutely fixed. Then the camera led me remorselessly beyond those borders into the perilous land of the exile. It has been a passage that feels less like a pilgrimage – more like transmigration.

Inexorably drawn to release from the strictures of the church, welcoming parts of myself that had lain dormant and dismissed for decades yet in abject free fall, I rapidly lost my sense of place, and the safety I had found in the arms of a hundred mothers and fathers within my evangelical church community was irretrievably lost. The ferocity of my leave-taking, which fractured the bonds of faith, family, marriage, and church, was marking me out. I was living outside the camp. Moreover, this was an exile embroiled in confusion, for there seemed to be no more freedom "outside" than "inside" – it was a cruel checkmate that was to hold me tight in its grasp for a decade to follow. It remained a checkmate because it is so difficult to leave. There are myriad reasons why we stay within what I eventually perceived to be a problematic faith community. This was a community that held me in ways I had not experienced as a child and the paradox is that I am grateful. My day-to-day life was enriched in what had been a lonely and isolating childhood. They gathered me in and held a steady space for me with kindness and an offering of relationship I had sorely lacked. This has been a tricky exit journey and my camera has been my traveling companion.

The photographic image entitled *Creed*, with its circular form punctured by the breaching of negative space, mirrors a long-held fascination with a particular kind of Irish burial site known as a *cillín*. The *cillíni* (pl.) speak to a sense of exile, the fear of punishment and the loss of place within the world. These forlorn landscapes of the dead, windswept, solitary and housed in border-type locations – streams, ditches or on the outskirts of many an Irish cemetery – situated their occupants firmly on the periphery. To be buried in one of Ireland's many *cillíni* was to be categorized as one of the "dangerous dead." These were stigmatized souls, whose taxonomy spread its net wide to include adult and child alike – the footloose criminal, those cursed by insanity, the haplessly shipwrecked, the suicidal and the unbaptized stillborn infant. Tender tales of fathers swaddling small, tragically lifeless babies under their coats at midnight, a bottle of milk the only accompaniment to the next world, reveal the tragic and transitory state of the unconsecrated. Why? Because holy burial and interment within holy earth depends upon purity and upon the ritual cleansing that takes place in the sacrament that is baptism. Without priestly intervention, a life dies with the historical stain of Eve and of Adam, and with this stain comes inevitable banishment both from divine embrace and from heavenly rest. The soul rests in an in-between state, a liminal existence. Incurring neither suffering nor sublimity. It hovers. Floats. Waits for its soul to be claimed. Thus, its resting place exists eternally on the periphery.

So, what happens on the periphery, on the outside? These sorrowful souls supposedly lived outside the sacred. Their designated burial sites are located on the periphery and thus without full acceptance by their communities. Their manner of both living and dying is in abject contrast to the accepted order of spiritual and physical place. It is to be as close to the boundary of unbelonging as you can be. The banished space, whether chosen or inflicted, has long played a part in human experience and is nothing new. Contemporary liminal "holding" spaces are to be found in the life of the refugee, the interned, those living on the margins of our cities under cardboard, denied integration and acceptance into communities and thus thrust into the unfamiliar. In our urban cities, it signifies the outskirts, the "not in the center." In a conversation, it is the "not important," the "surplus to requirement," the "no longer relevant." Existing near to or outside the border means we are deep in strangerland. Perhaps most frightening – as it relates to our anatomy – it is the site of the body where the nerves end and where feeling, focused attention and sensation is "no more." That sounds like death to me, and it is terrifying. I need an alternative to terror. I need the location of safe spaces within which to hide, to unfold my limbs which still stiffen with panic. To escape catatonia. Because there are still days when I cannot move and cannot rouse myself. I am told it is fear and I think that is probably true.

Yet, as I begin to dig deeper, I find a paradox. There is a strange and delicate mystery to be found in the exiled space. On the one hand, there is Golgotha, a desperately inhumane site where Jesus, the forever-outsider, underwent the horror of crucifixion and a terror beyond human imagining. The site lay outside the city of Jerusalem – outside consecration. Nonetheless, for the Christian church, it is a place replete with holiness. It is the banished, neglected, and unsanctified space embraced. I am beginning to wonder more about exile and what it may mean for a life.

Holy space. Profane space. Space of abject dejection and loneliness. Space of tender communion.

Moses' holy interactions with God also seem to have been outside community space. The Israelites, knee-deep in unknown territory and an accompanying despair, are required to wait for the return of Moses from beyond the camp. There seems to be an understanding. It is outside the camp that Moses communes with the Divine. This place of retreat was necessary both for communion with the Sacred and, it seems, a holy site. Intimate conversation and the reception of holy wisdom required separateness and exclusion from the whole. It was the outward journey that preceded a return to the collective. And it could be survived.

Kenneth Krushel describes how the one on the outside stands before a threshold, a limit, a passage to the liminal, an "axis of dignity" containing elements of "deliverance."[10] Did the Israelites know that? Did Jesus' followers intuit an alternative semiotic meaning in a culturally derided location?

I hope Krushel is right, for if he is, there just might be hope in hell.

Film: Anxiety, Emptiness, and Liminal Space

Mary Farrell

> But to his surprise he saw that the door was open, and the more he looked inside the more Piglet wasn't there.
> > from A.A. Milne, *The House at Pooh Corner*, 1928

I have chosen three films that may help us to explore the effect that scenic emptiness might have on subjects/spectators. According to Manolo Dos, film commentator: "The space is not actually empty, rather a setup forcing the thrust of attention toward the possibilities of that which lies outside the image."[11] I want to call attention to the experience of film audiences in regard to the nothingness framed within these works. Is this apparent emptiness on the screen significant or even important? These questions are part of a larger enquiry into the use of binary silence/non-silence in various artistic approaches.

How does the spectator look through frames (the geometrical form encompassing the so-called content through the camera's eye) into even deeper archetypal frames, especially windows, doors, stairways, and even rooms? How does the search for meaning consider a something

---

[10.] Kenneth Krushel, "Three Spaces and an Excursus," in Timothy Carson (ed.), *Neither Here nor There: The Many Voices of Liminality* (London: The Lutterworth Press, 2019), p. 221.

[11.] Manolo Dos, personal interview, Castellón, Spain, 21 September 2011.

rather than a nothing? What is suggested or implied in the off-screen of the film? Is there simply the horror of a vacuum? Or do we find more – anxiety, dread, threat, adventure, or peace?

Subject, Threshold, and the Liminal

From the *Sixth International Seminar on Liminality and Text*, I take up this idea: "the Subject itself – wherever it be and whatever it does – as defined in relation to lines of demarcation that can be viewed as ontological thresholds, the Subject would appear to have an essentially liminal nature."[12] In his studies on frames and subjects, the sociologist Erving Goffman suggests that a subject moves into and out of multiple situations, thus entering different frames.[13] From the viewpoint of neuroscience, we are becoming more and more aware that humans, as biosocial animals, operate within the domain of mirror neurons and pheromones. We are crossing chemical thresholds constantly. By our very biological makeup, we are essentially liminal creatures.

In many film stills and clips, viewers are left on their own to face the ambiguity of silence and apparent lack of human presence. Of course, in the so-called "under-consciousness", we know there has been a director and a team, but in our experiential consciousness, we are left alone. That emptiness is intended to provoke anxiety.

Goffman suggests that we unconsciously understand the way in which we are to decode the framed signs. Most often, they set up expectations that are related to our culture, history, gender, and other factors. With limited information, the brain fills in the elements that are lacking. Depending on who we are, we carry out this operation in various ways. As Eugenio Trías, Catalan philosopher of the subject and the limit, says: "art and religion try to formalize the beyond."[14]

[12.] Belén Piqueras, Esteban Pujals and Manuel Aguirre, "Seminar Proposal," ISLT 6: The Subject on the Threshold, Madrid 2012, http://limenandtext.com/islt_theislt6.html (accessed 4 October 2021).

[13.] This is a theme throughout Goffman's books such as *Frame Analysis: An Essay on the Organization of Experience* (Cambridge: Harvard University Press, 1974).

[14.] Eugenio Trías Sagnier, *Ciudad Sobre Ciudad* (Barcelona: Ediciones Destino, 2001).

Off-screen in Films

To return to Manolo Dos and the effect of off-screen shooting: "That something is the Important Thing beyond the experience of the scene.... Both the emotion and the significance of the scene rely on the highly conscious design of the director meant to influence the somewhat 'under-consciousness' of the spectator/subject."[15] "Under-consciousness" because we know what a film is. Coleridge's dictum "the willing suspension of disbelief" is in play when we interact with a fictional world. This suspension of disbelief allows us to cross one threshold after another into a liminal zone that is eventually abandoned upon leaving the cinema.

Consider two frightening scenes from so-called thrillers or horror movies and a third scene that utilizes a device that keeps the suspense going. All three scenes are empty of visual human agency while at the same time an off-screen contains what might be an undesirable presence. The question is this: Who is the subject? Is it the main character, the spectator, or an amalgam of audience viewer and the main character?

The off-screen technique places value on "suggestion and not on transparency, a filming that conceals the greater part of its components, yet at the same time unveils a sufficient number of elements that give the spectator an important role in understanding the filmic artifact."[16]

First under scrutiny is *M: Eine Stadt Sucht einen Mörder* (1931) by Fritz Lang, an Austrian-American filmmaker. This film lasts 117 minutes, and the scenes that occur only ten minutes into the film are particularly unsettling. The first disquieting moment comes with a high angle shot of an empty stairway, which should be the passage for a little girl to find her warm lunch and her waiting mother. The scene is not silent, but dependent on certain diegetic sound effects, especially the mother calling "Elsie."

What is disturbing is the series of shots that show the mother's voice growing fainter and fainter down the stairwell while we have a very long-lasting shot of the child's empty place and plate at the table. It dwells on this emptiness for seven seconds. Then, we have two metonymic shots regarding Elsie's fate: a rolling ball (five seconds) in a clearing near some bushes and a floating balloon (also five seconds) in the shape of a child,

---

[15.] Manolo Dos, personal interview.

[16.] Francisco Javier Gómez Tarin, *Discurso de la Ausencia: Elipsis y Fuera de Campo en el Texto Fílmico* (Valencia: Ediciones do la Filmoteca, 2006), p. 216.

first caught in the telephone lines, then freed into the sky. The rest of the film might be said to border on parody.

Next is another sequence also set relatively close to the beginning of Roman Polanski's 135-minute-long film *Rosemary's Baby* (1968). The French-Polish director has calculated an off-screen scene 27 minutes into the film where the only visible action is smoke coming from beyond the arching threshold. The shot lasts barely two seconds. The unfolding menace is only slightly perceived by Rosemary. A quizzical expression forms on her face as she turns to look through the arch to the living room. From now on the subject/spectator must decide how to meander through the soon-to-begin terror of the ambiguous state of Rosemary. Off-screen is where the story lies. A state of anxiety is created about the story to follow.

Finally, much lighter, is the comic detective story by Woody Allen. This New York director has a full bag of stock tricks, so we almost know what to expect in the off-screen ruse inserted at 96 minutes into his 105-minute film, *Manhattan Murder Mystery* (1993). Here we have another archetypical threshold passage – the empty hall, the woman going to change in the bathroom

M, the Vampire of Düsseldorf. Lang, Fritz, *M, Eine Stadt sucht einem Mörder*, 1931. (*M, the Vampire of Düsseldorf* 1931) Produced by Seymour Nebenzel. Distributed by Vereningte Star-Film GmbH in Germany, and in the USA by Paramount Pictures.

Rosemary's Baby. Polanski, Roman, *Rosemary's Baby*, 1993. Produced by William Castle. Distributed by Paramount Pictures.

Manhattan Murder Mystery. Allen, Woody, *Manhattan Murder Mystery*, 1993. Produced by Robert Greenhut. Distributed by TriStar Pictures.

with shower curtain included. A mere two-second shot, but worth its suspense for our narrative. Stock predictions are what the viewer is likely to make.

Thresholds, liminal zones, and frames act as border markers, especially with special regard to the possible reactions of the subject/ spectator. As the *Border Poetics Group* puts it, "Because border zones are places of negotiation and hybrid interpretation, they can also become contact zones between the real and the imaginary."[17] These images act as frames within frames, especially the archetypical frames used as thresholds to or from some imagined place – windows, doors, stairs, or hallways. The passage into and out is often interpreted through narrative or symbols. Emptiness is often a difficulty, a critical challenge for meaning. The notion of liminal emptiness is described so very well by an eighth-century poem by Wang Wei, where "with very simple words and images, [the Classical Chinese painters and poets] shape a wide space of associations, [they] use emptiness as a basic means for their composition. The rest is entrusted to the reader:"[18]

> In Wei the morning rain
> washes off the light dust
>
> green, newly green are
> the willows at the inn
>
> I urge you, my friend, to take
> another cup of wine
>
> to the west of Yang Pass
> there are no old friends

According to the translator, in the third verse, "leaving the Yang Pass for the West" literally means leaving civilization and everything familiar and entering the unknown, a liminal zone that may be either promising or threatening.

[17.] Johan Schimanski and Stephan Wolfe (eds), "Key Terms," Border Poetics, http://borderpoetics.wikidot.com/border-zone (accessed 27 September 2021).

[18.] Wang Wei, "Casa de Poesía China," *Poemas del Río Wang*, http://riowang .blogspot.com/2008/04/blog-post.html (accessed 6 February 2012).

Music: *Sea,* Saudade, *and Liminality*

Júlia Coelho

Haunting thirteenth-century *cantigas* of Martin Codax represent an essential contribution to medieval Galician-Portuguese secular music and poetry: the collection of seven *cantigas de amigo* (lit. "song of the friend/lover") from his *Pergamiño Vindel* is one of the few examples of medieval secular song from the northwestern Iberian peninsula whose musical notation survived almost in its entirety to this day.[19] Following the *cantigas de amigo* conventions, these pieces give voice to a female poetic persona regarding her feelings of love and longing (*saudade*) towards her betrothed.[20]

Cantigas de Amigo. Pierpont Morgan Library, New York, Vindel MS M979.

[19.] The language of the *cantigas* reflects the vernacular language spoken in the northern and southern regions of the Minho River (the river that divides modern Galicia from Portugal). It was the preferred idiom of lyric poets in these regions during the medieval era. The genre *cantigas de amigo* stems from the Galician-Portuguese *trovador* tradition and is exclusive to the repertoire of the Iberian peninsula, although the *trovadorismo* is inspired by its earlier French *troubadourisme* counterpart.

[20.] See Thayane Gaspar, "O Feminino nas Identidades Brasileira e Galega," *Quilombo Noroeste: A Cultura Galega no Rio de Janeiro e no Universo Galego-Português-Brasileiro* (3 August 2014), https://quilombonoroeste.wordpress. com/2014/08/03/o-feminino-nas-identidades-brasileira-e-galega/ (accessed May 2021); and Ana Luiza Mendes, "O Sentido dos Diálogos entre as Mulheres e o Mar nas Cantigas de Amigo Galego-Portuguesas do Século XIII," dissertation, Universidade Federal do Paraná, 2013, p. 14. See also Ana Luiza Mendes, "O Sentido dos Diálogos entre as Mulheres e o Mar nas Cantigas de Amigo Galego-Portuguesas do Século XIII," in Anais do XIV Seminário Nacional Mulher e Literatura/V Seminário Internacional Mulher e Literatura (Brasília: Universidade de Brasília, Departamento de Teoria Literária e Literaturas, 2011).

Common to this musico-literary genre is the practice of addressing nature directly, treating it as a friend and confidant, hence engaging in its anthropomorphization. Nature becomes the medium between the maiden and the physically absent object of her love and, therefore, an essential part of the narrative.[21]

In the poetic representation and direct references to nature – including its water-related elements – the literal and symbolic meanings are often entwined. This applies to the *cantiga* sub-category called *"barcarola"* or *"marinha,"* where the *amiga* sings to the sea about her love predicaments and the pains of silence and *saudade*. At the same time, it is that same element that physically separates her from her fiancé.[22] Therefore, the sea takes a dual and ambiguous role in the musico-poetic narrative, on the one hand, as the agent, origin, and cause of such distance between the two lovers and, on the other, as the maiden's confidant that would, she hopes, provide the answers regarding her beloved's return.[23] The first and last pieces of the *Vindel Parchment* (entitled "Ondas do mar de Vigo" [I] and "Ay ondas que eu vin veer" [VII]) are of particular relevance in exemplifying how liminality can be expressed through poetry and music, with the sea as a representation and symbol of liminal space and time.[24]

[21.] See Clarice Zamonaro Cortez, "Relações entre as Imagens da Natureza e os Estados Sentimentais Femininos na Lírica Medieval," in Gladis Massini-Cagliari *et al.*, *Séries Estudos Medievais 2: Fontes* (Campinas, Brazil: Associação Nacional de Pós-Graduação em Letras e Linguística, 2009), pp. 30–31.

[22.] *Cantigas de amigo* that use sea as the maiden's confidant are called "barcarola" or "marinha." Giulia Lanciani and Giuseppe Tavani, define these terms in the *Dicionário da Literatura Medieval Galega e Portuguesa*: "é uma variedade de cantiga de amigo em que o mar, e por extensão rio … constituem o elemento da causa da separação e o meio para o reencontro dos apaixonados." See Giulia Lanciani and Giuseppe Tavani (eds), *Dicionário da Literatura Medieval Galega e Portuguesa* (Lisboa: Caminho, 1993), pp. 78–79, quoted in Mendes, "O Sentido dos Diálogos," p. 13.

[23.] Cortez, "Relações entre as Imagens da Natureza," p. 37.

[24.] After van Gennep, Victor Turner stated that the liminal concept is "to include both a personal and collective liminality, temporal as well as spatial;" Victor Turner, in Bjørn Thomassen, "Liminality," in Austin Harrington (ed.), *Encyclopedia of Social Theory* (Abingdon: Routledge, Taylor & Francis, 2006), p. 322.

The theme development of these pieces is based on the maiden's lament, whose *amigo* is absent on the high sea to fulfill his duties for an unknown (yet often extended) period.[25] For centuries, it was not unusual that such departures had no return, leaving many fiancées waiting for months and even years without closure. In the words of Mendes, "the relationship with the sea is often a symbol of departure.… [It becomes] an icon of *saudade*, transformed into a feeling expressed by the sonority of the 'barcarolas.'"[26] Uncertain of her betrothed's return, the *amiga* asks the sea waves of Vigo (Galicia) at the beginning of this collection if they had seen her beloved ("Ondas do mar de Vigo," *Vindel Parchment*, I):[27]

Ondas do mar de Vigo	*Sea waves of Vigo,*
se vistes meu amigo?	*have you seen my beloved?*
E ay Deus!, se verrá cedo?	*Oh God, will he return soon?*
Ondas do mar levado,	*O turbulent sea waves,*
se vistes meu amado?	*have you seen my lover?*
E ay Deus!, se verrá cedo?	*Oh God, will he be back soon?*
Se vistes meu amigo,	*Have you seen my beloved*
o por que eu sospiro?	*for whom I sigh?*
E ay Deus!, se verrá cedo?	*Oh God, will he be back soon?*
Se vistes meu amado,	*Have you seen my lover,*
por que ei gran coidado?	*whom I worry greatly?*
E ay Deus!, se verrá cedo?	*Oh God, will he be back soon?*

---

25. Several scholars, including Alexandre Guerra and Xosé Freixedo, argue that the seven pieces should be read as a unified narrative instead of separate *cantigas*. See Alexandre Rodríguez Guerra and Xosé Bieito Arias Freixedo (eds), *The Vindel Parchment and Martin Codax/O Pergamiño Vindel e Martin Codax, The Golden Age of Medieval Galician Poetry* (Amsterdam: John Benjamins Pub. Co., 2018).

26. "Essa identidade foi construída através da relação entre o mar que, muitas das vezes é símbolo de partida, transforma em um ícone da saudade que é transformado em sentimento presente pela sonoridade pelas barcarolas." Original in Mendes, "O Sentido dos Diálogos," p. 17.

27. All translations are made by me, unless otherwise specified.

The maiden repeats her question to the sea several times throughout the piece, with few modifications. Both couplet and refrain evoke the seascape as a liminal space, the lover's absence, and the concerns towards him. The music helps to reinforce such literal and veiled meanings with the ascending and descending, albeit repetitive, melodic contour. As Mendes suggests, the description of the back-and-forth sea waves symbolizes the desire for a safe return; it is also reflected in these pieces' musical and poetic form, with its recurring questions.[28] The clear musical and textual parallelism and strophic structure, however, help to underline the liminal time through the thoughts of anguish, of the 'in-between' state in which she finds herself, and the need to know about her betrothed's situation.[29] The explicit reference to time comes when the *amiga* asks "when" (i.e. "if soon") to the divine entity; the shift in the text is reflected in the music as well, as the main tone/harmony (usually performed by a drone instrument) temporarily changes. Shortly after, she resumes the direct monologue with the sea, continuing the seemingly now-perpetual emotional state.

An identical formal approach occurs with her final plead, with similar devices used in *cantiga* I (poetic parallelism, musical repetitions, melodic contour element). However, this time the number of stanzas is shorter, and there is no contrasting tone/harmony between sections, as the maiden directs her question only to the sea ("Ay ondas que eu vin veer," *Vindel Parchment*, VII):[30]

[28.] Mendes, "O Sentido dos Diálogos," p. 14.

[29.] "Dístico e refrão convocam simultaneamente a paisagem marítima, … a ausência do amigo, … a ansiedade da amiga pelo seu bem-estar e retorno." Guerra and Freixedo, "Estudo Literário das Cantigas de Martim Codax," in *The Vindel Parchment and Martin Codax*, p. 35.

[30.] As customary for medieval repertoire to have only the melodic line, the instrumental part is a musical arrangement, added to the written melody and text, for Gothic harp (a fourteenth-century harp replica) and drone. Together with the voice, my arrangement attempts to mirror the intricacies explored in this portion of the chapter: a long, sustained drone persists through the entire piece, reflecting the ongoing persistence of *saudade* and ignorance towards the maiden's lover situation. The harp patterns, continuous and pervasive, yet always moving, reflect the movement of the sea waves: in motion, yet ever-present, ubiquitous. The voice, written by Martin Codax, is the plead, the voiced pain and love through the constancy of a maiden's last lamentation for her beloved one at the end of this *cantigas*

Ay ondas que eu vin veer,	Oh, sea waves that I came to see,
se me saberedes dizer	Could you tell me
por que tarda meu amigo sen min?	Why does my beloved delay without me?
Ay ondas que eu vin mirar,	Oh, waves I came to gaze at,
se me saberedes contar	Could you say to me
por que tarda meu amigo sen min?	Why does my beloved delay without me?

Although with only two stanzas instead of four, in comparison to *cantiga* I, the lengthier and repeated melodic phrases, together with the use of the same tone/harmony throughout the piece, enhance the sense of expanded time, as if it has been dilated throughout the maiden's wait. The music reflects persisting uncertainty throughout time, the *in-betweenness* of living in doubt, and the poignancy of the feeling *saudade*.[31] At the end of this collection, the *amiga* expresses herself almost without any hope, which has been "taken by the winds and the waves," in the words of Mendes.[32] These *cantigas* represent, therefore, a lament of *saudade* within a liminal space and time.

* * *

While the sea symbolizes a source of life, creation, and subsistence, it is also connected to destruction, loss, and death – followed by grief for those who stayed.[33] However, whereas grief represents an individual or collective liminal stage experienced in a temporal dimension, the

---

de amigo collection. See Martin Codax, "Ay ondas que eu vin veer," Júlia Coelho (soprano, gothic harp, and drone - music video) YouTube, 5 April 2021, https://www.youtube.com/watch?v=AePv56hmS5s.

[31.] For liminal sound studies, see Peter Long, "The Sound of In-Between: Exploring Liminality in Popular Music Composition," thesis, School of Humanities and Communication Arts, University of Western Sydney, 2014.

[32.] "Nesta cantiga, a amiga dissipa-se já sem esperança, levada pelo vento e as ondas." Original in Mendes, "O Sentido dos Diálogos," p. 107. See also Hélder Macedo and Stephen Reckert, *Do Cancioneiro de Amigo* (Lisbon: Assírio e Alvim, n.d.), p. 162.

[33.] As Gaspar put it, "it is in the water that life transforms and its creation happens: "Na água que acontecem as transformações da vida, e sua geração." Original in Gaspar, "O Feminino nas Identidades."

unknown status of a loved one means that those who remain behind can neither celebrate (his or her) return/life nor be allowed to go through the grieving passage.[34] Hence, the sea becomes a liminal space and dual element between life and death, land and sky, and creates liminality in time by representing the beginning and the end, the hope and the despair, as well as the timeless waiting through extended time that might never provide closure. For these reasons, to those who were left on land, the sea was often a metaphor for endless tears and countless hours, an idea that is expressed still in modern Portuguese and Galician music and poetry:[35]

Ó ondas do mar salgado	*Oh, sea waves of this salty sea*
Donde vos vem tanto sal?	*Where is it from all this salt?*
Vem das lágrimas choradas	*It comes from the tears that were shed*
Nas praias de Portugal	*At the beaches of Portugal.*

However, the perception of the sea in the northwestern Iberian peninsula represented more than that in the post-medieval *trovadorismo* tradition: the sea became both a window to the abyss and a portal to infinity.

Although the Celtic influence on the northwest Iberian peninsula often goes unmentioned, the author of this entry sheds light on the extent to which Galician-Portuguese culture was strongly connected to it and its relationship with the natural elements. See also Filippo Lourenço Olivieri, "Os Celtas e os Cultos das Águas: Crenças e Rituais," *Brathair* 6, no. 2 (2006), pp. 79–88. For more information on overall Celtiberian culture and history, see Alberto Lorrio, *Los Celtíberos* (Madrid: Universidad Complutense de Madrid, 2005), and Sílvia Alfayé Villa, *Imagen y Ritual en la Céltica Peninsular* (Noia, A Coruña: Toxosoutos, 2011).

[34.] See Thomassen, "The Uses and Meanings of Liminality."

[35.] The connection between sadness and the sea in Portuguese and Galician literature extends outside of the *cantigas de amigo* repertoire and continues much beyond the medieval era. Portuguese poet Fernando Pessoa (1888–1935) wrote his poem "Mar Português" (Portuguese Sea) (1934) inspired by the *trova* made by António Correia de Oliveira, *Cantigas* (Lisbon: Livraria Ferin, 1902).

Conclusion

Timothy Carson

Paleontologist John Huntley does not think in years; he thinks in millions of years. When I first described the concepts of liminality to John and asked how they might relate to his field and research, he instantly replied, "In the Ediacaran Period, there's your interval." His academic research is in the fossil record of biotic interactions, stratigraphic paleobiology, conservation paleobiology, and the evolution of morphological disparity. For a scientific lay person like me, that translates into this: He goes back millions of years in the strata of the fossil record and identifies forms of life and everything that contributed to their beginnings and endings.

That is what led John to make the connection between liminality and the Ediacaran Period. It is the Ediacaran interval (the final period of the Proterozoic era) that preceded what is called the Cambrian Explosion (the first period of the Phanerozoic era). That so-called explosion contributed to the appearance and evolutionary diversification of most of the animal phyla in a geologically rapid event. In other words, most of the life forms we know today exploded into being during the Cambrian period. So, what set the stage for that?

What set the stage was a highly liminal time, the Ediacaran interval of millions of years. It included a whole series of biotic and abiotic events, a set of feedbacks, a series of switches that all came into play in such a way that they created a pyramid of everything necessary for the big boom of the Cambrian period.[1]

---

[1] James D. Schiffbauer *et al.*, "The Latest Ediacaran Wormworld Fauna: Setting the Ecological Stage for the Cambrian Explosion," *GSA Today* 26,

This extensively studied liminal interval reveals the mystery of life preparing for itself. It is the in-between things during a huge process that makes possible everything that comes next. Everything that developed during the grand interval of the Ediacaran Period set the stage for life to explode in the Cambrian period and beyond. Combined with the changing context of supercontinent breakup, it also set the stage for the human species. It is nearly impossible to imagine these long liminal periods of time in the millions of years, but the stratigraphy of the fossil record freezes that story in time, providing a snapshot.

If we are looking for explanations as to how the big transitions of life unfold, we need to look to the margins, intervals, edges, and boundaries. That is where we shall find our clues as to what may come next and how.

The liminal loop that describes the human experience of moving from the known across a threshold into the ambiguous liminal domain of uncertainty is also deeply embedded in the structure and process of the planet, a non-anthropocentric phenomenon that transcends our human experience. This is a pattern integral to the unfolding of the universe, and it remains highly important to human life and our understanding of it; the universal manifests itself in the very particular, and the particular often reveals the universal.

Not infrequently, forces beyond the human push humans into liminal places. For example, natural disasters do not ask permission of human inhabitants before erupting onto the scene; they operate according to their own rules, quite oblivious to the inconvenience or destruction they may cause humans. On the other hand, the Anthropocene now has an outsized impact on the entire global ecosystem, often precipitating the very forms of liminality that humans would rather avoid.

However a state of liminality is precipitated, human agency and response play definitive roles in both the intensity and ways in which it is experienced and even endured. World views, philosophies and language all contribute to determining how people and communities will traverse voluntary and involuntary liminal states. Through the centuries, societies have found ways to negotiate the great passages of life through defined rites and rituals. Today our awareness of the deep patterns of liminality will inform our healing models, methods of interpreting historical events, and approaches to teaching and learning.

no. 11 (November 2016), pp. 4–11, https://www.geosociety.org/gsatoday/archive/26/11/pdf/i1052-5173-26-11-4.pdf.

On a more transcendent level, liminality underlies the narratives and symbolism of living religious traditions, informs personal transformation, and provides a way to endure present uncertainty without relinquishing hope. Art, literature, and poetry explore all of these in their own evocative ways, frequently surprising us with what we have not noticed. As we find ourselves suspended on the rock face of life, dangling in a strange vertical world between heaven and earth, hidden dimensions are revealed.

In addition, new knowledge and practices emerge at liminal intersections – between disciplines, between the different but complementary, between traditions and cultures. The third spaces of life, the overlaps and connective tissue, the ecotones, are replete with new possibilities, offering solutions to old and thorny problems.

Most of all, we are reminded that liminal time and space may be purposeful. In the same way that the Ediacaran interval prepared life for the Cambrian explosion, so other liminal spaces are full of other kinds of potential. Seeds of the future gestate in liminal soil. Just how long that process takes, we never know. However, the fact that the liminal time and space holds a trajectory toward the future reminds us of its implicit hopefulness.

From unlikely bedfellows – ancient religious tradition and quantum physics – we hear a common truth, articulated differently: *space is not empty.* There is an active presence in what appears to be absent. What is most invisible to the eye is often the most determinative. That which is undetected continues to create a new reality whether we know it or not. Therefore, the ambiguous, uncertain, winding path of liminality does not lead us through wasted time and space. Even the grand pause of a pandemic may lead to a revisualization of common life. When liminal sojourners cross voluntary or involuntary thresholds, they are escorted through new realms of possibility, even when those realms contain some form of suffering.

The communities most affiliated with tribal, pre-industrial, and ancient traditions, both religious and nonreligious, recognized the power of these transitional times and spaces. As a result, they devised spaces, stories, rites, and rituals to assist in these passages. They provided ways for their communities to negotiate powerful change. This frequently included sacred aspects, and rites of passage were employed for almost every dimension of life – birth, coming of age, marriage, war, planting and harvest, crisis, disaster, and death.

Though many people today still access these rites and rituals through their cultural or religious traditions, the technological culture of the global north has been conspicuous in the ways it abandoned these traditions and replaced them with other ways of thinking and living. This shift has often expunged transcendent symbols, language, and ritual from its common life. In the absence of the traditions that helped their ancestors, people will often have trouble in negotiating world-shaking transitions. Though a thoroughgoing intellectual reformation shifted the world-view landscape, that does not mean that the long-evolved need for ritual has disappeared. To the contrary, people continue to create new rites and rituals to help them through liminal passages; if we lack predetermined rituals, then we make up new ones. The search for new language, rites and rituals continues, and we are often surprised to discover that the quest has taken us to somewhere vaguely familiar, to ways that resemble those of our ancient predecessors, in form if not in philosophical or theological content. No less than our ancestors, we discover ways to describe and enact what human beings have always experienced, the phenomenon of liminal space and how to pass through it.

Most certainly, some liminal space is filled with tragedy. It often seems to extend indefinitely, without resolution. The disasters and conflicts of the past secure their inhabitants in chains, resisting every effort to set its captives free. The way out of such seemingly intractable liminality often requires a process of healing and reconciliation that extends as long as or longer than the violations that created it in the first place.

Some have said that historical life is defined best as a string of liminal thresholds through which individuals and groups continually pass. It would be hard to dispute that assertion, considering the frequency of liminal eruptions. If that is so, and I believe that it is, much of the quality and depth of our personal and collective life will be determined by our ability to make sense of being suspended on that wall; and after making some sense of it, to respond; and in responding to create a way forward for ourselves and others. Some of our very best work will be done in these liminal spaces. Our effectiveness as guides and leaders may be directly correlated to our understanding of liminality. Moreover, on the most esoteric level, our spirituality, vocation, and acting in the world may be guided best by the awareness of an infinite liminal loop and how we fit into it.

Contributors

Phil Allen, Jr., MAT, is a PhD candidate and Pannell Center for Black Church Studies Fellow at Fuller Theological Seminary. His research in Black Church theology and ethics informs his perspectives on justice, healing racial trauma, and racial solidarity. He is the founder of the Racial Solidarity Project and author of *Open Wounds: A Story of Racial Tragedy, Trauma, and Redemption.*

Jonathan Best, PhD, is a practical theologian, the creator and curator of Liminal Theology (liminaltheology.org) and host of the *Liminal Theology Podcast.* Jonathan is also a founding member of the Guild for Engaged Liminality (engagedliminality.org). His areas of interest include postmodern philosophy, poetry, and hermeneutics.

J.D. Bowers, PhD, holds degrees in both history and government from the College of William & Mary and Indiana University, and has been a university professor, administrator, and program leader. For over 25 years he has studied, written about, and been an activist in the fields of human rights and post-atrocity justice. He has both lived and taught in Cyprus, the Netherlands, and Bosnia.

Timothy Carson, DMin, is the editor of this volume, and also author of *Liminal Reality and Transformational Power,* editor of *Neither Here nor There: The Many Voices of Liminality,* and co-author of *Crossing Thresholds: A Practical Theology of Liminality.* He serves as the curator of TheLiminalityProject.org, is a co-founder of the Guild for Engaged Liminality (engagedliminality.org) and teaches seminars and classes on liminality in the Honors College of the University of Missouri.

Júlia Coelho, MA, is pursuing a PhD in Musicology and DMA in Vocal Performance at the University of North Texas where she serves as the journal editor of *Harmonia*. Originally from Portugal, Júlia brings her academic background in philosophy, music, and languages to peer-reviewed publications in English, Italian and Portuguese on several master works. In addition to her research activity, she works as a professional musician and piano and voice teacher.

Elizabeth Coombes, PhD, teaches at the University of South Wales and has been a music therapist for over 20 years. The scope of her work has included in-patient adolescents in a mental health clinic and premature babies and their parents in special educational schools. She is the author of a variety of academic papers that explore the societal impact of music therapy for clients, caregivers, educators and other professionals, and her training in the Bonny Method of Guided Imagery and Music has integrated liminality into her personal and professional life.

Louise Fago-Ruskin, MA, is an artist, writer, and lecturer in Photography and Critical and Contextual studies at Plymouth College of Art in Devon, England. She has exhibited both nationally and internationally in exhibitions such as the Hyères International Festival of Fashion and Photography, the Arles Photography Open Salon, the Parallax Art Fair (La Galleria, London) and La Gallerie Sakura in Paris. Her works have also been nominated for a variety of awards, including *Foam* magazine's "What's Next?: A Search into the Future of Photography."

Mary Farrell, PhD, is a retired professor of English literature at the Universitat Jaume I, Castellón, Spain. She is a poet and essayist whose main research includes American literature, silence in communication, and cultural studies, especially related to microhistory and transculturation. Her publications include numerous books, reviews, essays, and poetry.

Susan Franck, MSW, is a practicing clinician and facilitates dream and other soul-centered groups in Columbia, Missouri. She has studied Jung since 2005 and is an Analyst in Training with the Inter-regional Society of Jungian Analysts.

Justine Huxley, PhD, is the CEO of St. Ethelburga's Centre for Reconciliation and Peace in London, a community that builds resilience for times of social and ecological breakdown. Justine's work centers on inspiring people to bridge divisions, love Earth, and recognize the links between those two most urgent tasks. She is the editor of *Generation Y, Spirituality and Social Change.* She is a follower of the Sufi tradition and has been leading meditation and dreamwork groups for many years.

Gabrielle Malfatti, EdD, is the Director of Global Engagement and Associate Teaching Professor of Educational Leadership at the University of Missouri. She is recipient of the 2019 Patrick J. Moreo Global Education Leadership Award, serves on the Editorial Review Board of the *Journal of Global Education and Research*, and as a founding board member for Vidyashilp University in Bangalore, India. She is the editor of *People Centered-Approaches Toward the Internationalization of Higher Education* published in 2020 by IGI Global.

David McGee, MS, is the Director of Development and Communication for ENLACE, a community development organization based in El Salvador. Though his professional degree is in Organizational Leadership, his interests have also included art, photography, biblical studies, surfing, and rock climbing. He is presently opening a community-based rock-climbing gym.

Jenny McGee, BA, studied with award-winning designer/illustrator Mirko Ilić and her mixed media paintings are displayed in numerous private galleries. Jenny's work focuses on the pathway through trauma to artistic beauty and self-knowledge where brokenness is transformed into wholeness.

Carrie Newcomer is a songwriter, recording artist, poet, performer, and activist. Described as a "prairie mystic" by *The Boston Globe*, she has nineteen nationally released recordings, two books of poetry and essays, earned an Emmy for her PBS special, *An Evening with Carrie Newcomer*, and is the recipient of the 2019 Shalem Institute's Contemplative Voices Award. Carrie has joined Parker J. Palmer on *The Growing Edge* podcast and was named by *Spirituality and Health* magazine as one of the top ten spiritual leaders for the next 20 years.

Katie Potapoff, MFA, is from Canada and currently completing her practice-led PhD at DJCAD, University of Dundee, Scotland. She works intuitively across mediums, such as drawing, installation, writing, fiber, and clay. At the center of her practice is an exploration of the space in-between. She was awarded the Canada Council for the Arts 'Explore and Create' grant to fund her residency on the Isle of Iona.

Mary Lane Potter, PhD, is the author of *A Woman of Salt, Strangers and Sojourners: Stories from the Lowcountry* and *Seeking God and Losing the Way*. Her essays have appeared in *River Teeth, Witness, Parabola, Tablet* magazine, *SUFI Journal, Spiritus, The Other Journal, Leaping Clear, Still Point Arts Quarterly, ARTS, Women's Studies Quarterly,* and *Feminist Studies in Religion*. Before receiving an MFA in creative writing, Potter taught and published academic theology.

Llewellyn Vaughan-Lee, Ph.D., is a Sufi teacher, author, and founder of the Golden Sufi Center in northern California. The recent focus of his writing has been on spiritual ecology and the need for a spiritual response to our present ecological crisis (*Spiritual Ecology: The Cry of the Earth*). He was also interviewed by Oprah Winfrey as a part of her Super Soul Sunday series. His most recent book is *Seasons of the Sacred: Reconnecting to the Wisdom within Nature and the Soul.*

Kate Weir, EdS, is a Licensed Professional Counselor-Supervisor (LPC-S) and is a Registered Play Therapist-Supervisor (RPT-S). She is in private practice, providing child-centered play therapy, child-parent relationship therapy, teacher/parent consultation, and professional supervision. She owns and directs the wellness center Kindred Collective, LLC, is an instructor with Heartland Play Therapy, and an adjunct instructor at Stephen's College, Columbia, Missouri.

Lisa Withrow, PhD, is an ordained clergywoman and author/scholar with 20 years' experience serving as a leadership professor. She is an ICF-certified coach and regular consultant for religious organizations and businesses. Withrow is the co-founder of the Guild for Engaged Liminality (engagedliminality.org) and the Catalytic Coaching Institute, author of *Leadership in Unknown Waters: Liminality as Threshold to the Future,* and co-author of *Crossing Thresholds: A Practical Theology of Liminality.*

Bibliography

Achinte, Adolo Albán, "Interculturalidad sin Decolonialidad? Colonialidades Circulantes y Practices de Re-Existencia," in Wilmer Villa and Arturo Grueso (eds), *Diversidad, Interculturalidad y Construcción de Ciudad* (Bogotá: Universidad Pedagógica Nacional/Alcaldía Mayor, 2008), found in Walter D. Mignolo and Catherine E. Walsh, *On Decoloniality: Concepts, Analytics, and Praxis* (Durham, NC: Duke University Press, 2018) (Kindle)

'Al-Arabî, Ibn, Proem to *The Universal Tree and the Four Birds*, trans. Angela Jaffray (Oxford: Anqa, 2006)

Alfayé Villa, Sílvia, *Imagen y Ritual en la Céltica Peninsular* (Noia, A Coruña: Toxosoutos, 2011)

Anderson, Benedict, *Imagined Communities: Reflections on the Origins and Spread of Nationalism*, rev. edn (New York and London: Verso, 1991)

Annan Plan (formally known as "Comprehensive Settlement of the Cyprus Problem"), final version, 31 March 2004, http://www.hri.org/docs/annan/Annan_Plan_Text.html

Attar, Farid ud-Din, *The Conference of Birds*, trans. Afkham Darbandi and Dick Davis (Auckland, New Zealand: Aziloth Books, 2011)

Banac, Ivo, "The Politics of National Homogeneity", in B. Blitz (ed.), *War and Change in the Balkans: Nationalism, Conflict and Cooperation* (Cambridge: Cambridge University Press, 2006)

Barton, Ruth Haley, *Sacred Rhythms: Arranging Our Lives for Spiritual Formation* (Downers Grove, IL: InterVarsity Press, 2009) (Kindle)

Bellah, Robert, *Religion in Human Evolution: From the Paleolithic to the Axial Age* (Cambridge, MA: Belknap, 2011)

Bendell, Jem, "Deep Adaptation: A Map for Navigating Climate Tragedy," IFLAS Occasional Paper 2, July 2018

Bennett, Christopher, *Bosnia's Paralysed Peace* (Oxford: Oxford University Press, 2016)

Camus, Albert, *The Plague* (New York: Vintage Books, 1991)

——, Quotes, Brainy Quote, http://www.brainyquote.com (accessed 2 April 2021)

Caputo, John D., *The Folly of God: A Theology of the Unconditional* (Salem, OR: Polebridge Press, 2016)

——, *The Insistence of God: A Theology of Perhaps* (Bloomington: Indiana University Press, 2013)

——, "Spectral Hermeneutics: On the Weakness of God and the Theology of the Event", in John D. Caputo and Gianni Vattimo, *After the Death of God*, ed. Jeffrey W. Robbins (New York: Columbia University Press, 2007)

——, *Truth: Philosophy in Transit* (New York: Penguin, 2014)

Carson, Timothy, Rosy Fairhurst, Nigel Rooms and Lisa Withrow, *Crossing Thresholds: A Practical Theology of Liminality* (Cambridge: The Lutterworth Press, 2021)

Chittick, William C., "Ibn 'Arabî", *Stanford Encyclopedia of Philosophy* (Spring 2020 edition), https://plato.stanford.edu/entries/ibn-arabi/#Bar

——, *Imaginal Worlds: Ibn al-ʿArabî and the Problem of Religious Diversity* (Albany, NY: SUNY Press, 1994)

Chodkiewicz, Michel (ed.), *The Meccan Revelations*, trans. William C. Chittick and James W. Morris (New York: Pir Press, 2002)

Codax, Martin, "Ay ondas que eu vin veer," Júlia Coelho (soprano, gothic harp, and drone – music video), *YouTube*, 5 April 2021, https://www.youtube.com/watch?v=AePv56hmS5s

Coleman, Will, *Tribal Talk: Black Theology, Hermeneutics, and African/American Ways of "Telling the Story"* (University Park: Pennsylvania University Press, 2000)

Cone, James, *The Cross and the Lynching Tree* (Maryknoll, NY: Orbis Books, 2011) (Kindle)

Corral, Esther, "Feminine Voices in the Galician-Portuguese *Cantigas de Amigo*," in Anne L. Klinck and Ann Marie Rasmussen (eds), *Medieval Woman's Song: Cross-Cultural Approaches* (Philadelphia: University of Pennsylvania Press, 2015)

Cortez, Clarice Zamonaro, "Relações entre as Imagens da Natureza e os Estados Sentimentais Femininos na Lírica Medieval," in Gladis Massini-Cagliari *et al.*, *Séries Estudos Medievais 2: Fontes* (Campinas, Brazil: Associação Nacional de Pós-Graduação em Letras e Linguística, 2009), pp. 19–45

Council of Europe, *Framework Convention for the Protection of National Minorities*, European Treaty Series No. 157, Strasbourg, 1995 (in effect 1998), https://rm.coe.int/168007cdac

Deely, John, and Inna Semetsky, "Semiotics, Edusemiotics and the Culture of Education," *Educational Philosophy and Theory* 49, no. 3 (2017), pp. 207–19

Defoe, Daniel, *A Journal of the Plague Year* (New York: Everyman, 1994)

DeGruy, Joy, *Post-Traumatic Slave Syndrome: America's Legacy of Enduring Injury and Healing* (Portland, OR: Joy DeGruy Publications, 2017)

Democker, Mary, "If Your House Is on Fire: On the Moral Urgency of Climate Change," interview of Kathleen Dean Moore, *Sun Magazine*, December 2012

Draper, Andrew T., "The End of 'Mission:' Christian Witness and the Decentering of White Identity," in Love Sechrest, Johnny Ramirez-Johnson and Amos Young (eds), *Can "White" People Be Saved? Triangulating Race, Theology, and Mission* (Downers Grove, IL: InterVarsity Press, 2018)

"Earth, Sea, and Sky: Liminality in Celtic Folklore," *Shapes in the Mist* (n.d.), https://www.shapesinthemist.com/liminality/ (accessed May 2021)

Eisenstein, Charles, *The More Beautiful World Our Hearts Know Is Possible* (Berkeley, CA: North Atlantic Books, 2013)

Estés, Clarissa Pinkola, *Women Who Run With the Wolves: Myths and Stories of the Wild Woman Archetype* (New York: Ballantine Books, 1992)

Ferreira, Manuel Pedro, *O Som de Martin Codax: Sobre a Dimensão Musical da Lírica Galego-Portuguesa (Séculos XII-XIV)* (Lisbon: UNISYS, 1986)

Fox, Everett (trans. and commentary), *The Five Books of Moses* (New York: Schocken, 1997)

Gaspar, Thayane, "O Feminino nas Identidades Brasileira e Galega," *Quilombo Noroeste: A Cultura Galega no Rio de Janeiro e no Universo Galego-Português-Brasileiro* (3 August 2014), https://quilombonoroeste. wordpress.com/2014/08/03/o-feminino-nas-identidades-brasileira-e-galega/ (accessed May 2021)

Gennep, Arnold van, *The Rites of Passage*, trans. M.B. Vizedom and Gabrielle L. Caffee (London: Routledge & Kegan Paul, 1960)

Giddens, Anthony, Mitchell Duneier, Richard P. Appelbaum and Deborah Carr, *Essentials of Sociology: A Down-To-Earth Approach*, seventh edn (New York: Norton, 2019)

Goffman, Erving, *Frame Analysis: An Essay on the Organization of Experience* (Cambridge, MA: Harvard University Press, 1974)

Gómez Tarin, Francisco Javier, *Discurso de la Ausencia: Elipsis y Fuera de Campo en el Texto Fílmico* (Valencia: Ediciones de la Filmoteca, 2006)

Gross, Jan T., *Fear: Anti-Semitism in Poland after Auschwitz* (New York: Random House, 2007)

Guerra, Alexandre Rodríguez, and Xosé Bieito Arias Freixedo (eds), *The Vindel Parchment and Martin Codax/O Pergamiño Vindel e Martin Codax*, The Golden Age of Medieval Galician Poetry (Amsterdam: John Benjamins Pub. Co., 2018)

Han, Byung-Chul, *The Scent of Time: A Philosophical Essay on the Art of Lingering*, trans. Daniel Steuer (Cambridge: Polity, 2017)

Healy, Ciara, "Thin Place: An Alternative Approach to Curatorial Practice," thesis, University of the West of England, Bristol, 2016, http://eprints.uwe. ac.uk/26057/68/Ciara%20Healy%20Thin%20Place%20PhD%20Thesis%20 for%20Repository%20%281%29.pdf (accessed 20 April 2021)

Hickel, Jason, "A Letter to Steven Pinker (and Bill Gates, for that Matter) about Global Poverty," 4 February 2019, https://www.jasonhickel.org/blog /2019/2/3/pinker-and-global-poverty

"History of the Blues," BBC Bitesize, https://www.bbc.co.uk/bitesize/articles /zkbh2v4 (accessed 21 May 2021)

"Improvise," Dictionary.com, https://www.dictionary.com/browse/improvise

Johnson, Mark, *The Aesthetics of Meaning and Thought* (Chicago: University of Chicago Press, 2018)

Johnson, Steven, *The Ghost Map: A Street, an Epidemic and the Hidden Power of Urban Networks* (New York: Penguin, 2006)

Keats, John, "On Negative Capability: Letter to George and Tom Keats, 21, ?27 December 1817," Selections from Keats' Letters, https://www.poetry foundation.org/articles/69384/selections-from-keatss-letters

Ketcham, Christopher, "The Fallacy of Endless Economic Growth: What Economists Around the World Get Wrong about the Future," *Pacific Standard*, 22 September 2018, https://psmag.com/magazine/fallacy-of -endless-growth

King, Kathleen P., *Handbook of the Evolving Research of Transformative Learning* (Charlotte, NC: Information Age Publishing, 2009)

King, Martin Luther, Jr., "The Case against Tokenism," in Martin Luther King, Jr., *A Testament of Hope: The Essential Writings and Speeches of Martin Luther King, Jr.*, ed. James M. Washington (New York: Harper One, 1986)

———, "Suffering and Faith," in Martin Luther King, Jr., *A Testament of Hope: The Essential Writings and Speeches of Martin Luther King, Jr.*, ed. James M. Washington (New York: Harper One, 1986), p. 41

Klee, Paul, *Pedagogical Sketchbook*, trans. Sibyl Moholy-Nagy (New York: Prager, 1972)

Kretchmer, Harry, "Global Hunger Fell for Decades, But It's Rising Again," 23 July 2020, https://www.weforum.org/agenda/2020/07/global-hunger -rising-food-agriculture-organization-report/

Krushel, Kenneth, "Three Spaces and an Excursus," in Timothy Carson (ed.), *Neither Here nor There: The Many Voices of Liminality* (London: The Lutterworth Press, 2019)

Langermann, Y. Tzvi (trans.), *Yemenite Midrash: Philosophical Commentaries on the Torah* (San Francisco: Harper San Francisco, 1996)

Lartey, Emmanuel Y., *Postcolonializing God: An African Practical Theology* (Norwich: SCM Press, 2013) (Kindle)

Lederach, John Paul, *Building Peace: Sustainable Reconciliation in Divided Societies*, tenth edn (Washington, DC: US Institute of Peace Press, 2013)

Lévi-Strauss, Claude, *Structural Anthropology* (New York: Anchor Books, 1967)

Lewis, Thomas, "Transatlantic Slave Trade," *Encyclopedia Britannica*, 18 August 2021, https://www.britannica.com/topic/transatlantic-slave -trade

Lippman, Peter, *Surviving the Peace: The Struggle for Postwar Recovery in Bosnia-Herzegovina* (Nashville, TN: Vanderbilt University Press, 2019)

Long, Peter, "The Sound of In-Between: Exploring Liminality in Popular Music Composition," thesis, School of Humanities and Communication Arts, University of Western Sydney, 2014

Lorrio, Alberto, *Los Celtíberos* (Madrid: Universidad Complutense de Madrid, 2005)

Losal Rinpoche, Yeshe, *From a Mountain in Tibet: A Monk's Journey* (New York: Penguin, 2020)

Macedo, Hélder, and Stephen Reckert, *Do Cancioneiro de Amigo* (Lisbon: Assírio e Alvim, n.d.)

Macy, Joanna, *Greening of the Self* (Berkeley, CA: Parallax Press, 2013) (Kindle)

Manhattan Murder Mystery, film, directed by Woody Allen (US: TriStar Pictures, 1993)

McNeil, Brenda Salter, "Foreword,", in Soong-Chan Rah, *Prophetic Lament: A Call for Justice in Troubled Times* (Downers Grove, IL: InterVarsity Press, 2015) (Kindle)

M: Eine Stadt Sucht einen Mörder, film, directed by Fritz Lang (Germany: Vereningte Star-Film GmbH; US: Paramount Pictures, 1931)

Menakem, Resmaa, *My Grandmother's Hands: Racialized Trauma and the Pathology to Mending Our Hearts and Bodies* (Las Vegas: Central Recovery Press, 2017)

Mendes, Ana Luiza, "O Sentido dos Diálogos entre as Mulheres e o Mar nas Cantigas de Amigo Galego-Portuguesas do Século XIII," in *Anais do XIV Seminário Nacional Mulher e Literatura/V Seminário Internacional Mulher e Literatura* (Brasília: Universidade de Brasília, Departamento de Teoria Literária e Literaturas, 2011)

———, "O Sentido dos Diálogos entre as Mulheres e o Mar nas Cantigas de Amigo Galego-Portuguesas do Século XIII," dissertation, Universidade Federal do Paraná, 2013

Merleau-Ponty, M. Maurice, *Phenomenology of Perception*, trans. Colin Smith (New York: Routledge & Kegan Paul, 1962)

———, *The Visible and the Invisible*, ed. Claude Lefort, trans. Alphonso Lingis (Evanston, IL: Northwestern University Press, 1968)

Mezirow, Jack, *Transformative Dimensions of Adult Learning* (San Francisco: Jossey-Bass, 1991)

"Midrash on Exodus 5:9," in *Genesis Rabbah*, in Hayim Nahman Bialik and Yehoshua Hana Ravnitzky (eds), *The Book of Legends: Sefer Ha-Aggadah: Legends from the Talmud and Midrash*, trans. William G. Braude (New York: Schocken, 1991)

Mitrović, Miloš, "Mladen Grujičić: Dete Srebrenice," *Dnevni list Danas*, 05 October 2016, https://www.danas.rs/ljudi/mladen-grujicic-dete-srebrenice/ (accessed 23 June 2021)

Moore, Robert, "Contemporary Psychotherapy as Ritual Process: An Initial Reconnaissance," *Zygon* 18 (1 September 1983), pp. 283–94

Nacouzi, Pavlos, administrator and post author, Κύπρος βάθρο Μαρωνίτη (Cyprus Maronite Podium) (accessed 21 June 2021)

NAFSA: Association of International Educators, "Trends in U.S. Study Abroad," 2018–19, https://www.nafsa.org/policy-and-advocacy/policy -resources/trends-us-study-abroad

Nannup, Noel, "A Piece of the Path," Gaia Journey Webinar, Presencing Institute Global Forum, 9–11 July 2020, presencing.org/gaia (accessed 9–11 July 2020)

Office of the High Representative, "Decisions in the Field of Property Laws, Return of Displaced Persons and Refugees and Reconciliation," http://www.ohr.int/cat/hrs-decisions/decisions-in-the-field-of-property-laws-return-of-displaced-persons-and-refugees-and-reconciliation/

Olivieri, Filippo Lourenço, "Os Celtas e os Cultos das Águas: Crenças e Rituais," *Brathair* 6, no. 2 (2006), pp. 79–88

Organization for Security and Cooperation in Europe Mission to Bosnia and Herzegovina, "Hate Monitor," https://www.osce.org/hatemonitorbih (accessed 23 June 2021)

Ouaknin, Marc-Alain, *Symbols of Judaism* (New York: Assouline, 2000)

Perera, Sylvia Brinton, *Descent to the Goddess: A Way of Initiation for Women* (Toronto: Inner City Books, 1981)

Petrila, Ann, and Hasan Hasanović. *Voices from Srebrenica: Survivor Narratives of the Bosnian Genocide* (Jefferson, NC: McFarland Press, 2021)

Pettigrew, David, "Statement Concerning the January 23, 2014 Desecration of the Stražište Memorial," Bosnian American Genocide Institute & Education Center, https://www.baginst.org/denial-of-genocide.html (accessed 28 June 2021)

Piqueras, Belén, Esteban Pujals and Manuel Aguirre, "Seminar Proposal," International Seminar on Liminality and Text 6: The Subject on the Threshold, Madrid, 2012, http://limenandtext.com/islt_theislt6.html (accessed 4 October 2021)

Puryear, Mark, "Tell It Like It Is: A History of Rhythm and Blues," *Folklife Magazine* (Smithsonian Center for Folklife and Cultural Heritage) (20 September 2016), https://folklife.si.edu/magazine/freedom-sounds-tell-it-like-it-is-a-history-of-rhythm-and-blues (accessed 21 May 2021)

Rah, Soong-Chan, *Prophetic Lament: A Call for Justice in Troubled Times* (Downers Grove, IL: InterVarsity Press, 2015) (Kindle)

Report Submitted by the Republic of Cyprus to the UN International Convention on the Elimination of All Forms of Racial Discrimination, CERD /C/299/Add.19, 15 October 1997, http://www.bayefsky.com/reports/cyprus_cerd_c_299_add.19_1997.php

Republic of Cyprus, Constitution, August 1960, https://www.constituteproject.org/constitution/Cyprus_2013.pdf?lang=en

Rosemary's Baby, film, directed by Roman Polanski (US: Paramount Pictures, 1993)

Said, Edward W., "Reflections on Exile," in *Reflections on Exile and Other Literary and Cultural* Essays (London: Granta Books, 2000), pp. 173–186

Santos, Dulce Oliveira Amarante dos, "Caminhos e Atalhos da Historiografia Sobre as Mulheres Medievais," *História Revista* 1, no. 2 (1996), pp. 69–78

Scharmer, Otto C., *The Essentials of Theory U: Core Principles and Applications* (Oakland, CA: Berrett-Koehler Publishers, Inc., 2008)

Scharmer, Otto C., *Theory U: Leading from the Future as It Emerges* (Oakland, CA: Berrett-Koehler, 2016)

Schiffbauer, James D., John Warren Huntley, Gretchen R. O'Neil, Simon A.F. Darroch, Marc Laflamme and Yaoping Cai, "The Latest Ediacaran Wormworld Fauna: Setting the Ecological Stage for the Cambrian Explosion," *GSA Today* 26, no. 11 (November 2016), pp. 4–11, https://www .geosociety.org/gsatoday/archive/26/11/pdf/i1052-5173-26-11-4.pdf

Schimanski, Johan, and Stephan Wolfe (eds), "Key Terms," *Border Poetics*, http://borderpoetics.wikidot.com/border-zone (accessed 27 September 2021)

Scholem, Gershom, *The Messianic Idea in Judaism: And Other Essays on Jewish Spirituality* (New York: Schocken, 1971)

Schouten, John W., "Personal Rites of Passage and the Reconstruction of Self," *Advances in Consumer Research* 18 (1991), pp. 49–51

Sechrest, Love, Johnny Ramirez-Johnson and Amos Young, "Introduction," in Love Sechrest, Johnny Ramirez-Johnson and Amos Young (eds), *Can "White" People Be Saved? Triangulating Race, Theology, and Missions* (Downers Grove, IL: InterVarsity Press, 2018)

Sen, Somdeep, "Cyrillization of Republika Srpska," *Perspectives on Global Development and Technology* 8, no. 2-3 (April 2009), pp. 509–30

Shepherd, Nan, *The Living Mountain: A Celebration of the Cairngorm Mountains of Scotland* (Edinburgh: Canongate, 2011)

"Sinking: eadar dà lionn," *Am Faclair Beag* online Gaelic-English Dictionary, https://www.faclair.com/ViewEntry.aspx?ID=EB40E2CF8150CF510DC818 B7BDBC98E9 (accessed 30 April 2021)

Smith, James K.A., *Desiring the Kingdom: Worship, Worldview, and Cultural Formation: Cultural Liturgies Volume 1* (Grand Rapids, MI: Baker Academic, 2009) (Kindle)

Smith, Roger W., "American Self-Interest and the Response to Genocide," *The Review: The Chronicle of Higher Education*, 30 July 2004, https:// www.chronicle.com/article/american-self-interest-and-the-response-to -genocide/

Solnit, Rebecca, *A Paradise Built in Hell: The Extraordinary Communities That Arise in Disaster* (New York: Penguin, 2010) (Kindle)

Sorguc, Albina "Bosnian Mosques Threatened by Vandalism, Srebrenica Threats," in *Balkan Insight / Balkan Transitional Justice*, 14 June 2019. https://balkaninsight.com/2019/06/14/bosnian-mosques-targeted-by -vandalism-srebrenica-threats/ (accessed 04 October 2021)

Stein, Jan, and Murray Stein, "Psychotherapy, Initiation and the Midlife Transition," in Louise Carus Mahdi (ed.), *Betwixt and Between: Patterns of Masculine and Feminine Initiation* (La Salle, IL: Open Court Pub. Co., 1987)

Stewart, Susan, *The Poet's Freedom: A Notebook on Making* (Chicago: University of Chicago Press, 2011)

"Swag," Slangit.com, https://slangit.com/meaning/swag

Szakolczai, Arpad, "Liminality and Experience: Structuring Transitory Situations and Transformative Events," *International Political Anthropology* 2, no. 1 (2009), pp. 141–72

TED: The Economics Daily, 22 May 2020, https://www.bls.gov/opub/ted/2020 /66-point-2-percent-of-2019-high-school-graduates-enrolled-in-college-in -october-2019.htm

Tharp, Twyla, *The Creative Habit: Learn It and Use It for Life* (New York: Simon & Schuster, 2003)

Thomason, Sarah G., *Endangered Languages: An Introduction* (Cambridge: Cambridge University Press, 2015)

Thomassen, Bjørn, "Liminality," in Austin Harrington (ed.), *Encyclopedia of Social Theory* (Abingdon: Routledge, Taylor & Francis, 2006)

——, *Liminality and the Modern: Living Through the In-Between* (New York: Routledge, 2018)

——, "The Uses and Meanings of Liminality," *International Political Anthropology* 2, no. 1 (2009), pp. 5–28

"Threshold," Etymonline.com, https://www.etymonline.com/search?q=thresh old&ref=searchbar_searchhint.

Trebilcock, Michelle, "Hope in a Dark Passage," in Timothy Carson (ed.), *Neither Here nor There: The Many Voices of Liminality* (Cambridge: The Lutterworth Press, 2019)

Trías Sagnier, Eugenio, *Ciudad Sobre Ciudad* (Barcelona: Ediciones Destino, 2001)

Turner, Victor, "The Center out There: Pilgrim's Goal,' *History of Religions* 12, no. 3 (1973), pp. 191–230

——, *The Ritual Process: Structure and Anti-Structure* (New York: Aldine Pub. Co., 1969)

Ukpokodu, Omiunota N., "Teacher Preparation for Global Perspectives Pedagogy," in Binaya Subedi (ed.), *Critical Global Perspectives: Rethinking Knowledge about Global Societies* (Charlotte, NC: Information Age Pub., 2010)

Varnava, Andrekos, Nicholas Coureas and Marina Elia (eds), *The Minorities of Cyprus: Development Patterns and the Identity of the Internal-Exclusion* (Newcastle upon Tyne: Cambridge Scholars, 2009)

Vasconcellos, Carolina Michaelis de, *A Saudade Portuguesa: Divagações Filológicas e Literar-Históricas em Volta de Inês de Castro e do Cantar Velho "Saudade Minha – Quando te Veria?"* (Porto: Renascença Portuguesa, 1922)

Vaughan-Lee, Llewellyn, *A Handbook for Survivalists: Caring for the Earth: A Series of Meditations* (Point Reyes, CA: Golden Sufi Center, 2020)

Volf, Miroslav, *Exclusion and Embrace*: *A Theological Exploration of Identity, Otherness, and Reconciliation* (Nashville, TN: Abingdon Press, 1996)

Warren, Calvin L., *Ontological Terror: Blackness, Nihilism, and Emancipation* (Durham, NC: Duke University Press, 2018) (Kindle)

Wei, Wang, "Casa de Poesía China," *Poemas del Río Wang*, http://riowang. blogspot.com/2008/04/blog-post.html (accessed 6 February 2012)

Weyhenmeyer, Gesa, Will Steffen *et al.*, "A Warning on Climate and the Risk of Societal Collapse", *The Guardian*, 6 December 2020, https://www.theguardian.com/environment/2020/dec/06/a-warning-on-climate-and-the-risk-of-societal-collapse

White, J.M., "Maintaining the Fire," *Parabola* (Winter 2020–2021)

White, Michael, and David Epston, *Narrative Means to Therapeutic Ends* (New York: W.W. Norton & Co., 1990)

Wilczek, Frank, *A Beautiful Question: Finding Nature's Deep Design* (New York: Penguin Books, 2015)

Wray, John, "Haruki Murakami: The Art of Fiction No. 182," *The Paris Review* 170 (Summer 2004), https://www.theparisreview.org/interviews/2/the-art-of-fiction-no-182-haruki-murakami

Zornberg, Avivah Gottlieb, *The Murmuring Deep: Reflections on the Biblical Unconscious* (New York: Schocken, 2009)

Index

Crossing Thresholds
A Practical Theology of Liminality

By Timothy Carson, Rosy Fairhurst,
Nigel Rooms and Lisa Withrow

An inter-disciplinary study of the phenomenon of liminality and its relevance to theology, worship and mission.

"Holding a pluralistic vision about the significance of liminality, readers are invited into an ever-expanding sense of a God at work in the world."
– **Joretta L. Marshall**, Brite Divinity School

First published by The Lutterworth Press, 30 January 2021

Paperback ISBN: 978 0 7188 9346 0
PDF ISBN: 978 0 7188 4237 6
ePub ISBN: 978 0 7188 4239 0

Liminal Reality
and Transformational Power
Revised Edition: Transition, Renewal and Hope

By Timothy Carson

An important study of the varieties of liminality, illuminating in particular the liminal aspects of pastoral leadership.

"Equipped with liminality, this book takes the reader on a voyage into the heart of theology, and into the human search for meaning. It is worth a read for scholars and non-scholars alike." – **Bjørn Thomassen**, Roskilde University

First published by The Lutterworth Press, 28 April 2016

Paperback ISBN: 978 0 7188 9401 6
PDF ISBN: 978 0 7188 4400 4
ePub ISBN: 978 0 7188 4401 1

BV - #0036 - 140122 - C0 - 234/156/12 - PB - 9780718895839 - Gloss Lamination